Celebrating the 100th Anniversary of Madame Marie Sklodowska Curie's Nobel Prize in Chemistry

CELEBRATING THE 100TH ANNIVERSARY OF MADAME MARIE SKLODOWSKA CURIE'S NOBEL PRIZE IN CHEMISTRY

Edited by

M. -H. Chiu
Graduate Institute of Science Education, National Taiwan Normal University

P. J. Gilmer
Department of Chemistry and Biochemistry, Florida State University

D. F. Treagust
Science and Mathematics Education Centre, Curtin University

SENSE PUBLISHERS
ROTTERDAM/BOSTON/TAIPEI

A C.I.P. record for this book is available from the Library of Congress.

ISBN: 978-94-6091-717-2 (paperback)
ISBN: 978-94-6091-718-9 (hardback)
ISBN: 978-94-6091-719-6 (e-book)

Published by: Sense Publishers,
P.O. Box 21858,
3001 AW Rotterdam,
The Netherlands
www.sensepublishers.com

Printed on acid-free paper

TABLE OF CONTENTS

PETER MAHAFFY

FOREWORD

It wasn't easy, I thought, as I wound my way down the narrow steps from the 2nd floor museum in Marie Sklodowska Curie's home in Warsaw. It was April, 2011, a third of the way through the International Year of Chemistry, and I was deeply moved by the story of her life and scientific work told by the simple displays set in her home that was reconstructed after the levelling of Warsaw during World War II. Sklodowska Curie's words, spoken a century ago, stuck in my mind: "It has not been easy." They describe her challenges in maintaining a balance between two things she cared deeply about – scientific career and family. "I have frequently been questioned, especially by women, of how I could reconcile family life with a scientific career. Well, it has not been easy," she said.

My thoughts turned back to meetings in Paris, five years earlier, where the International Union of Pure & Applied Chemistry (IUPAC) and UNESCO's Division of Basic & Engineering Sciences agreed to work together to seek declaration by UNESCO and the United Nations of an International Year of Chemistry (IYC). We were pleased to learn that 2011, the first available year for consideration, coincided with important anniversaries of events that helped to shape the discipline and profession of chemistry, including the centenary of Mme Sklodowska Curie's Nobel Prize in Chemistry, the founding of the International Association of Chemical Societies (the predecessor of IUPAC), and the bicentenary of the publication of Amadeo Avogadro's ground-breaking memoir in *Journal de physique*. We recommended that these be highlighted in activities and events during IYC–2011. In the final wording of the UN resolution and in the implementation of the year, two themes emerged as being of particular importance to the International Year of Chemistry: The essential contributions of chemistry to sustainable development and the celebration of the contribution of women to science, in honor of Mme Sklodowska Curie.

The volume you have opened on Mme Sklodowska Curie's groundbreaking work in radiochemistry is one of several IYC–2011 legacy contributions that resulted from implementing those two themes. The profession of chemistry seeks to better understand the stories of those vital and often unrecognized contributions of women to the creative science of chemistry. But that understanding has a purpose: to learn from the past in tackling the important challenges that lie ahead for the next generation of scientists and for society.

As you will discover in reading each chapter, it certainly was not easy for Sklodowska Curie. At every step along the way (Chapter 1) she broke new ground. "She was the first woman to receive a doctorate in France and the first woman anywhere to earn that doctorate in physics. She was the first female professor at that great Parisian university, the Sorbonne. She was the first woman to win a Nobel Prize, for [physics] ---in 1903---. Eight years later, she became the first scientist, male or female, to be awarded a second Nobel Prize-----" (Angier, 2001, p. xiii, quoted in Chapter 7 of this book).

And it did not seem to get easier, even when she was well established as a scientist. Her juggling act in her roles as both scientist and mother became even more challenging after the tragic horse-and-carriage accident in 1906 that snuffed out the life of her husband and scientific collaborator, as well as fellow 1903 Nobel Prize in Physics recipient, Pierre Curie (Chapter 2). Her story shows that Sklodowska Curie, like many women scientists of her day and beyond, had to fight for the opportunities to do the work she was passionate about, and then again to receive appropriate recognition for that work. This included her need to insist on receiving the Nobel Prize in Chemistry that had been awarded to her, despite the advice of a prominent Swedish scientist on the committee that she ought to decline the award until such time as the public scandal over her romantic involvement with Paul Langevin abated.

But the creative genius, diligent work habits, and scientific accomplishments of Mme Sklodowska Curie built a legacy that opened doors for other women to rise to the pinnacles of science. And their stories are both informative and inspiring (Chapters 2, 5, and 6). Included in this book are stories of the only three other female Nobel Laureates in Chemistry: Marie's daughter, Irène Joliot-Curie, Dorothy Crowfoot Hodgkin, and Ada Yonath, as well as that of chemical immunologist Ruth Arnon, who recently was elected as the first woman president of the Israel Academy of Sciences and the Humanities. Popular historical accounts would sometimes lead us to believe that Sklodowska Curie was the only woman of her time working in chemistry and nuclear science. Some of the many less well known stories are also recorded here (Chapters 5, 8 and 9).

This collection of essays also challenges us to look at the present and into the future (Chapters 10 and 11). Understanding life in the past (Chapters 3 and 4) is always helpful in living life into the future. The stories, experiences, and insights here are a resource to help the chemistry profession and the public find ways toward creating supportive cultures of science that are truly inclusive. And I can almost hear Mme Sklodowska Curie say, 100 years after her Nobel Prize in Chemistry: "It will not be easy"!

Peter Mahaffy
Chair, IUPAC Committee on Chemistry Education
Professor of Chemistry, The King's University College
Edmonton, AB, Canada
peter.mahaffy@kingsu.ca

MEI-HUNG CHIU, PENNY J. GILMER, AND DAVID F. TREAGUST

INTRODUCING THE BOOK

BACKGROUND TO THE DEVELOPMENT OF THIS BOOK

Research in elementary and secondary school science shows that male and female students have similar interests and motivation, albeit, with those males interested in science tending to prefer physical sciences and females biological sciences. However, at the university level, gender differences appear when examining the intended majors of all first-year US college students: 15.1% of women and 29.3% men plan to major in engineering, and in the physical sciences 2.0% of women and 2.8% of men plan to major in the physical sciences (Hill, Corbett, & St. Rose, 2010). Gender differences continue throughout university as evidenced by the percentage of US undergraduate women graduating with various majors: women graduate with only 20.5% of the physics majors and 19.5% of the engineering majors in the US in 2006 (Hill et al., 2010). Women in 2006 were the majority (51.8%) of majors in undergraduate chemistry (Hill et al., 2010); in 2007, US colleges and universities enrolled 57.2% women overall (National Center for Educational Statistics, 2009). Doctoral degrees are awarded in the physical sciences to males and females in the US at a rate of 2.6 to 1, respectively (Chapter 1, in this volume, Chiu & Wang). Clearly much female academic potential is lost to science.

Not surprisingly, these gender differences have a long history. Female scientists and their contributions have long been downplayed and in some cases even ignored by both western and eastern science traditions. Female students, for a great part of history, were not considered of suitable constitution to be permitted even to study the sciences. Once this barrier began to come down, women who were passionate about the sciences found themselves delegated to the role of assistant to male mentors and teachers who were considered the true scientists. This underrepresentation and imbalance has left an incomplete picture of how the history of science and scientific discoveries should be portrayed. This book hopes to begin to rectify this perception.

Marie Curie's receipt of her second Nobel Prize for her independent work in chemistry stands as a watershed moment in the history of science. Marie Curie has inspired many girls and women to study and pursue careers in science—and not just because she was a female scientist but also because she broke the rule that said women could not "do" good science. Having experienced firsthand the discrimination and obstacles that women encounter on the path to scientific careers, Marie Curie established the first Radium Institute (Institut du Radium, now the Institut Curie) in Paris in 1909 and also initiated the Radium Institute in Poland in 1923 during the celebration of the 25th anniversary of the discovery of radium. These institutes

M. -H. Chiu, P. J. Gilmer, and D. F. Treagust (Eds.), Celebrating the 100th Anniversary
of Madame Marie Sklodowska Curie's Nobel Prize in Chemistry. 1–6.

supported both female and male students in their pursuit of science education and science-related careers. Despite Marie Curie, along with a few other female scientists, being sparsely sprinkled throughout contemporary science textbooks and historical accounts, the manner in which the abilities and accomplishments of female scientists are portrayed differs from how these same elements are portrayed for male scientists. When mentioned, the female scientist is too often characterized as hard working and as achieving her results solely because of the sheer number of repeated trials she made, while male scientists are credited with being creative thinkers and systematic researchers. We hope this work will challenge these stereotypes and demonstrate that female scientists' brilliance and creativity have advanced our understanding in a number of science domains.

In December 2008, the United Nations declared 2011 as the International Year of Chemistry (IYC) and placed the International Union of Pure and Applied Chemistry (IUPAC) and the United Nations Educational, Scientific, and Cultural Organization (UNESCO) at the helm of the event. The IYC–2011 aims to increase the public's appreciation of chemistry, encourage young people's interest in chemistry, generate enthusiasm for the creative future of chemistry, enhance international cooperation on information sources for activities in chemistry, and emphasize the importance of chemistry in sustaining natural resources throughout the world (IYC–2011, 2011). Marie Curie seemed a most fitting model for the book because 2011 marked the 100th anniversary of her Nobel Prize in Chemistry.

THREE BOOK SECTIONS AND CHAPTERS

This book is a companion to the IYC–2011 celebration. The eleven chapters are organized into three sections: Section 1: Marie Curie's Impact on Science and Society, Section 2: Women Chemists in the Past Two Centuries, and Section 3: Policy Implications.

The authors invited to contribute to this book were asked to orient their chapter around a particular aspect of Marie Curie's life such as the ethical aspects of her research, women's role in research or her influence on the image of chemists. As a consequence we have 11 very different chapters celebrating Marie Curie's life but, almost by necessity, there is overlap between chapters when referring to the same historical events. As editors, the authors had freedom to write as they wished and we did not attempt to prevent this overlap.

Section 1: Marie Curie's Impact on Science and Society

In the first section, Marie Curie's Impact on Science and Society, all four chapters shed light on Marie Curie's life and discuss the impact of her research from a number of different perspectives. Chapter 1 concerns Marie Curie and science education, co-authored by Chiu and Wang. Their chapter draws upon the critical events of Marie Curie's life describing her creative contributions to both research and her role in inspiring young women to pursue science careers. Chiu and Wang highlight Marie and Pierre Curie's gift to the world of giving up their patent rights associated with the production of radium. This unselfish decision to abandon the patent rights captured the world's attention and was received with high respect across the globe. The entire Curie family is unique and holds a special place in the history of science. However, the topic of Marie Curie as science educator or as subject of textbooks might offer an innovative angle for the Centennial. In Chapter 2, Gilmer provides insightful perspectives on Irène Joliot-Curie, the daughter of Nobel laureates in Physics—Marie and Pierre Curie, and of Nobel laureate in Chemistry—Marie Curie. In 1935 Irène also received the Nobel Prize in Chemistry, 24 years after her mother, and jointly with her husband, Frédéric Joliot-Curie. In this chapter, Gilmer describes Irène's personal life, her scientific achievement, and also her political involvements during her life. From her earliest days, Irène's parents and parental grandfather influenced her learning of science and her scientific orientation. In Chapter 3, Des Jardins elaborates on the visits of Madame Curie to the United States, via the help of Marie Mattingly Meloney (known as Missy Meloney). The public relations blitz surrounding Marie's visit to America influenced both men and women's perceptions of women scientists, even to this day. In the public relations surrounding her trip, Marie was painted in domestic terms whose science was maternally motivated to help rid the world of cancer. The ultimate paradox for a woman is she needs to look maternal, but then she looks incompetent in science—which Des Jardins dubs '*the Marie Curie complex*'. In Chapter 4, Catherine Milne delves into the ethics related to Marie Curie's research findings, the role that ethics play in scientific research and the existing ideologies that frame ethics associated with the practice and outcomes of scientific research. Of particular importance was Curie's desire, by not taking out patents, to ensure the longevity of research associated with the chemistry, physics, and biomedical applications of radium. With this decision, Curie's research provides a context for considering the nature and role of ethics in scientific and chemical research.

Section 2: Women Chemists in the Past Two Centuries

The second section with four chapters takes readers on a journey through the life and times of significant female scientists. The first two chapters in this section attend more to the scientific work of women scientists while the second two chapters deal more with the influence on public education by women scientists and science educators. In Chapter 5, Ogilvie draws our attention to the barriers to women's success in science, barriers that continued throughout the 19th and early 20th centuries. Ogilvie claims that two strategies existed that were accepted by male scientists and were normally used by women scientists who hoped to pursue a scientific career. The first strategy was to become involved in those scientific fields—so-called *women's work*—that men did not care to pursue—such as radioactivity. The second strategy was for women to collaborate with a spouse in order to enter the sciences. However, in the latter case, women scientists' contributions have been difficult or even impossible to ascertain and is contentious In Chapter 6, Mamlok-Naaman, Blonder, and Dori examine the work of five women scientists (four with Nobel Prizes in Chemistry, with the fifth famous for developing a medical drug) and highlight their roles in changing the face of science over the last 100 years. They propose women could create social networking groups in order to assist themselves with becoming accepted into the science community and forming an outlet for collaboration and informal mentorship. In Chapter 7, Gilbert focuses on the role of women chemists in the evolution of public education about chemistry and describes the nature of the contributions made by prominent women chemists and Nobel laureates in Chemistry—Marie Curie, Irène Joliot-Curie, and Dorothy Crowfoot Hodgkin—to 'chemistry and the public'. Gilbert claims that the importance of equity demands that an access to careers in chemistry be gender-neutral. However, for women, the challenge is to draw a balance between the commitments of home and research as well as working in a male-dominated environment. Gilbert points out that avenues of promoting 'green chemistry' should attract positive engagement and awareness by a public that includes both women and men. Finally in Chapter 8, Palmer discusses some of the reasons why women scientists and science authors have been generally overlooked and provides a detailed account of the productivity and influences of an early, largely unrecognized science textbook author, Mary Amelia Swift. Palmer points out that Swift's work should be given more recognition than it is in current biographies because of her books' usefulness and popularity for younger children in understanding science.

Section 3: Policy Implications

The third and final section with three chapters examines how policies influence female students to enter the field of science. In Chapter 9, Hussenius and Scantlebury discuss how images of chemists have changed very slowly over time. They present a wide range of perceptions of chemists from witches, alchemists, poisoners, to scientists that showed an evolutionary path gradually moving toward a positive image of chemists/scientists. However, the images of chemists/scientists are still dominated by men, including the images and text in school chemistry books. Also, studies on students' attitudes towards chemistry reveal significant differences in liking chemistry, with males preferring to study chemistry more often than females. Needless to say, this phenomenon is universal. In Chapter 10, Pnina Abir-Am raises the issue of how scientific societies often fail—intentionally or unintentionally—to celebrate women scientists' accomplishments, particularly in this year of the centennial of Marie Curie's Nobel Prize in Chemistry. Abir-Am points out that in the history of science, scientists and scholars often refer to the scientific work of Marie Curie with feminine qualities rather than her scientific accomplishments. In this manner, Marie Curie and other women scientists and their *female topics* are relegated to the margins of both science and its commemorative practices. Finally in Chapter 11, Southerland and Bahbah comment that while women have made tremendous progress in terms of their participation in science over the past century, their continued underrepresentation in science, technology, engineering, and mathematics fields is still perplexing. They suggest that an accountability system (i.e., alignment of standards, assessment and professional development) might provide useful information to inform instruction for supporting females in becoming scientists. These three chapters frame a wide scope of actions that we, as science educators, could take to change the trend and stereotypes of female scientists and provide more opportunities for females in scientific practice.

OUR GOALS FOR THIS BOOK

Our hope is that this book will positively influence young women's minds and decisions they make in learning of chemistry/science like Marie Curie's biography. But we do hope this book opens an avenue for young women to explore the possibility of being a scientist, or at least to appreciate chemistry as a human enterprise that has its merit in contributing to sustainability in our world. Also we hope that both men and women will realize that women are fully competent and capable of conducting creative and fascinating scientific research.

In sum, we thank all of the authors who contributed to this work and supported the celebration of the 100th Anniversary of Madame Marie Sklodowska Curie's Nobel Prize in Chemistry. We thank Dr. Armond Cognetta who provided us with his original copy of the caricature of Marie and Pierre Curie that is on the cover of our book, from the December 22, 1904 issue of Vanity Fair. We would also like to express our appreciation to Sense Publishers who joined us in marketing this book during the International Year of Chemistry-2011. In particular, Mei-Hung Chiu wants to express her appreciation to Penny Gilmer and David Treagust who have been supportive to serve as co-editors of this book with her.

Finally, we hope this book ignites people's interest in chemistry across the globe, and begins in some small way to validate the significant scientific sacrifices and contributions of women who prove science is indeed *women's work.*

REFERENCES

Hill, C., Corbett, C., & St. Rose, A. (2010). *Why so few? Women in science, technology, engineering and mathematics.* Washington, DC: American Association for University Women.

International Year of Chemistry—2011 (IYC–2011). Retrieved from http://www.chemistry2011.org/

National Center for Institute for Education Statistics, Institute of Education Sciences (2009). Retrieved from http://nces.ed.gov/fastfacts/display.asp?id=98

Mei-Hung Chiu
Professor
Graduate Institute of Science Education
National Taiwan Normal University
mhchiu@ntnu.edu.tw

MEI-HUNG CHIU, PENNY J. GILMER, AND DAVID F. TREAGUST

Penny J. Gilmer
Professor Emerita
Department of Chemistry and Biochemistry
Florida State University
gilmer@chem.fsu.edu

David F. Treagust
Professor
Science and Mathematics Education Centre
Curtin University
d.treagust@curtin.edu.au

SECTION 1: MARIE CURIE'S IMPACT ON SCIENCE AND SOCIETY

MEI-HUNG CHIU AND NADIA Y. WANG

1. MARIE CURIE AND SCIENCE EDUCATION

Nothing in life is to be feared, it is only to be understood. Now is the time to understand more, so that we may fear less. (Marie Curie, cited in Langevin-Joliot, 2011, p. 5)

INTRODUCTION

It is not a surprise that when one is asked to think of a woman scientist, Marie Curie often comes to mind (Ogilvie, 2004). Not only was she a female scientist but also her scientific accomplishments made her as famous as any scientist, male or female, past or present. Marie Curie received her first Nobel Award in Physics with Henri Becquerel and Pierre Curie in 1903, only three years after the inauguration of the Nobel Award. Eight years later, she received her second Nobel, a solo award in Chemistry. When Marie Curie's daughter, Irène Joliot-Curie, was awarded the Nobel Prize for Chemistry in 1935 with her husband, Frédéric Joliot-Curie for the discovery of artificial radioactivity, the two women became the first and only mother-daughter Nobel Prize awardees in the history of science.[1] Marie Curie's generosity in relinquishing the patents she held for producing radium brought her admiration even from outside of the scientific community. In her lifetime she received 15 gold medals, 19 degrees, and enormous honors from all over the world. Years after her death in 1934 Marie Curie was the first woman, for her own accomplishments in science, laid to rest under the famous dome of the Pantheon in Paris in 1995.

One hundred years has passed since Marie Curie received her Nobel Prize in Chemistry but people still remember her as an influential scientist and not just as a female chemist. Being a woman working in a discipline that had been dominated by men for centuries, she broke many barriers and showed her creativity, intelligence, and persistence to be equal to that of any man. Marie Curie's scientific achievements provided evidence that gender did not confine one's interests and abilities, and that science must be made accessible to men and women. Her beliefs and achievements have inspired many students and scientists to devote their lives to scientific research. Marie Curie's professional accomplishments and her personal struggles continue to impact students across the globe. In this chapter, we highlight Marie Curie's influence on science education from different perspectives (e.g., philosophical, pedagogical, historical, etc.).

M.-H. Chiu, P. J. Gilmer, and D. F. Treagust (Eds.), Celebrating the 100th Anniversary of Madame Marie Sklodowska Curie's Nobel Prize in Chemistry. 9–39.

MARIE CURIE AND HER LIFE

There are countless records and commentaries that discuss Marie Sklodowska Curie's life and contributions to science and humanity. This chapter could hardly cover all her achievements in science, her influences on the field of radioactivity, as well as her relationships with other scientists, her students, and her family. In this section, we will highlight several relevant events that shaped Marie Curie's life. In the appendix, we summarize the major events during her life.

Marie Curie's Childhood and Education

Marie Sklodowska was born on November 7, 1867, in Warsaw, Poland, which at the time was ruled by Russia. Marie's parents were Vladislav Sklodowski[2] and Bronislawa Sklodowska. Mr. Sklodowski was a professor and vice-president in a boys school where he taught physics and mathematics. Mrs. Sklodowska was a principal at a private primary girls school in Warsaw. Marie was first sent to school at the age of 10. At the time she was the youngest student in the class but she excelled and showed promise even at this young age. One time the Russian supervisor visited Marie's school to monitor that the Polish schools were teaching in Russian. Marie, who had memorized all the names of the Russian emperors, and who spoke Russian with a St. Petersburg accent,[3] dazzled the supervisor. This was a conflicting experience for Marie who craved learning, but did not want to forsake her Polish heritage.

Figure 1. Portrait of Marie Curie as a young woman.

In the Sklodowski family, all four children did well at school; three of them received gold medals at their graduation ceremonies and the other received a silver medal. However, no matter how much the Sklodowska girls wanted to pursue higher education at the University of Warsaw, the university's policy restricted female students. Instead, Marie and her sister, Bronya, tutored students around the city. In Poland, Marie Curie realized that few of the neighborhood children could read. She became determined to change this and in 1886 Marie held a small class to teach the local children how to read and write. With a merciful heart and patriotic pride, Marie sought to expand the right to learn for all people everywhere.

There were two additional events in Marie Curie's education that deserve mention. One was that after being a governess for five years, Marie joined the Floating University[4] at which 1000 female students obtained an academic education despite a ban by the Russian authorities (Friedrich & Remane, 2011, p. 4754; Curie, 1937, p. 53), to study the sciences and satisfy her curiosity and passion. Marie Curie once mentioned that she developed her interest and experimental work during her time at the Floating University. The other was that Marie's cousin, Josef Boguski, was educated in St. Petersburg under the great Russian scientist Dmitri Mendeleev. Boguska also worked as a laboratory assistant for Mendeleev, the father of the periodic table (Ham, 2002–2003, p. 33; Serri, 2007). With this special connection, when Marie became famous in science, she wrote to Boguska who forwarded her letters to Mendeleev. Mendeleev's ideas about undiscovered elements intrigued Marie and later played an important role in guiding her work.

Figure 2. The Floating University in Warsaw
(with the permission from Prof. Dr. Christoph Friedrich).

Marie Curie and Her Scientific Journey

Marie never gave up her dream of enrolling in a university and she eventually devised a plan where she and her sister could travel to Paris and study there. This would be a turning point in Marie's life.

In 1893, at the Sorbonne in Paris with Mlle Dydynska's help, Marie was granted the Alexandrovitch Scholarship for six hundred rubles that was designed for students to pursue their efforts abroad. Marie Curie returned the scholarship some years later when she had saved the amount of the scholarship. Marie Curie initially accepted the scholarship "as testimony of confidence in her, a debt of honor" (Curie, 1937, p. 116) and later returned the funds because she believed the scholarship would help another poor young Polish students to go abroad. In this 1893, Marie passed her first master's examination, which was in physics, and of course did superior work. Marie got the highest grade on the examination. As a result, Marie received a scholarship that enabled her to study further and she received her second master's degree in mathematics. This poem written by Marie describes her early days in Paris.

Ah! How harshly the youth of the student passes,

While all around her, with passions ever fresh,

Other youths search eagerly easy pleasures!

And yet in solitude

She lives, obscure and blessed,

For in her cell she finds the ardor

That makes her heart immense.

But the blessed time is effaced.

She must leave the land of Science

To go out and struggle for her bread

On the grey roads of life.

Often and often then, her weary spirit

Returns beneath the roofs

To the corner ever dear to her heart

Where silent labor dwelled

And where a world of memory has rested

(Marie Curie, cited in Curie, 1937, p. 117)

During her studies in Paris, Marie met her future husband, Pierre Curie, in 1894. The love story between Marie and Pierre began over their desire to establish a laboratory for their work. Marie had wanted to have a place to conduct experiments and a mutual friend introduced Marie to Pierre who was also looking for laboratory space. In Pierre's diary he wrote that during their time together in the laboratory, they discussed their work and their common interest in research, they understood each other and in time a love developed between the two. Before Pierre met Marie, he did not believe in love; in his words, women only distracted men from their work. Once, he said women are the enemy of science and ... "women of genius are rare..." (Curie, 1937, p. 120). This bias disappeared soon after meeting Marie. Marie was a smart, elegant, and hard-working student. During the time they were in each other's lives, Pierre wrote love letters to Marie whenever they were separated. After Marie's initial hesitation and Pierre's insistence, in the summer of 1895, they married, and had a honeymoon bicycling in the countryside. Both of them loved Mother Nature so they had beautiful memories of rural areas. Later in Marie Curie's life, she displayed passion for gardening, hiking and swimming.

Figure 3. Wedding photo of Pierre and Marie Curie, 1895.
Copyright © Association Curie Joliot-Curie (from nobelprize.org).

In 1897–98, Pierre stopped his own research on the properties of crystals to work full time with Marie on her research into radioactivity (Mould, 1998, p. 1233). Toward the end of 1897, Marie had a shed laboratory where she and Pierre would discover new elements. The shed laboratory used to be a storage site for cadavers for medical students. Before having the shed laboratory, Marie Curie conducted her experiments on the ground floor of the school, where the temperature was extremely hot in the summer and freezing cold in the winter. But the Curies' efforts and sacrifices were not in vain. In July 1898, they submitted the newly found element for analysis and the outcome proved to be a new radioactive element, which Marie named polonium for her native country of Poland. On December 26, the Curies with Gustave Bémont identified another now famous radioactive element, radium. They published their findings in the *Proceedings for the Academy of Science* and announced the existence of a second new element found in pitchblende. In the announcement, they stated the following:

> The various reasons we have just enumerated lead [led] us to believe that the new radioactive substance contains a new element to [for] which we propose to give the name of RADIUM.

The new radioactive substance certainly contains a very strong proportion of barium; in spite of that its radioactivity is considerable. The radioactivity of radium therefore must be enormous. (Curie, 1937, p. 164)

Figure 4. Shed laboratory where the Curies discovered their new elements.

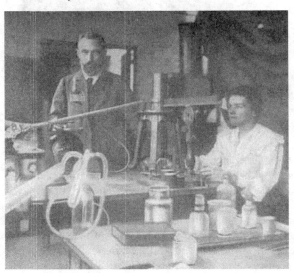

Figures 5. Pierre and Marie Curie in the "hangar" at l'Ecole de physique et chimie industrielles in Paris, France, where they made their discovery (photo taken 1898.) Copyright © Association Curie Joliot-Curie (from nobelprize.org).

In this same year, the couple welcomed their first daughter, Irène, who would go on to earn her own Nobel Prize with her husband Frédéric Joliot-Curie in 1935. In 1904 Pierre and Marie welcomed a second daughter, Eve, whose husband Henry R. Labouisse would receive the Nobel Peace Prize in 1965. What a legendary family that Pierre and Marie Curie created! (See Figure 6 for the Curies' family tree.)

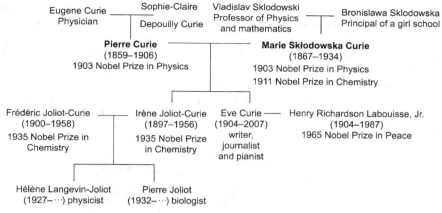

Figure 6. Curies' family tree.

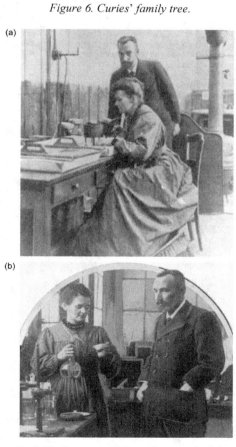

Figures 7a & 7b. Pierre and Marie Curie in the laboratory.

After discovering the new radioactive elements, the Curies decided to dedicate themselves to this field and its role in the treatment of cancer patients. Through their generosity, the Curies provided their raw material to all those who were also working with these elements and continued with their own research. The two worked tirelessly even endangering their own lives in the name of science. Pierre applied the element, radium, to his own skin to see the effect. His skin burned red, but strangely did not cause him pain. Scientists at that time did not know the harmful effects that radioactivity caused. The ability of radium to kill cancer cells would soon be established.

Figure 8. Marie Curie and her daughters Eve and Irène sitting on a bench in the garden (1908). Copyright © Association Curie Joliot-Curie (from nobelprize.org).

Figure 9. Marie Curie and four of her students. (Photo taken between 1910 and 1914.) Source: US Library of Congress (from nobelprize.org).

Marie chose the topic of radioactive substances for her doctorate in 1897 but she did not receive her doctorate for research on radioactive substances until 1903. In 1898, the Curies published their stunning research. People saw the usefulness of radioactivity of which the Curie's work was at the center. In 1901, the Curies had mentioned that lead-plate could defend against the radiation from radium but they never really put this safety measure into practice. In 1903,[5] along with Becquerel, the Curies received the most prestigious award—the Nobel Prize in Physics—in recognition of their contributions to science and the world. However, while Pierre and Marie did not attend the Nobel Award ceremony in 1903 due to their poor health, Pierre did deliver a Nobel Lecture on June 6, 1905.

One of Marie Curie's biographers, Susan Quinn once commented in an interview:

> Pierre was very much an outsider, he did not play the game... Marie wanted results, she wanted recognition. Pierre once said that it does not matter who gets the credits as long as the discovery is made. She pushed Pierre to finish things and to follow through, for example, the isolation of radium. Their daughter said that, left to Pierre, he would not have bothered about it. (Bragg, 1998, p. 251)

Although the Curies presented their research as a collaboration between equal partners, to outsiders Marie was often relegated to the status of assistant simply because she was a woman.[6] As a result, Pierre went to great lengths to publicly recognize Marie's contribution to their joint experiments and to support her independence in designing and carrying out her own research. The following three events reveal his love and respect for Marie's work. First, Pierre thought it important for Marie alone to sign the note after measuring radiation using a quartz piezoelectroscope, designed by Pierre and his brother, to investigate minerals and to compare the activity of natural chalcolite to the artificial one. Second, the nomination for the Nobel Prize in 1903 did not initially include Marie Curie's name. Pierre protested and Marie was added as a prize recipient. In his letter replying to the Swedish Academy of Sciences, Pierre wrote, "If it is true that one is seriously thinking about me, I very much wish to be considered together with Madame Curie with respect to our research on radioactive bodies.... Don't you think it would be more satisfying, from an artistic point of view, if we were to be associated in this manner?" (Quinn, 1995, p. 189). This lyric and artistic analogy not only revealed the deep love of Pierre for Marie, but it also showed his respect for and recognition of Marie's contribution to their work in radioactivity. Finally, in Pierre's Nobel Lecture,[7] he mentioned Marie Curie's name no less than 12 times to acknowledge her contribution to the properties of the radioactive substances and those of radium. Pierre explicitly stated that "Its [radium's] atomic weight as determined by Mme. Curie is 225" to further recognize her contribution in the area of radioactivity research.

Marie Curie and Her New Life

After Pierre's death, Marie recalled that Pierre had once said, "Whatever happens, even if one has to go on like a body without a soul, one must work just the same..." (Curie, 1937, p. 254). Marie lived by these words especially during her later life. Pierre was a great man. He gave all he had to science, and encouraged Marie to pursue her own dream. In their marriage, Pierre was the person to cheer Marie when they struggled with their experiments. Both shared good moments in their lives as a couple and worked collaboratively on their research as colleagues. Pierre's personality made Marie more approachable and helped her to be better understood by other colleagues. The loss of Pierre in 1906 from a carriage accident was devastating for Marie—both personally and professionally.

There was a long period during which Marie felt her life had faded away after Pierre's death. However, the world moved on. When the new semester began, Marie was asked to conduct the class that Pierre had left behind. In her diary, she wrote:

> I am offered the post of successor to you, my Pierre: your course and the direction of your laboratory. I have accepted. I don't know whether this is good or bad. You often told me you would have liked me to give a course at the Sorbonne. And I would like at least to make an effort to continue your work. Sometimes it seems to me that this is how it will be most easy for me to live, and at other times it seems to me that I am mad to attempt it. (Curie, 1937, p. 254)

This was the first time that a position in French higher education had been given to a woman. Her classes were always filled with students. People were eager to know what this Nobel Prize-winning scientist had to say. Marie began her first class from where Pierre had left off by saying,

> When one considers the progress that has been made in physics in the past ten years, one is surprised at the advance that has taken place in our ideas concerning electricity and matter..." (cited in Curie, 1937, p. 259)

Of course, she returned with new zeal to her laboratory as well.

To prove that she had the competence to work by herself, Marie worked harder than ever and tried to accomplish alone what she and Pierre had hoped to accomplish together. Her solo work on radioactivity brought her a second Nobel Prize in Chemistry in 1911.

Figure 10. Marie Curie's 1911 Nobel Prize certificate Insert Figure 10.

Even with the international fame from two Nobel Prizes, Marie Curie was still lacking research funds, equipment, and radium for her experiments partly because of her prior decision not to apply for patents. Her trip to the US in 1921, arranged by Missy Meloney, an American editor of a popular woman's magazine, made a significant impression on Marie. Marie Curie (1923b) wrote:

> I got back to France with a feeling of gratitude for the precious gift of the American women, and with a feeling of affection for their great country tied with ours by mutual sympathy which gives confidence for a peaceful future for humanity. (p. 242)

On this trip, not only did Marie Curie receive one gram of radium (valued at more than $100,000 at the time), mainly paid by donors in the US, but she also had extraordinary opportunities to visit women's colleges and to meet with doctors and physiologists. Scientists researching cancer treatments met with Marie and discussed the effects of radium. In 1929, Marie took her second trip to the US. This time she received $50,000 to continue her research and met with US President Hoover who expressed his great appreciation for her service to humanity. In addition, Marie purchased a gram of radium for the research institute she was establishing in Poland.

In 1922, in a rebuke to the Académie des sciences (The French Academy of Sciences), which had rejected Marie's membership application 11 years prior,[8] the Académie de médecine made Marie Curie the first Frenchwoman to enter the Institute in recognition of the role of radium in cancer therapy. Her brother-in-law, Jacques Curie, wrote to Marie: "The Académie des Sciences would learn its lesson and call you now to its bosom" (Quinn, 1995, pp. 421–422).

In 1932, Marie took what would be her last trip to Poland and officially opened the Radium Institute of Warsaw. Shortly thereafter, in 1934, she died. "Mme Curie can be counted among the eventual victims of the radioactive bodies which she and her husband discovered," Professor Regaud wrote (Curie, 1937, p. 384). "The disease was an aplastic pernicious anemia of rapid, feverish development. The bone marrow did not react, probably because it had been injured by a long accumulation of radiations," reported by Dr. Tobé (Curie, 1937, p. 384), the director of the Sancellemoz sanatorium in the Haute-Savoie, where she had been hospitalized a few days beforehand. Long term exposure to radiation led to the premature death of the learned woman scientist of the time.

MARIE CURIE AND SCIENTIFIC INQUIRY

I am among those who think that science has great beauty...A scientist in his laboratory is not a mere technician: he is also a child placed before natural phenomena which impress him like a fairy tale. We would not allow it to be believed that all scientific progress can be reduced to mechanisms, machines, gearings, even though such machinery also has its own beauty.

Neither do I believe that the spirit of adventure runs any risk of disappearing in our world. If I see anything vital around me, it is precisely that spirit of adventure, which seems indestructible and is akin to curiosity.... (Marie Curie, cited in Curie, 1937, p. 341)

Pierre and Marie worked together closely. As already mentioned earlier in this chapter, by April 1898, the Curies announced their discovery of one of two new elements, the polonium. Curie's associate, Gustave Bémont, described additional findings eight months later. The first described barium and its compounds as not ordinarily radioactive. They wrote, "Radioactivity appears to be an atomic property...the radioactivity of our substance, not being due to barium, must be attributed to another element" (Ham, 2002–2003, p. 41). The second concluded, "When these chlorides are dissolved in water and partially precipitated by alcohol, the part precipitated is much more [radio]active than the part remaining in solution...chlorides had an activity 900 times greater than that of uranium...these facts can be explained by the presence of a radioactive element whose chloride would be less soluble in alcohol and water than that of barium" (Ham, 2002–2003, p. 41). Third, the researchers declared, Demarcay has found one line in the spectrum which does not seem due to any known element because "the intensity of this line increases, then, at the same time as the radioactivity; that, we think, is a very serious reason for attributing it to the radioactive part of our substance" (Ham, 2002–2003, p. 41). These various forms of evidence led the Curies to believe in the existence of new radioactive element, which they proposed to give the name of radium.

In 1899 and 1900, Marie wrote two papers alone updating her effort to isolate radium, and Pierre wrote one alone on the effect of a magnetic field on radium emissions (Quinn, 1995). Marie and Pierre jointly authored three papers, including groundbreaking reports on induced radioactivity and on the electric charge of certain radium rays (Quinn, 1995, p. 158). The "induced" radioactivity was from the formation of radon, the first of the decay products of radium, as radon was also radioactive with its own half-life, and from other decay products resulting from radon's decay. One could not present one's work at the Academy unless one was a member of the Academy. Pierre and Marie were fortunate to be asked to compile their radioactivity studies and present their research in front of a gathering of scientists from all over the world (Quinn, 1995, p. 158). This action proved to be an important event that raised their stature within the international scientific community.

In the couple's ongoing efforts to ensure Marie received equal recognition for their discoveries, they relied upon the plural, "we" in their professional writings.

When the Curies were constrained by fact to distinguish between their parts, they employed this moving locution:

> Certain minerals containing uranium and thorium (pitchblende, chalcolite, uranite) are very active from the point of view of the emission of Becquerel rays. In a preceding communication, *one of us* [emphasis added] showed that their activity was even greater than that of uranium and thorium, and stated the opinion that this effect was due to some other very active substance contained in small quantity in these minerals. (Pierre and Marie Curie: *Proceedings of the Academy of Science*, July 18, 1898, cited in Curie, 1937, p. 160)

With all these achievements, the next most difficult challenge was how to isolate this minute quantity of intimately mixed matters, polonium and radium. Marie naïvely expected the radium content of pitchblende to be one per cent, but the radiation of the new elements was so powerful that a tiny quantity of radium easily observed and measured. The pressure to conduct additional research became heavier and heavier because of the quick development of radioactivity in Europe. Pierre was about to abandon this repetitive work of treating tons and tons of pitchblende residues although it did not mean that he would give up the dream of radium and radioactivity. However, "Marie wanted to isolate radium and she would isolate it" (Curie, 1937, p. 173). In 1902, almost four years after Marie announced the probable existence of radium, she succeeded in preparing a decigram of pure radium, and made a first determination of the atomic mass of the new substance, which was 225. As Eve stated:

> The incredulous chemists—of whom there were still a few—could only bow before the facts, before the superhuman obstinacy of a woman.

> Radium officially existed. (Curie, 1937, p. 175)

Not only did the radium exist, but it also gave off spontaneous luminosity with its phosphorescent bluish outlines in the night. Marie once wrote: "This luminosity cannot be seen by daylight but it can be easily seen in a half darkness. The light emitted can be strong enough to read by, using a little of the product for light in darkness... " (Curie, 1937, p. 196). The results from Marie's experiments opened a completely new avenue for the theories and applications of radioactivity.

Marie Curie's life was devoted to scientific endeavors; her passion, persistence, and intellect in science could be seen in her notebooks.

Sometimes my courage fails me and I think I ought to stop working, live in the country and devote myself to gardening. But I am held by a thousand bonds, and I don't know when I shall be able to arrange things otherwise. *Nor do I know whether, even by writing scientific books, I could live without the laboratory.* (Curie, 1937, p. 373)

Also, from Marie's lectures, it is clear that her teaching style relied upon experimental demonstration at the Sorbonne because she believed scientific concepts should be taught in a hands-on manner.

I [Marie] am among those who think that science has great beauty [she told her interlocutors]. A scientist in his laboratory is not only a technician: he is also a child placed before natural phenomena which impress him like a fairy tale. We should not allow it to be believed that all scientific progress can be reduced to mechanisms, machines, gearings, even though such machinery also has its own beauty.

Neither do I believe that the spirit of adventure runs any risk of disappearing in our world. If I see anything vital around me, it is precisely that spirit of adventure, which seems indestructible and is akin to curiosity... (Curie, 1937, p. 341)

All my mind was centred on my studies. I divided my time between courses, experimental work and study in the library. In the evening I worked in my room, sometimes very late into the night. All that I saw and learned that was new delighted me, it was like a new world opened to me, the world of science which I was at last permitted to know. (cited in Bragg, 1998, p. 249)

Before discussing Marie scientific achievement, we would like to introduce some background on Pierre Curie. Pierre was born on May 15, 1859, a second son of Dr. Eugéne Curie and Sophie-Claire Depouilly Curie. Pierre had informal education mainly from his father and a private tutor because Dr. Curie believed Pierre was brilliant yet different in his learning from others. Pierre went to the university at age 16 and received his master's degree at age 18. In 1880, Pierre and his brother, Jacques, studied the piezoelectric effect and discovered the quartz piezoelectroscope (also called the electrometer), which can accurately measure very tiny electrical currents[9] (Ham, 2002–2003, p. 34).

On March 18, 1898, as recounted by Marie, "Pierre abandoned his work on crystals (provisionally, he thought) to join me in the research" (Quinn, 1995, p. 148).[10] This perfect combination afforded them the skill necessary to uncover the new elements.

Wisdom on Facing Anomaly in Science

Marie's discovery of radioactivity should not be described as an accident in the history of science. Chinn and Brewer (1993) categorize seven distinct responses to anomalous data. They include a) ignore the anomalous data, b) reject the data, c) exclude the data from the domain of theory A, d) hold the data in abeyance, e) reinterpret the data while retaining theory A, f) reinterpret the data and make peripheral changes to theory A, and g) accept the data and change the theories. In Marie's case, the anomalies played an important role in her discovery of new elements that brought her the two Nobel Prizes in science. Becquerel was concerned about uranium salts that might emit X-rays when exposed to sunlight. In 1896, while studying properties of fluorescent materials, Becquerel wrapped some photographic plates in his black cloth, covered it with aluminum foil, and then placed the crystals of potassium uranyl sulphate on top of the aluminum. Even though it was not a sunny day, he still found the salts emitted rays on the photographic plate (Ham, 2002–2003, p. 36; Curie, 1937, p.196). With this observation, Becquerel discovered the spontaneous emission of radiation without exposure to light, which Marie Curie interpreted later as radioactivity. Becquerel did not show any interest in finding what caused this phenomenon and put it aside in the laboratory. Becquerel's case was just like what Chinn and Brewer's category d) holding the data in abeyance. However, Marie decided to study it for her doctoral thesis. This was a crucial decision and would lead to her first Nobel Prize in Physics in 1903.

The approach Marie took was to see whether this property of "radiation" existed in the other known elements of the periodic table. She tested over and over again but nothing was found except uranium, which came from pitchblende and chalcolite from which the uranium was extracted. However, she found that pitchblende's electrical conductivity was four times greater than that of uranium and twice that of chalcolite. The question for Marie was why this occurred and which substance contributed to its occurrence. It is important to understand that pitchblende is a mixture of about 30 elements. In order to rule out the possibility of existing elements (by then there were 78 elements in the periodic table), Marie Curie had to do the experiments multiple times, 5677 times for crystallization from eight tons of pitchblende, spanning almost four years (Madame Curie (film), 1943, 1 hr: 22 min: 36 s). Originally, she hypothesized radium might be 1% of the pitchblende, at the end of almost four years, they found that "an enormous radioactivity of an order of magnitude 2 million times greater than that of uranium" (Curie, 1905) ! Without a passion for doing this research and a passion for finding the truth, how could anyone have worked so tirelessly, for so long, repeating the same experiments, and under such uncomfortable conditions?

Marie Curie and Creativity

In many cases, successful female scientists are described as hard working, diligent, patient, and pain-suffering persons, while the male scientists are described as creative and critical. The topic of "creativity" chosen for this section is to reveal that we have to admit working hard is not enough to make a great scientist if one does not have creativity in one's nature in pursuing scientific research. Therefore, in this section, we are pursuing Marie's creative side.

Being the first and only individual to receive two Nobel Awards in different areas of science, Marie Curie's intellectual aptitude was only enhanced by her creativity. Curie's perseverance helped her reach her potential as a scientific genius (Ogilvie, 2004, p. 143). Marie used novel methods to separate and purify the pitchblende. On March 18, 1894 Marie wrote to her brother:

One never notices what has been done; one can only see what remains to be done, and if one didn't like the work it would be very discouraging... Life is not easy for any of us. But what of that? We must have perseverance and above all confidence in ourselves. We must believe that we are gifted for something, and that this thing, at whatever cost, must be attained. (Curie, 1937, p. 116)

According to a fellow scientist's observations,

Marie often sat before her laboratory apparatus, making measurements in the half darkness of an unheated room to avoid variations in temperature. The series of operations—opening the apparatus, starting the chronometer, lifting the mass, etc.—were carried out by Marie Curie with admirable discipline and harmony of movement. No pianist could accomplish what Marie Curie's hands accomplished with greater virtuosity. It was a perfect technique, which tended to reduce the coefficient of personal error to zero. (Curie, 1937, p. 373)

Not only did she require herself to be as precise as possible in her laboratory work, but she also passed her rigor of science onto future scientists. For instance, once she taught her apprentices, "Don't tell me you will clean it afterward, one must never dirty a table during an experiment" (Curie, 1937, p. 374).

Mayer (1999) identified two major defining features of creativity—originality and usefulness. From this perspective, Marie's research qualified as creativity in science research. Becquerel discovered uranium rays and had no clue what radioactivity was. Marie Curie chose this new phenomenon observed by Becquerel (i.e., uranium rays) at a time there was relatively little interest in the radiation of uranium. As Badash (1966) stated, "few scientists [of the late nineteenth century] thought radioactivity had much of a future" (cited in Pycior, 1997, p. 38). Marie formulated her distinctive approach to radioactivity (Pycior, 1997, 1989). First, she developed a technique for measuring the intensity of radiation. Second, she developed the hypothesis that radioactivity was an atomic property. Third, she found that the measurements produced an anomaly probably not restricted to two elements (uranium or thorium). Fourth, Marie made a bold hypothesis that there was a new (undiscovered) element in the pitchblende. The most important part was to conduct an experiment to prove that one of the three new elements (including polonium, radium, and thorium) was contained in pitchblende. Fifth, explanations for the experiment were needed. Finally, radium was successfully used to cure cancer in later days.[11] Her work "was instrumental in opening up most fruitful avenues of research in a previously untrodden field" (Pycior, 1997, p. 39). Marie

Curie's creative thinking led her to eventually make one of the most significant contributions to the area of radioactivity.

Marie Curie was both an experimental and theoretical scientist and believed to be the first in the primacy of ideas (Ham, 2002–2003, p. 36). Goldsmith (2004) stated that people tended not to remember her important contribution on measurement and on setting the international radium standard. She combined her knowledge in physics and chemistry to measure the quantity of radioactive substance. In this field, she is the best in the world. In 1904, the "American Century Magazine published an article by her, which leaves no room for doubt of her genius for hypothesis formation and her rigor for experimental proof" (Ham, 2002–2003, p. 36).

> This discovery of the phenomena of radioactivity adds a new group to the great number of invisible radiations now known, and once more we are forced to recognize how limited is our direct perception of the world which surrounds us, and how numerous and varied may be the phenomena which we pass without a suspicion of their existence until the day when a fortunate hazard reveals them... (*Century Magazine,* 1904, cited in Ham, pp. 36–37)

MARIE CURIE AND WOMEN IN SCIENCE

Marie Curie deeply believed that women and men were equal in their potential intellectual capabilities. (Langevin-Joliot, 2011, p. 5)

Women in Science

Before detailing Marie Curie's influences on women in science, we would like to draw attention to some contributions from females before 1900 that have not been well recognized in the history of science. According to Houlihan and Wotiz (1973), women perfumer-esses were the earliest chemists whose names were found on cuneiform tablets of ancient Mesopotamia dating back to about 2,000 B.C. However, in the following thousand years women had very little direct influence on the evolution of chemistry until the 17th century. Palmer (2011, in this volume, chapter 8) and Hussenius and Scantlebury (2011, in this volume, Chapter 10) discuss women in science education largely unrecognized for their achievements. Several historical events might shape our understanding of the evolution of chemistry. The following examples were drawn from Houlihan and Wotiz. For instance, in 1666 Marie Meurdrac published *La Chymie Charitable et Facile, en Faveur des Dames* (*Charitable and Easy Chemistry for Ladies*) which is probably the first chemistry book written by a woman in which she covered topics like laboratory operations and weights, separations, preparation of medicinals, metals, and the preservation and enhancement of the beauty of ladies.

In 1789, Marie Anne Pierrette Paulze (later referred to as the famous Madame Lavoisier) accomplished 13 illustrations for Antoine Lavoisier's book, *Traité de Chimie* (*Elementary Treatise of Chemistry*) in Paris. She also published Lavoisier's

Memoires de Chimie (Chemistry Essays) after the French revolutionists executed him in 1794. Few people knew that Madame Lavoisier gave her husband a great deal of assistance in his scientific work (i.e., Houlihan & Wotiz, 1973; Badilescu, 2001). For instance, she translated the work of many contemporary British chemists into French (Duveen, 1953). With all these accomplishments, it is evident that she had sufficient knowledge and experiences in chemical theories and experimental work and played an important role in Lavoisier's life in chemistry. However, many people considered her as merely an assistant to Lavoisier.

In addition, in 1805, Jane Marcet (wife of a distinguished Swiss physician and chemist who worked on several ideas with Berzelius) published (anonymously) a textbook entitled *"Conversation on Chemistry"* which was used in Great Britain and the US for 30 years. Another of her contributions was "her method of teaching chemistry to beginners through experimental demonstrations, a practice that was not yet accepted as a teaching method" (Houlihan & Wotiz, 1973, p. 363).

There were supporters of women engaging in science. For instance, the Braggs, William, H. Bragg and his son, William L. Bragg, welcomed gifted women into their research groups (Julian, 1990, as cited in Rayner-Canham & Rayner-Canham, 1996). Sir Gowland Hopkins, later Nobel Laureate in Physiology or Medicine in 1921, encouraged women researchers to join research groups conducting laboratory work and provided valuable moral support (Rayner-Canham & Rayner-Canham, 1996). Early supporters of women taking a more active role in the field of science included T. P. Smith:

> I shall now present you with the last and most pleasing revolution that has occurred in chemistry. Hitherto we have beheld this science entirely in the hands of *men*; we are now about to behold *women* assert their just, though too long neglected claims, of being participators in the pleasures arising from a knowledge of chemistry. (Smith, 1914, cited in Houlihan & Wotiz, 1973, p. 364)

In a recent report from the National Science Foundation (2011), the statistics for doctorate recipients in the physical sciences for males and females in 1979, 1989, 1999, and 2009 revealed that the ratios were 7.7:1, 4.4:1, 3.3:1, and 2.4:1, respectively. According to UNESCO statistics (2011), female tertiary graduates as percentages of all graduates in science in 1999 and 2008 were from the following countries: 41% and 36% for Australia, 45% and 47% for Finland (ranked as first in PISA), 31% and 44% for Germany, 24% and 26% for Japan, 42% and 37% for Korea, 20% and 37% for Taiwan (DGBAS, 2008, 2011), and 43% and 41% for the US, respectively. A relatively low percentage of women graduate from higher education in Asia compared to countries in Europe and the US. Efforts to promote female participation in the sciences is a continuing focus in education reform. Although the gender gap persists, an increasing tendency of females receiving higher degrees in the physical sciences is observed. Even with these achievements and contributions and the growing support for the participation of female scientists, obstacles and biases still exist. The evolution in science from a male-centered domain to one that is gender free is still ongoing today.[12]

This section could hardly cover the important topic of women in science. Related information can be found in the following sources: *Uneasy Careers and Intimate Lives: Women in Science, 1789–1979* (Abir-Am & Outram, 1989), *Creative Couples in the Sciences* (Pycior, 1996), *A Devotion to their Science: Pioneer Women of Radioactivity* (Rayner-Canham & Rayner-Canham, 1997), *Women in Chemistry: Their changing roles from alchemical times to the mid-twentieth century* (Rayner-Canham & Rayner-Canham, 2001), Ogilvie (Chapter 5 in this book), Mamlok-Naaman, Blonder, & Dori (Chapter 6 in this book), Gilbert (Chapter 7 in this book), Palmer (Chapter 8 in this book), and Hussenius and Scantlebury (Chapter 10 of this book) also provide more information on depictions of women in chemistry, in particular Marie Curie.

Marie Curie's Interest in Girls' Education and Challenges

Marie Curie taught science to women in a Normal School called Ecole Normale Supérieure de Jeunes Filles in Sèvres near Paris, and she said:

I became much interested in my work in the Normal School, and endeavoured to develop more fully the practical laboratory exercises of the pupils. These pupils were girls of about twenty years who had entered the school after severe examination and had still to work very seriously to meet the requirements that would enable them to be named professors in the lycées. All these young women worked with great eagerness, and it was a pleasure for me to direct their studies in physics. (Curie, 1923, p. 189)

Marie's father, M. Vladislav Skłodowski was a teacher of physics and mathematics and her mother also received a good education in a private school in Warsaw and then devoted herself to teaching, becoming a teacher and the director of the same institution (Curie, 1937, p. 6). Pierre's father, Eugéne Curie, was a physician who loved nature and physics. Coming from intellectual families, both Pierre and Marie Curie shared similar interests in science and family activities.

The following events reveal the value Marie placed on education. The first event, already mentioned earlier in this chapter, was to initiate a private tutoring school for her and other scientists' children. The Curies were passionate about educating young people. In Eve's book, she recorded there were many students who remembered the Curies and their novel way of instructing them. This might be one of the reasons why Irène did not attend regular school. Marie set up an experimental school and put Irène and other scientists' children into the laboratory instead. These children were taught directly from the professionals, who were Sorbonne professors. Pedagogy and music were emphasized as well as poetry and languages, and in particular, the scientific subjects. The second event occurred during World War I when Marie, including Irène, and a group of medical doctors trained hundreds of young women in radiological science. Over a two-year period, Marie provided a course on basic education in elementary mathematics, physics, and anatomy to 150 young women including nurses, maids, and even rich women, and then sent them to hospitals near the frontlines. Meanwhile, more than 200

X-ray cars were recruited by Marie and put into service in the battlefields. During the period of 1917–1918, 100,000 men were treated through these radiological posts (Ham, 2002–2003, p. 48). The third event was establishing Institutes to allow more women scientists to join scientific research.

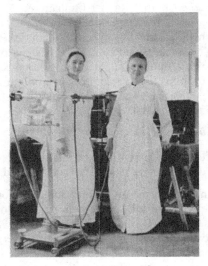

Figure 11. Marie Curie and her daughter Irène at the Hoogstade Hospital in Belgium, 1915. Radiographic equipment is installed. Copyright © Association Curie Joliot-Curie.

Figure 12. Marie Curie and The Little Curie.

Even well known scientists of Marie's generation dismissed female intelligence and wisdom and deemed women unfit to carry out scientific experiments. For instance, J. J. Thomson maintained for many years that radioactivity was nothing more than a simple physical or chemical phenomenon rather than a completely new field of science (Sinclair, 1988, cited in Rayner-Canham & Rayner-Canham, 1996). In his letter to *The Times* of London, a famous scientist of the day, Ernest

Rutherford, publicly questioned whether women should be admitted to the university with the same privileges as men (Rayner-Canham & Rayner-Canham, 1996). Francoise Balibar, Professor of Physics at Paris University, indicated his prejudice of females by saying, "It is complicated because they did not think of her [Marie Curie] as a thinker, but they did not think of her as a woman either. Because a woman must not think and a thinker must not be a woman" (Bragg, 1998, p. 250)!

With all the obstacles and prejudices incurred in that era and the following years, many female scientists consider Marie Curie a pioneer and role model for pursuing their careers in science. According to statistics from the Nobel Prize organization, the Nobel Prizes (including those in Economics) have only been awarded to women 41 times out of 776 (5.3%) between 1901 and 2010 (Nobelprize.org, 2010). Among them, there were only two women in physics, four in chemistry (4 out of 156 awardees in chemistry equals to 2.6%), and 10 for Physiology or Medicine. Marie also educated Irène to be a successful scientist who subsequently played an important role as a daughter and a collaborator in Curie's science world. Gilmer (2011 in this volume, chapter 2) focuses on Irène Joliot-Curie, Nobel laureate in Chemistry in 1935 with her husband, Frédéric Joliot, for discovering artificial radioactivity.

Figure 13. Marie and Irène Curie in the laboratory
(from nobelprize.com).

Marie Curie in Science Textbooks

It is not a surprise to see male scientists appear in science textbooks as exemplars for stimulating students to study science. In some cases, Marie Curie is presented as a pioneer for finding new elements and also as a role model in science. However,

Schiebinger (1987) studied science textbooks and found that women are depicted differentially compared to male scientists. Brush (1985, as cited in Milne, 1998) called this "the Marie Curie syndrome…in which the scientist, regardless of her abilities to be intuitive, imaginative, and creative, and a leader in her field, is presented as someone who painstakingly carried out tedious observational experimental work." Milne (1998), expanding on Murphy and Smoot's (1982) study, found emotional descriptions were linked to female scientists such as Marie Curie while logical and mathematical thinking were linked to male scientists such as Galileo.

Limited studies have been conducted in investigating the topic of this section, so comparisons of textbooks from different countries (e.g., Kahveci, 2010) and periods (e.g., Milne, 1998) are worthwhile being developed further.

MARIE'S VIEWS OF SCIENCE AS A HUMAN ENTERPRISE

We must not forget that when radium was discovered no one knew that it would prove useful in hospitals. The work was one of pure science. And this is a proof that scientific work must not be considered from the point of view of the direct usefulness of it. It must be done for itself, *for the beauty of science* [emphasis added], and then there is always the chance that *a scientific discovery may become like the radium a benefit for humanity* [emphasis added]. (Curie, 1921, unnumbered)

The price of radium is very high since it is found in minerals in very small quantities, and the profits of its manufacture have been great, as this substance is used to cure a number of diseases. So it is a fortune which we have sacrificed in renouncing the exploitation of our discovery, a fortune that could, after us, have gone to our children. But what is even more to be considered is the objection of many of our friends, who have argued, not without reason, that if we had guaranteed our rights, we could have had the financial means of founding a satisfactory Institute of Radium, without experiencing any of the difficulties that have been such a handicap to both of us, and are still a handicap to me. *Yet, I still believe that we have done right* [emphasis added]. (Curie, 1923b, pp. 226–227)

Marie believed passionately that science is necessary for the betterment of the world and sacrificed personally and financially in the name of research.

Humanity, surely, needs practical men who make the best of their work for the sake of their own interests, without forgetting the general interest. But it also needs dreamers, for whom the unselfish following of a purpose is so imperative that it becomes impossible for them to devote much attention to their own material benefit. No doubt it could be said that these idealists do not deserve riches since they do not have the desire for them. It seems, however, that a society well organized ought to assure to these workers the means for efficient labor, in a life from which material care is excluded so that this life may be freely devoted to the service of scientific research. (Curie, 1923b, p. 227)

During the last paragraph of his acceptance speech at the Nobel Prize ceremony in 1905 Pierre Curie said he believed that more good than evil could come from scientific discoveries.

It can even be thought that radium could become very dangerous in criminal hands, and here the question can be raised whether mankind benefits from knowing the secrets of Nature, whether it is ready to profit from it or whether this knowledge will not be harmful for it. The example of the discoveries of Nobel is characteristic, as powerful explosives have enabled man to do wonderful work. They are also a terrible means of destruction in the hands of great criminals who are leading the peoples towards war. I am one of those who believe with Nobel that mankind will derive more good than harm from the new discoveries. (Curie, 1905, p. 78)

Marie had contended, "in science we must be interested in things, not in persons" (Curie, 1937, p. 347). However, the years had taught her that the public, and even governments did not know how to be interested in things except through persons. Whether or not she wished to do so, she had to use her prestige to honor and enrich science—to "*dignify*" it, as the Americans said—and she allowed her own legend to be the voice for a cause that was dear to her (Curie, 1937).

It is easy to understand how important for me is the conviction that *our discovery is a blessing for humanity* [emphasis added] not only by its scientific importance but also because it permits the reduction of human suffering and treatment of a terrible disease. This is indeed a great reward for the years of our enormous effort (Marie Curie, as cited in Mould, 1989, p. 1236).

(a)   (b)

14a & 14b (from nobelprize.com)

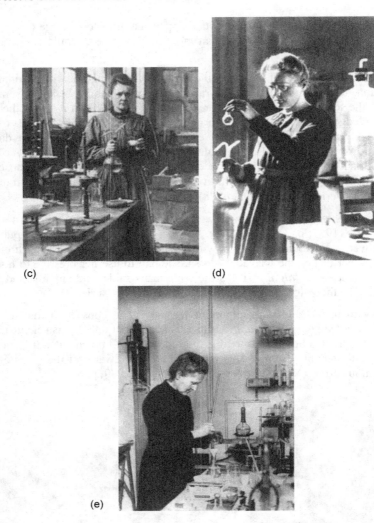

14c, 14d & 14e (from nobelprize.com)

Figure 14a-e. Marie Curie's every day (1867–1934).

Figure 15. Marie Curie on Polish bills.

In Eve Curie's biography of her mother, she quoted Pierre's words about her parents' decision not to apply for patents for their discovery. Pierre had remarked, "The recent cures of malignant tumors have been radium have been conclusive; in a few years the whole world will be wanting radium" (Curie, 1937, p. 203). However, both Marie and Pierre had thought: "It is impossible [to patent the technique to assure their right], it would be contrary to the scientific spirit" (Curie, 1937, p. 203). Marie further stated, "radium is going to be of use in treating disease... It seems to me impossible to take advantage of that" (Curie, 1937, p. 204). Pierre was appeased and added, "I shall write tonight, then, to the American engineers, and give them the information they ask for...." (Curie, 1937, p. 204).

During her first visit to the US in 1921, US President Warren Harding met her at the White House and delivered in his speech the following:

It has been your fortune, Mme. Curie, to accomplish an immortal work for humanity. But with it all we bring something more. We bring to you the meed [reward] of honor which is due to preeminence in science, scholarship, research and humanitarianism. But with it all we bring something more. We lay at your feet the testimony of that love which all the generations of men have been wont to bestow upon the noble woman, the unselfish wife, the devoted mother... I have liked to believe in an analogy between the spiritual and the physical world. I have been very sure that which I may call the radioactive soul, or spirit, or intellect—call it what you choose—must first gather to itself, from its surroundings, the power that it afterward radiates in beneficence to those near it. I believe it is the sum of many inspirations, borne in on great souls, which enables them to warm, to scintillate, to radiate, to illumine and serve those about them... (Harding, 1921, pp. 509–510)

However, within his speech, President Harding never referred to Marie Curie as a women scientist or scientist, instead, he used "noble woman", unselfish wife", and "the devoted mother" to refer to this great scientist. The true respect to a scientist was not revealed in his speech!

From the preceeding discussions, the following are evident. First, that Marie Curie's decision to relinquish her patent had a significant impact on science discoveries across the globe. It was a decision she never regretted and one that brought her world-wide respect. Second, Marie Curie believed that science was the key to improving the quality of life for all people (e.g., eliminating cancer patients' pain). This "scientific spirit" comes across in all of Marie Curie's work and is what made her a role model and hero to many. Finally, her Nobel Prizes thrust her into the international limelight and brought formal recognition which gave countless women and men the courage to follow in her steps.

As we think about Marie Curie's contributions to humanity, we also need to remember that she was never spoiled by the fame she owned and the love from the public. As Einstein stated: "Marie Curie is, of all celebrated beings, the only one whom fame has not corrupted" (cited in Curie, 1937, p. xvii).

At last, we would like to use Eve's description of Marie:

Marie's idea was simple—simple as the stroke of genius. At the crossroads where Marie now stood, hundreds of research workers might have remained, nonplussed, for months or even years. After examining all known chemical substances, and discovering as Marie had done—the radiation of thorium, they would have continued to ask themselves in vain whence came this mysterious radioactivity. Marie, too, questioned and wondered. But her surprise was translated into fruitful acts. She had used up all evident possibilities. Now she turned toward the unplumbed and the unknown. (Curie, 1937, p. 156)

This description explained why Marie Curie could be so outstanding and inspiring to many women as well as men scientists all over the world. Don't be afraid of being different! Follow your dream/passion and not let the narrow-mindedness of the time limit your potential.

Look for the clear light of Truth;

Look for the unknown, new roads...

Even when man's sight is keener far than now,

Divine wonder will never fail him...

Every age has its own dreams,

Leave, then, the dreams of yesterday;

You—take the torch of knowledge,

Perform a new work among the labors of the centuries

And build the palace of the future…

(Marie Curie, cited in Curie, 1937, p. 55)

CONCLUDING REMARKS

We were thrilled to have this opportunity to present Marie Curie's life and delve into the obstacles she overcame as well as the creative ways of thinking she applied to her scientific work. When Marie discovered the great benefit radium could bring to the world, she and Pierre decided to share this treasure with every human being. Marie Curie was a noble woman who gave much of herself, including her life, in order to advance science. She sought the truth not for her own material betterment, but the betterment of humankind. Although she lived in Paris, France, for most of her adult life, she never forgot her home country, Poland, by establishing the Institute of Radium in Warsaw and providing scholarships for Polish students to study at her institute in Paris. She named the new element she discovered, polonium, in memory of Poland. Even though she had close bonds with France, Poland, and the US, Marie Curie belongs to the world.

As a brilliant and visionary scientist, her wisdom in selecting research topics, forming hypotheses, conducting scientific experiments, and providing profound explanations and new theories, has inspired us in numerous ways. More importantly, we have been touched by her engagement in education as a creative science educator to guide not only her own but also other children and women from different ages and from different parts of the world. She demonstrated persistence and unselfishness, and displayed a strong set a high standard for her followers. We believe Marie Curie's story can be taught from various perspectives in textbooks, lectures, and storybooks not only for inspiring young minds to love and respect science as a human enterprise but also for combating gender stereotypes in science and society.

The United Nations declared 2011 as the International Year of Chemistry in as we commemorate the 100th anniversary of Marie Curie's Nobel Prize in Chemistry. We are honored to be part of this worldwide celebration by contributing this chapter.

NOTES

[1] William Henry and William Lawrence Bragg, father and son, shared the Nobel in Physics in 1915; (scientists from UK & Australia) and Arthur and Roger Kornberg, father and son (US) received the Nobel in 1959 and 2006, respectively, the former in physiology or medicine and the latter in chemistry; Niels and Aage Bohr, father and son, received the Nobel in 1922 and 1975, respectively, in physics (Abir-Am, 2011).

[2] In this chapter, we used the Polish form of the last name for Marie's parents.

[3] Marie Curie's accent might have come from her cousin Josef Boguski who worked in St. Petersburg.

[4] This was an "underground" college, known as the Floating University, where young men and women could study with trained individuals. Polish patriots who considered this "a pathway to eventual freedom for their nation" ran the university. Apparently, this was an important opportunity for young women to receive an education in philosophy, progressive politics, chemistry, physics, and physiology (Ham, 2002–2003, p. 33).

[5] Ironically, because the Nobel Prize in Physics in 1903 did not refer to the discovery of radium, it left the door open for her to win a second Nobel Prize in Chemistry in 1911 (Langevin-Joliot, 2011, p. 5).

[6] We have to be aware that after Marie Curie's notebooks published, there were pieces of evidence revealing some solo and important contributions in radioactivity initiated and completed by Marie Curie.

[7] Pierre and Marie Curie did not attend the Nobel Award ceremony in 1903 because of their poor health. However, Pierre Curie did have an opportunity to deliver his Nobel lecture in 1905.

[8] In 1911, Marie Curie fell one vote shy in the competition for a seat at the French Academy of Science. The "Institut de France" which represents the five French Academies, had publicly expressed the desire to maintain its male status quo. She never applied again to the French Academy of Sciences (Langevin-Joliot, 2011, p. 6).

[9] In 1898, Marie used a quartz piezoelectroscope to see if her sample, after fractional crystallization, carried an electrical charge. Her hypothesis was that if a sample has an electrical charge, it might contain a radioactive substance (Ham, 2002–2003, p. 38).

[10] In Irène Joliot-Curie's Nobel official address in Stockholm, she insisted on sharing the talk with Frédéric, her husband, because she felt her father had never been given enough credit for his part in the isolation of radium (Crossfield, 1997, p. 114).

[11] For instance, in 1902, radium had been used successfully to treat a pharyngeal carcinoma in Vienna. In 1904, patients in New York were undergoing implantation of radium tubes directly into tumors, representing some of the first interstitial brachytherapy treatment (Connell & Hellman, 2009, p. 383).

[12] Statistics on the underrepresentation of women in science can be found from National Association for Scholars (2007, 2009) at http://www.nas.org/polarticles.cfm?doc_id=422

REFERENCES

Abir-Am, P. G. (2011). Personal communication.

Abir-Am, P. G., & Outram, D. (Eds.) (1989). *Uneasy careers and intimate lives: Women in science, 1789–1979*. New Jersey: Rutgers University Press.

Badash, L. (1966). The discovery of thorium's radioactivity. *Journal of Chemical Education, 43*, 219–220.

Badilescu, S. (2001). Chemistry for beginners. Women authors and illustrators of early chemistry textbooks. *The Chemical Educator, 6*, 114–120.

Bragg, M. (with Balibar, F., Gribbin, J., Pestre, D., & Quinn, S.) (1998). Marie Curie (1867–1934). In M. Bragg (Ed.), *On giants' shoulders: Great scientists and their discoveries from Archimedes to DNA* (pp. 243–271). London: Hodder and Stoughton.

Brush, S. G. (1985). Women in physical science: From drudges to discovers. *The Physics Teacher, 23*, 11–19.

Chinn, C. A., & Brewer, W. F. (1993). The role of anomalous data in knowledge acquisition: A theoretical framework and implications for science instruction. *Review of Educational Research, 63*, 1–49.

Curie, E. (1937). *Madame Curie: A biography*. New York: Doubleday, Doran & Company, Inc.

Curie, M. (1911, December 11). Nobel lecture. Retrieved from http://nobelprize.org/nobel_prizes/chemistry/laureates/1911/marie-curie-lecture.html.

Curie, M. (1921). Radiology and the war, Lecture at Vassar College, May 14.

Curie, M. (1923a). *Pierre Curie*, translated by Charlotte and Vernon Kellogg. The Macmillan Company.

Curie, M. (1923b). *Marie Curie*. New York: J. J. Little & Ives Company.

Curie, M. (1928). A speech at the 25th anniversary celebration of the discovery of radium.

Curie, P. (1905). Nobel Lecture: Radioactive substances, especially radium. June 6, 1905. Retrieved from http://nobelprize.org/nobel_prizes/physics/laureates/1903/pierre-curie-lecture.html

Duveen, D.I. (1953). Madame Lavoisier. *Chymia: Annual Studies in the History of Chemistry, 4*, 13–29.

DGBAS (2008). Directorate-General of Budget, Accounting, and Statistics, Executive Yuan, ROC (Taiwan). Retrieved from http://www.dgbas.gov.tw/

DGBAS (2011). Directorate- General of Budget, Accounting, and Statistics, Executive Yuan, ROC (Taiwan). Retrieved from http://www.stat.gov.tw/ct.asp?xItem=835&ctNode=531.

Friedrich, C., & Remane, H. (2011). Marie Curie: Recipient of the 1911 Nobel Prize in Chemistry and discoverer of the chemical elements polonium and radium, *Angewandte Chemie International Edition, 50*, 4752–4758.

Gilbert, J. K. (2011). Women chemists informing public education about chemistry during the 20th century, In M.-H. Chiu, P. J. Gilmer, & D. F. Treagust (Eds.), *Celebrating the 100th anniversary of Madame Marie Sklodowska Curie's Nobel Prize in Chemistry* (pp. 141–166). Rotterdam: Sense Publishers.

Gilmer, P. J. (2011). Irène Joliot-Curie, a Nobel laureate in artificial radioactivity. In M.-H. Chiu, P. J. Gilmer, & D. F. Treagust (Eds.), *Celebrating the 100th anniversary of Madame Marie Sklodowska Curie's Nobel Prize in Chemistry* (pp. 41–57). Rotterdam: Sense Publishers.

Goldsmith, B. (2004). *Obsessive genius: The inner world of Marie Curie.* New York: W. W. Norton.

Ham, D. (2002–2003). Marie Sklodowska Curie: The woman who opened the nuclear age. *21st Century*, Winter issue, pp. 30–68.

Harding,W. G. (1921). President Harding's presentation address to Mme. Curie. *Science*, New Series, *53*(1379), 509–510.

Houlihan, S., & Wotiz, J. H. (1973). Women in chemistry before 1900. *Journal of Chemical Education, 52*(6), 362–364.

Hussenius, A., & Scantlebury, K. (2011). Witches, alchemists, poisoners and scientists:changing image of chemistry. In M.-H. Chiu, P. J. Gilmer, & D. F. Treagust (Eds.), *Celebrating the 100th anniversary of Madame Marie Sklodowska Curie's Nobel Prize in Chemistry* (pp. 191–204). Rotterdam: Sense Publishers.

Julian, M. M. (1990). Women in crystallography. In G. Kass-Simon, & P. Farnes (Eds.), *Women of science: Righting the record* (pp. 335–384). Bloomington: Indiana University Press.

Kahveci, A. (2010). Quantitative analysis of science and chemistry textbooks for indicators of reform: A complementary perspective. *International Journal of Science Education, 32*, 1495–1519.

Langevin-Joliot, H. (2011). *Marie Curie and her time. Chemistry International, 33*(1), 4–7.

Madame Curie (film, 1943). MGM released the movie staring Greer Garson and Walter Pidgeon.

Mamlok-Naaman, R., Blonder, R., & Dori, Y. J. (2011). One hundred years of women in chemistry in the 20th century: Sociocultural developments of women's status. In M.-H. Chiu, P. J. Gilmer, & D. F. Treagust (Eds.), *Celebrating the 100th anniversary of Madame Marie Sklodowska Curie's Nobel Prize in Chemistry* (pp. 119–139). Rotterdam: Sense Publishers.

Mayer, R. E. (1999). Fifty years of creativity research. In R. J. Sternberg (Ed.), *Handbook of creativity* (pp. 449–460). New York: Cambridge.

Meurdrac, M. (1666). Retrieved from http://www.womenalchemists.com/Marie_Meurdrac.html

Milne, C. (1998). Philosophically correct science stories? Examining the implications of heroic science stories for school science. *Journal of Research in Science Teaching, 35*(2), 175–187.

Mould, R. F. (1998). The discovery of radium in 1898 by Marie Sklodowska-Curie (1867–1934) and Pierre Curie (1859–1906) with commentary on their life and times. *The British Journal of Radiology, 71*, 1229–1254.

Murphy, J. T. & Smoot, R. C. (1982). *Physics: Principles and problems.* Columbus, OH: Charles E. Merrill.

National Association for Scholars (2007, 2009). Retrieved from http://www.nas.org/polarticles.cfm?doc_id=422

National Science Foundation (2011). Doctorate recipients from the U.S. universities: 2009. Retrieved from http://www.nsf.gov/statistics/nsf11306/appendix/pdf/tab12.pdf

Nobelprize.org (2011). Create a list. Retrieved from http://nobelprize.org/nobel_prizes/lists /all/create.html

Ogilvie, M. B. (2004). *Marie Curie: A biography*. London: Greenwood Press.

Ogilvie, M. B. (2011), Marie Curie, women and the history of chemistry. In M.-H. Chiu, P. J. Gilmer, & D. F. Treagust (Eds.), *Celebrating the 100th anniversary of Madame Marie Sklodowska Curie's Nobel Prize in Chemistry* (pp. 105–118). Rotterdam: Sense Publishers.

Palmer, B. (2011). Forgotten women in science education: The case of Mary Amelia Swift. In M.-H. Chiu, P. J. Gilmer, & D. F. Treagust (Eds.), *Celebrating the 100th anniversary of Madame Marie Sklodowska Curie's Nobel Prize in Chemistry* (pp. 167–187). Rotterdam: Sense Publishers.

Pycior, H. M. (1997). Marie Curie: Time only for science and family. In M. F. Rayner-Canham & G. W. Rayner-Canham (Eds.), *A devotion to their science: Pioneer women of radioactivity* (pp. 31–50). Philadelphia: Chemical Heritage Foundation.

Pycior, H. M. (1989). Marie Curie's "anti-natural path": Time only for science and family. In P. G. Abir-Am & D. Outram (Eds.), *Uneasy careers and intimate lives: Women in science, 1789–1979*. Rutgers: Rutgers University Press.

Pycior, H. M., Slack, N. G., & Abir-Am, P. G. (1996, Eds.). *Creative couples in the sciences*. New Jersey: Rutgers University Press.

Quinn, S. (1995). *Marie Curie: A life*. Reading, MA: Perseus Books.

Rayner-Canham, M. F., & Rayner-Canham, G. W. (1996). Women's fields of chemistry: 1900–1920. *Journal of Chemical Education, 73*(2), 136–162.

Rayner-Canham M., & Rayner-Canham, G. (2001). *Women in Chemistry: Their changing roles from alchemical times to the mid-twentieth century*. Philadelphia, PA: Chemical Heritage Foundation.

Schiebinger, L. (1987). The history and philosophy of women in science: A review essay. *Journal of Women in Culture and Society, 12*(2), 305–332.

Serri, E. (2007). *The periodic table: Its story and its significance*. Oxford, England: Oxford University Press.

Sinclair, S. B. (1988). J. J. Thomson and radioactivity: part I. *Ambix, 35*(2), 91–104.

Smith, E. P. (1914). *Chemistry in America. Chapters from the history of the science in the United States* (p. 35). New York: D. Apleton and Co.

Southerland, S. A., & Bahbah, S. U. (2011). Educational policy of accountability and women's representation in science: The specter of unintended consequences. In M.-H. Chiu, P. J. Gilmer, & D. F. Treagust (Eds.), *Celebrating the 100th anniversary of Madame Marie Sklodowska Curie's Nobel Prize in Chemistry* (pp. 225–238). Rotterdam: Sense Publishers.

UNESCO (2011). Female tertiary graduates by field of education. Retrieved from http://stats.uis.unesco.org/unesco/TableViewer/tableView.aspx?ReportId=3350&IF_Language=eng

UNESCO Institute for Statistics (2011). Retrieved from http://stats.uis.unesco.org/unesco/TableViewer/tableView.aspx?ReportId=3350&IF_Language=eng

APPENDIX

MAJOR EVENTS IN PIERRE AND MARIE CURIE'S LIVES

1867 November 7, birth of Marie Sklodowska (future Marie Curie) in Warsaw (Poland).

1880 Pierre and his brother Jacques discovered quartz piezoelectroscope.

1883 Marie Sklodowska graduated (gold medal winner) from high school in Poland.

1891 Marie arrived in Paris to study physics and mathematics at the Sorbonne.

1893 Marie graduated top in her class with a master's degree in physics.

1894 Pierre and Marie met in the spring. That summer, Marie passed her mathematics examination with the second highest score.

1895 Pierre and Marie married on 26 July at Sceaux (near Paris).

1896 Becquerel's discovery of the phenomenon of spontaneous radioactivity.

1897 Birth of Irène, their first daughter. In December, Marie started her thesis work on "uranium rays" discovered by Becquerel. Pierre gave up his own research and helped Marie.

1898 On April 12 1898 Marie showed that thorium emits the same type of radiation as uranium (natural radioactivity). On July 18, Pierre and Marie announced the discovery of a new radioactive element - polonium. On 26 December, in collaboration with Gustave Bémont, they announced the discovery of radium.

1900 On October 26, Marie was appointed teacher at the Ecole Normale Supérieure de Jeunes Filles in Sèvres. Pierre started teaching physics to medical students in the annex of the Faculty of Sciences, on the rue Cuvier.

1902 Marie calculated the atomic mass of radium (chemical symbol, Ra) equal to 225.

1903 Marie defended her thesis on radioactive substances other than uranium and thorium, entitled "Research on radioactive substances." On December 10, Pierre and Marie Curie shared with Henri Becquerel the Nobel Prize in Physics for the discovery of natural radioactivity.

1904 On December 6 Eve was born, their second daughter. Marie was appointed to be the director of laboratory of radioactivity.

1906 Pierre died on April 19, at age 47. Marie started to teach at the Sorbonne physics department; she was the first woman to teach there. The university entrusted Marie with full authority over the laboratory on May 13. In November, Marie Curie replaced her husband as professor of physics at the Sorbonne. She was appointed full professor in 1908.

1910 Marie had a success on isolation of pure radium.

1911 Nobel Prize in chemistry by the discovery of the elements radium and polonium, for the isolation of radium and the study of the nature and compounds of this remarkable element

1914 Construction of the Radium Institute was complete.

1914–1918 Director of the physics and chemistry laboratory in the newly completed Radium Institute (started in 1909). "Little Curies" with radiology equipment served the army at the frontlines of World War I.

1917–1918 150 women trained, 1.1 million people benefited from X-ray treatments.

1921 First visit to the US under the invitation from Missy Meloney who raised 100,000 US dollars to purchase one gram of radium for the Radium Institute in Paris.

1922 Marie was appointed to be a member of the Académie de médecine.

1929 Second visit to the US. Received 50,000 US dollars. Donated the gift of a second gram of radium to the Radium Institute in Warsaw.

1934 Died from of pernicious anemia on July 4 aged 67. In 1935, Marie's daughter, Irène and her husband, Frédéric Joliot, received the Nobel Prize Award in Chemistry for their discovery of artificial radioactivity.

1995 Pierre and Marie's ashes were transferred to the Panthéon in April. Marie was the first woman, for her own accomplishments, to be buried with other famous French male heroes, such as Victor Hugo, Voltaire, Émile Zola, etc.

Mei-Hung Chiu
National Taiwan Normal University
Graduate Institute of Science Education
Taipei, Taiwan
mhchiu@ntnu.edu.tw

Nadia Yutin Wang
Kaohsiung Medical University
Department of Public Health
Kaohsiung, Taiwan
nwcrazigg@gmail.com

PENNY J. GILMER

2. IRÈNE JOLIOT-CURIE, A NOBEL LAUREATE IN ARTIFICIAL RADIOACTIVITY

INTRODUCTION

This chapter provides a biographical profile of Irène Joliot-Curie, the daughter of Nobel laureates Marie and Pierre Curie, and details of her personal life and professional accomplishments. Growing up with internationally renowned parents, Irène led a life marked by both expectations and obligations. Irène, like her mother, chose to marry a scientist, Frédéric Joliot, with whom she would collaborate successfully (leading eventually to a joint Nobel Prize in Chemistry) and have two children, both of whom would become part of the next generation of scientists. Even with all of her successes, the difficulties of being a woman in the sciences affected Irène, as they had her mother. Denied memberships and honors given to men with equal successes, both Marie and Irène fought for their place, respectability and research opportunities.

IRÈNE'S EARLY LIFE

Marie and Pierre Curie had their first child, Irène, when Marie was starting her doctoral work on radioactivity. Marie and Pierre worked jointly on this research project—Marie focused on the chemistry-related aspects while Pierre concentrated on the physics. After Marie and Pierre had taken a strenuous bicycle ride in the country Marie went into labor one month early, and Irène was born on September 12, 1897. A few weeks later, Pierre's mother died. Marie and Pierre invited Pierre's father, Dr. Eugène Curie, to live with them at the edge of Paris in their small house with an attached garden. During this time, Marie was heavily involved in her doctoral research on the emissions from radioactivity of natural sources, so it was difficult to be both taking care of her infant daughter and conducting her research on newly identified radioelements. The presence of Eugène aided Marie as he could help take care of baby Irène (Curie, 1923). Still, Marie doted on her daughter's progress and recorded in a notebook her daughter's daily events.

Dr. Eugène Curie "loved her [Irène] tenderly and [his] own life was made brighter by her" (Curie, 1923, p. 179). He delighted in caring for his granddaughter until his death when Irène was 12 years old. He taught Irène, much like he taught his son Pierre, "to love nature, poetry, and radical politics" (McGrayne, 1998, p. 121). Later in life, Irène said, "My spirit had been formed in great part by my

M.-H. Chiu, P. J. Gilmer, and D. F. Treagust (Eds.), Celebrating the 100th Anniversary of Madame Marie Sklodowska Curie's Nobel Prize in Chemistry. 41–57.

grandfather, Eugène, and my reactions to political or religious questions came from him more than from my mother" (cited in McGrayne, 1998, p. 121).

When Irène was just six years old, her family life changed significantly. The radiochemical research conducted by her parents led to Marie and Pierre's shared Nobel Prize in Physics, together with Becquerel, in 1903. With this announcement they became well known, and family life was no longer so private. A year later, Irène's sister, Eve, was born. Then, however, in 1906, tragedy struck the family. Pierre was killed in an accident when he was hit by a horse-drawn carriage and died instantly. For many years, Marie did not even mention Pierre's name to her children. Irène became very close to her mother after Pierre's death and remained close for the rest of Marie's life.

For two and a half years after Pierre's death, Marie Curie and some of her academic colleagues formed a cooperative schooling arrangement for their children, ten in all, which included Irène. Eve was too young to be part of it. Marie Curie said that each of the colleagues took "charge of the teaching of a particular subject to all of the young people... With a small number of classes we yet succeeded in reuniting the scientific and literary elements of a desirable culture" (Curie, 1923, p. 195). Marie Curie and Paul Langevin taught the children physics while Jean Perrin taught them chemistry. Henriette Perrin taught French literature and history and took the children on visits to the Louvre. Isabel Chavannes, wife of a professor, taught them German and English. Henri Mouton taught natural science, and sculptor Jean Magrou taught drawing and modeling (Crossfield, 1997; Physicist of the week, 2011). Irène profited enormously from this type of education, especially because it included practical exercises.

With both of her daughters, Marie believed that physical education was critical for their development. In the summers, the daughters went to the French coast in Brittany to swim in the Atlantic Ocean and in the winters to ski areas for vigorous exercise. At home the children did gymnastics on a regular basis. Marie and her two daughters exercised and also relaxed by hiking and riding bicycles together.

IRÈNE'S TEENAGE YEARS

Dr. Eugène Curie, Irène's grandfather, died on February 25, 1910, after a yearlong illness. This was another trauma for Irène, especially after losing her father in 1906, and she worried that she would also lose her mother. Eugène was also not there to help her through another trauma in 1911 when the newspapers published reports that Marie Curie had an affair with Paul Langevin. Though Langevin was the one who was married, these reports were much more critical of Marie. She and her family were verbally antagonized and threatened by the general public.

Later that year, Marie Curie received word that she was to be the sole awardee of a second Nobel Prize. Because of the publicity surrounding the affair Marie had with Paul Langevin, the Nobel Committee even wrote Marie shortly afterward, advising that because of the affair, she perhaps ought not to accept the award. Marie adamantly refused this suggestion, writing a fiery letter back that the award had nothing to do with her personal life, only with her scientific discovery. In

October 1911, now a hundred years ago this year (2011), she and 14-year old Irène traveled to Stockholm for Marie Curie to accept the Nobel Prize in Chemistry as the sole recipient for the discovery and isolation of polonium and radium. "Irène was dazzled. For the first time, she sensed her mother's fame and importance and her standing in the scientific community" (McGrayne, 1998, p. 124).

Though she did travel to Sweden, to give her Nobel lecture and receive her award, the scandal devastated Marie. At the lecture itself, Marie was sick, in part because of the stresses of the scandal, but also because of the disappointment earlier in 1911 of not being elected to the Academy of Sciences of Paris, even though she had already become a Nobel laureate in physics in 1903. This trip and the emotional turmoil surrounding this time of Marie's life exhausted her so much that she went into seclusion for a year. She did not even see her children and instead had a governess care for them.

Meanwhile, Irène continued to excel in her studies. With her excellent education in the cooperative, Irène entered the independent school, the Collège Sévigné, in Paris in 1912, finishing her high school education in 1914. In that same year, Irène started her college education at the Sorbonne University, but preambles of the European war got in the way of her continued education.

Earlier in the summer of 1914, World War I started, and on August 1st, Germany declared war on France. During that summer Marie had two Polish maids supervise both Irène and Eve on the French coast in l'Arcouest with war on the horizon. Meanwhile Marie stayed at the Radium Institute in Paris as most of the men who worked there had been mobilized for war following the preambles to war starting with the assassination of Archduke Franz Ferdinand of Austria on June 28, 1914. During that time Marie Curie worried about losing her precious supply of radium and decided to transport it from Paris to Bordeaux. She did this herself by carrying the radium in a lead-lined suitcase on a train. After the trip, Marie wrote for Irène and Eve to return home to Paris, as occupation of the city did not seem imminent following the successful Battle of the Marne, which ended on September 12, 1914.

In the same year, when Irène was just 17 years of age, she started helping her mother teach surgeons and doctors in the battlefield how to use X-rays to find the bullets and shrapnel in the wounded soldiers, to aid in their extractions. With so much need for this type of service to the injured French soldiers, Marie Curie organized 20 radiologic cars, which were equipped with X-ray equipment. Irène and her mother trained other women to go into the battlefields to help the surgeons on site. Irène "did ambulance work between Furnes and Ypres, and also at Amiens, receiving, from the Chiefs of Service, testimonials of her work satisfactorily performed and, at the end of the war, a medal" (Curie, 1923, pp. 213–214). Irène reflected later about the experience, "My mother had no more doubts about me than she doubted herself" (cited in McGrayne, 1998, p. 117). During this time Irène and Marie formed a true collaboration, much like that Marie experienced with her husband Pierre. About this collaboration, Irène said reflectively, years later, "[I am] more like my father and, perhaps, this is one of the reasons we understood each other so well" (cited in Pflaum, 1989, p. 201).

Despite the war, during the bombardment of Paris by the Germans, Irène and Eve stayed in town with their mother. Irène continued with her undergraduate studies with the Faculty of Science at the Sorbonne University in October 1914. Even while bringing X-ray equipment and know-how to the staff at an Anglo-Belgian hospital, a few kilometers from the battlefront, Irène studied for her baccalaureate examinations in physics and mathematics. After four years of war, French people and countryside were devastated. In 1918, when Irène was 21 years old, the armistice finally brought the war to an end.

IRÈNE'S START TO HER DOCTORAL RESEARCH IN THE RADIUM INSTITUTE

Marie Curie created the Radium Institute that opened in Paris in 1914, at the start of World War I. After the war, Irène worked side-by-side with her mother in the Radium Institute. The composition of the laboratory in which Marie had worked changed over the years. For instance from 1904 to 1914, ten of the 58 workers were women, mostly from countries other than France. In the two years after the war, the majority of the workers were women as many of the men had died in the war, with the percentage of women stabilizing at 30% years later (Boudia, 2011).

Irène was one of 47 women in all who worked in Marie Curie's laboratory (Boudia, 2011) between 1904 and 1934. There, Irène "simply studied science for the personal pleasure of understanding nature's beauty" (McGrayne, 1998, p. 126). She loved chemistry, including seeing a brightly colored precipitate or the glow of a radioelement. But her life was not only science. Irène and Eve moved back with their mother during this time in order to help her with the household chores. They also spent much time discussing poetry and music, as well as the laboratory work. Eve was particularly interested in music.

Marie had always encouraged athletic ability and intellectual development for her daughters. To her colleagues in the laboratory, though, these traits made Irène seem "intimidating and robust, both intellectually and physically. Her imperturbability and her knowledge of physics and math seemed well-nigh incredible for someone age[d] twenty-five" (McGrayne, 1998, p. 127). Her nickname in the laboratory was "Crown Princess," in part because others were jealous of her and recognized her privileged position with her mother as Director. In the laboratory, Irène was known for behaving more like a man in that she was short-tempered, direct, and sometimes brutally honest with colleagues, and did not take the time for niceties of conversation. Perhaps Irène's tough posture developed from the scandals and frustrations endured by her mother as Marie struggled for her place within the mostly male world of scientific research.

IRÈNE AND EVE'S TOUR OF AMERICA WITH MARIE CURIE

In May of 1921, Irène interrupted her doctoral research, to go with Marie and Eve on a two-month tour of America organized by Marie (Missy) Mattingly Meloney, editor of the well-known New York women's magazine, *The Delineator*. The purpose of the tour was to gather funds from American women for the purchase of one gram of radium for the "Marie Curie Radium Fund," for her Radium Institute in Paris.

Years earlier, Marie and Pierre had purposefully decided not to patent the method to purify radium as they felt the discovery belonged to the public. Marie commented on this decision: "No detail was kept secret, and it is due to the information we gave in our publications that the industry of radium has been rapidly developed" (Curie, 1923, p. 226). One outcome of this decision though was the lack of financial support that the patent could have provided them— both personally and for the Radium Institute. Therefore, this trip to America would help Marie purchase the radium needed for new experiments.

On the trip through America, Marie received honorary degrees at a number of universities and attended receptions at the Museum of Natural History, the National Museum, and Carnegie Hall of New York, among others. The American Chemical Society had Marie present a lecture on the Discovery of Radium in Chicago at their annual meeting. Marie did not visit as many laboratories as she wanted because of her health; however, she did see the Bureau of Standards in Washington (now known as the National Institute of Standards and Technology), which is known for measurements. Employees of the Bureau packaged the radium supply for Marie to take back to France for her Radium Institute's research.

At times Marie was so exhausted from the travels and tension of meeting so many people that Irène occasionally gave the addresses on radium. In her best English, she spoke to the audiences and accepted honorary degrees for her mother. Marie received the gift, presented by U.S. President Warren G. Harding at the White House, from Americans for the supply of radium for her Parisian Radium Institute. The trip was not solely speeches, awards and meetings. The Curies also were able to visit many famous places across the American continent, from riding ponies down the Grand Canyon to a spectacular visit to Niagara Falls. Marie wrote of her daughters' trip: "my daughters enjoyed to a full extent the opportunities of their unexpected vacation and the pride in the recognition of their mother's work" (Curie, 1923, p. 255).

RETURN TO PARIS TO CONTINUE HER RESEARCH

After the trip to America, Irène returned to Paris to continue her doctoral research at the Radium Institute. At this time, in the 1920s, Irène was one of the few trained radiochemists in the world. Perhaps led by her mother's 1898 discovery of the element polonium, named after Marie's native country of Poland, Irène decided to study polonium for her doctoral studies. Polonium had the advantage that essentially only α–particles are given off in radioactive decay (actually one in 100,000 decays emits a γ-ray, International Atomic Energy Agency, 2011). Her major doctoral professor at the Sorbonne University was Paul Langevin, who had been supervised by her father Pierre, in his doctorate, and who had been one of Irène's teachers in the cooperative. Her doctoral studies focused on α-particles emitted from polonium during natural radioactive decay.

At Irène's doctoral defense in 1925, journalists filled the audience to see the daughter of Marie Curie. As Bensaude-Vincent (1996, p. 62) notes, they perceived her "to be a future star scientist and a potential Nobel Prize winner, even before she had done any work on her own. Irène, unlike Marie, never had to fight for recognition." Even across the ocean, the *New York Times* reported on her thesis defense.

Following in her parents' footsteps made Irène's life easier than other women of the day who were interested in pursuing science. However, she also lived in the shadow of her parents, particularly her mother. Irène stayed at the Radium Institute for the rest of her professional career after graduating with her doctorate, continuing her study of radioelements and radioactivity but also examining the structure of the atom. Shortly after defending her doctorate, upon the recommendation of Paul Langevin, her mother hired Frédéric Joliot at the Radium Institute. Initially, Irène was both his supervisor and teacher. Although Irène and Fred had opposite personalities, each had expertise that complemented the other, much like the way Marie and Pierre worked together in the laboratory and in life. Irène and Fred also had some things in common, like an interest in sports and leftish politics. "Fred's sociability softened and humanized Irène. Most important, they loved science and each deeply respected the other's abilities" (McGrayne, 1998, p. 129).

Fred Joliot said about Irène,

I discovered in this girl, whom other people regarded somewhat as a block of ice, an extraordinary person, sensitive and poetic, who in many things gave the impression of being a living replica of what her father had been. I had read much about Pierre Curie. I had heard teachers who had known him talking about him and I rediscovered in his daughter the same purity, his good sense, his humility (cited in McGrayne, 1998, pp. 129–130).

Irène and Fred married on October 9, 1926 when Irène was 29 years old and Fred was 27. Shortly after their marriage, they both changed their surname to Joliot-Curie, although they often published with their given names. They had two children, Hélène and Pierre, and Irène felt her life was complete with both research and children. "She was a feminist who defined her role as a woman in terms of both work and children. At home, she remained a traditional wife and mother" (McGrayne, 1998, p. 131). Publicly, Irène served on the National Committee of the Union of French Women (Comité National de l'Union des Femmes Françaises) and on the World Peace Council and promoted women's education. She may have been influenced by her trip to America with her mother when Marie raised funds for securing a supply of radium, as they visited two of the "seven-sisters" women's colleges, Vassar College and Smith College (Ham, 2002–03).

Irène and Fred were a powerful collaborative team with her focusing more on the chemistry (although she had her doctorate in physics) and him concentrating more on the physics (although his doctoral degree was in chemistry). They were different in their thinking patterns as well. Irène processed ideas more slowly, with a more logical methodology, while Fred was quicker and often took a variety of positions in an argument. Both were experimentalists, however, and having less expertise in theory hurt them in their earlier joint studies, as they did not always see the implications of their research. Still, they enjoyed great success after a few early disappointments. Their collaboration resulted a very important discovery for radiochemistry—the discovery of artificial radioactivity.

JOINT RESEARCH OF IRÈNE AND FRÉDÉRIC JOLIOT-CURIE

In the early 1930s, the structure of the atom was understood to have a positively-charge nucleus, based on Rutherford's gold foil experiment.[1] However, the atom was not fully understood, as the neutron had not yet been discovered. Fred and Irène Joliot-Curie were competing with Lise Meitner from Berlin's Kaiser Wilhelm Institute, the New Zealander Ernest Rutherford from McGill University in Canada, and Niels Bohr from Copenhagen University in Denmark. All were hot on the trail of fully understanding the structure of the atom.

To keep up, Irène and Fred needed to increase their supply of polonium (atomic number 84). Polonium is a very dangerous element with which to work, but the two of them purified polonium by a method developed by Marie Curie to produce more of the element. They accomplished this purification using ampoules that originally held radium, with the chemical symbol, Ra. The radium undergoes radioactive decay to form radon, Rn, gas and an α-particle. The α-particle had been shown to be the helium nucleus, symbolized by $^{4}_{2}He$, with two positive charges (note subscript) and a mass of four (note superscript). This nuclear reaction, shown with the most stable radium isotope of mass 226, is as follows (written in the form used in Fred Joliot's Nobel lecture, 1935):

$$^{226}_{88}Ra = {}^{222}_{86}Rn + {}^{4}_{2}He$$

Note that the sum of masses (indicated by the superscripts) and the sum of the positive charges (indicated by the subscripts), respectively, are equal on both sides of the nuclear reaction $226 = 222 + 4$, and $88 = 86 + 2$. Then some of the radon undergoes further nuclear decay, to yield, polonium, Po, by this nuclear reaction, releasing another α-particle:

$$^{222}_{86}Rn = {}^{218}_{84}Po + {}^{4}_{2}He$$

When polonium undergoes radioactive decay, a particular isotope of the element lead, Pb, forms, with release of another α-particle:

$$^{218}_{84}Po = {}^{214}_{82}Pb + {}^{4}_{2}He$$

Therefore, here in a series of three nuclear reactions, starting with radium, one radioelement decays into another, releasing an α-particle with each radioactive decay, finally ending with a particular isotope of lead.

Marie Curie had carefully collected these spent radium ampoules, obtained from physicians around the world (Weart, 1979). Irène and Fred used these samples to obtain highly purified polonium. With the world's best supply of highly purified polonium, they had ready access to this powerful tool of polonium-emitted α-particles in their hands. Using this polonium, with an abundant supply of high-energy α-particles, Irène and Fred could examine the structure of the atom.

In 1930, Irène read a paper by Walter Bothe and H. Becker in which they studied the bombardment of beryllium with α–particles from the nuclear disintegration of polonium. Bothe and Becker thought they had discovered a more penetrating form of radiation than γ–rays that was not deflected by a magnetic field. Irène and Fred repeated Bothe and Becker's study and found the same energetic radiation. They allowed this strange radiation to hit a thin piece of paraffin (which is rich in hydrogen atoms that bond to carbon atoms) and found very fast hydrogen nuclei were ejected from the paraffin. Unfortunately, Irène and Fred misunderstood their experiments. Since γ–rays do not have any mass, they could not have ejected the hydrogen nuclei that contain mass from the paraffin. In further experiments, Chadwick and Rutherford demonstrated that the radiation that the Joliot-Curie's mistakenly had thought to be γ–rays was actually neutrons. Consequently, Irène and Fred were incorrect in their inference of the type of radiation emitted.

Chadwick and Rutherford published their explanation in 1932. Earlier, in 1920, Rutherford had predicted the existence of neutrons, so he was looking for evidence of them. The neutron is the uncharged subatomic particle of approximately the same mass as the proton and found within the nucleus. Chadwick alone received the Nobel Prize in Physics in 1935 for his discovery of the neutron (Nobelprize.org, 1935b). The discovery of the neutron opened further the fields of nuclear chemistry and nuclear physics, which ultimately led to the discovery of fission of uranium by slow-moving neutrons, with the concomitant release of enormous amounts of energy—the same process of fission used to make atomic bombs.

Irène and Fred also misinterpreted part of their data on the study of some lighter atomic nuclei that used a Wilson cloud chamber[2] in which charged particles could be monitored and recorded using photography. Although their experiments provided proof of the positron, which was predicted in theory by Paul Dirac in 1928, the Joliot-Curies failed to see the significance of the track of the movement of the particle in the Wilson cloud chamber. Soon after, Carl D. Anderson and Victor Hess in 1932 discovered the positron by studying cosmic rays interacting with a lead plate in the presence of a magnetic field (Nobelprize.org, 1936). Particles, which had the same mass as electrons, were emitted but they moved toward the negatively charged plate in the magnetic field; thus the particles had to be positively charged. Anderson received the Nobel Prize in Physics in 1936 for the discovery of the positron, and again Irène and Fred were disappointed that they had missed a great discovery.

In their next experiment, Irène and Fred used their polonium source to bombard aluminum (atomic number 13) foil with α-particles, produced by polonium undergoing radioactive decay. First, they observed radioactive phosphorus (atomic number 15) plus a neutron. This isotope of phosphorus had never before been seen, as it is not the naturally occurring form of phosphorus but an artificially-made form generated through this nuclear reaction:

$$^{27}_{13}\text{Al} + {}^{4}_{2}\text{He} = {}^{30}_{15}\text{P} + {}^{1}_{0}\text{n}$$

Many people at the Solvay Conference in 1934, including Lise Meitner, however, expressed reservations or doubts about the scientific accuracy of Irène and Fred's observation that neutrons were formed. The Joliot-Curies both felt discouraged by this reception, though they did get some private encouragement at this same conference from Niels Bohr and Wolfgang Pauli, two scientists who thought their observations were important.

Their observations this time turned out to be correct. The first nuclear reaction is as cited above, so the total mass $27 + 4 = 30 + 1$ and the total number of protons equals $13 + 2 = 15 + 0$ (Joliot, 1935). Following this reaction was a subsequent nuclear reaction in which a positron, p, of mass zero and charge positive one, was ejected from the phosphorus isotope, leading to stable silicon (atomic number 14):

$$^{30}_{15}P = {}^{30}_{14}Si + {}^{0}_{1}p$$

As a positron is eliminated, a proton in phosphorus becomes a neutron, so the element changes from phosphorus with 15 protons to silicon with 14 protons, with constant mass of 30. Therefore, in the series of the two nuclear reactions, overall, aluminum converts to stable silicon, with release of a neutron in the first step and a positron in the second step. This is transmutation of elements, from one element, aluminum, to a radioactive and artificial isotope of phosphorus, to stable silicon. Even though Irène and Fred had not discovered either the neutron or the positron (both reported in 1932), they realized that the artificial radioactivity that they did discover in 1934 involved both the release of a neutron in the first step and of a positron in the second step. Therefore, these discoveries by others catalyzed their own discovery of artificial radioactivity.

They became more certain of their results when Fred removed the bombarded aluminum from the polonium source and could still detect the positrons being emitted. Irène developed a chemical test for the short-lived phosphorus radioisotope, artificially made, so they could verify their hypothesis. Fred said I felt "a child's joy. I began to run and jump a round in that vast basement... I thought of the consequences which might come from the discovery" (quoted in Quinn, 1995, p. 429). The Geiger counter showed that they had created an artificial radioelement, in this case, radioactive phosphorus, with a 3.5-minute half-life. They had created a radioactive element, a short-lived atom of phosphorus, from a naturally stable element, aluminum, by bombardment with helium nuclei with release of neutrons. Fred then showed the experiments to Marie Curie and Paul Langevin that evening, and all were jubilant.

> Afterward, Frédéric Joliot recalled that moment. 'I will never forget the expression of intense joy which overtook her [Marie] when Irène and I showed her the first 'artificially produced' radioactive element in a little glass tube. I can see her still taking this little tube of the radioelement, already quite weak, in her radium-damaged fingers. To verify what we were telling her, she brought the Geiger-Muller counter up close to it and she could hear the numerous clicks... This was without a doubt the last great satisfaction of her life.' (cited in Quinn, 1995, p. 430)

"For a brief moment [Fred and Irène] had achieved the ancient alchemists' dream, transmutation—changing one chemical element, aluminum, into another, phosphorus, then into silicon" (Brian, 2005, p. 240).

This time Irène and Fred had been correct with the results that they had presented at the 1934 Solvay Conference. This work led to their joint Nobel Prize in Chemistry in 1935 for the discovery of artificial radioactivity induced by α-particles (Nobelprize.org, 1935a). Unfortunately, by this time, Marie Curie had passed away, so she did not know of the third Nobel Prize added in their family. Irène and Fred each gave an individual Nobel Prize lecture. Irène discussed the chemistry and Fred on the physics part of their discovery of artificial radioactivity. Irène in her Nobel Prize lecture (Joliot-Curie, 1935) gave credit to Rutherford for first reporting spontaneous transmutation of a radioactive element (Rutherford, 1919), thorium (atomic number of 90) to radium (atomic number of 88). Even though Irene was celebrated by the press when she received her doctorate in 1925, on the Joliot-Curie's joint Nobel Prize in Chemistry in 1935, Goldsmith (2005) notes, "Some things had not changed [since Marie Curie received her Nobel Prizes]. The press coverage almost universally attributed the prize to Frédéric's talent while Irène was relegated to an assistant's role" (p. 220). Pycior (1989) notes, "The Joliot-Curies' discovery was a fitting culmination of Marie Curie's life, in which science and family were the most important elements" (p. 213).

Irène and Fred's discovery of artificial radioactivity was an important discovery for subsequent research in medicine, chemistry and biology. Irène's daughter, Hélène Langevin-Joliot, a nuclear physicist, and Radvanyi (2006) say that Irène and Fred's discovery "suggested that the natural radio-elements were only the rare survivors of the very numerous radio-elements, which must have been formed at the beginning of the Earth's history" (p. 139). The ones with shorter half-lives were long since gone.

With this discovery, it became possible to make artificial isotopes that could be used to follow chemical and biochemical reactions. This procedure allowed scientists to understand the sequential steps of complicated series of reactions, using tracer amounts of the artificially made radioisotopes. In 1935, G. Hevesy and O. Chiewitz in Copenhagen "used radioactive phosphorus-32 to study the metabolism of phosphorus in rats" (Langevin-Joliot & Radvanyi, 2006, p. 140). Also Rosalyn Yalow's use of radioisotopic tracers to develop the radioimmunoassay, recognized with the 1977 Nobel Prize in Physiology or Medicine, was possible because of Irène and Fred's research on artificial radioactivity (Nobelprize.org, 1977).

The usefulness of the Joliot-Curies' discovery continues to this day. As a more personal example, Gilmer, the author of this chapter, once used ^{35}S-labeled amino acid methionine to follow membrane-bound proteins that coursed through the endoplasmic reticulum to the Golgi, and out to the cell surface of tumor cells from mice, using intact ^{35}S-cell-labeling (Gilmer, 1982). She purchased the ^{35}S-labeled methionine, sold industrially, but probably made by a process similar to one described in an experiment with yeast (Gajendiran, Jayachandran, Rao, Unny & Thyagarajan, 1994). Gajendiran et al., (1994) used ^{35}S-labeled sulfate obtained from a nuclear reaction, much like that discovered by Irène and Fred. Therefore, without the use of artificial radioactivity in Gilmer's experiment, the movement of membrane-bound molecules through various internal membranes to the plasma membrane could not have been followed. Indeed, much of the current understanding of biochemistry was determined using artificial radiotracers, discovered originally by Irène and Fred.

During the time of their discovery of artificial radioactivity and just before being awarded the Nobel Prize, as previously mentioned Marie Curie passed away on 4 July 1934. Her passing generated press and publicity—including Hollywood screenwriters who "believed that elements of her story would appeal to Americans during the anxious years of the Depression and World War II" (Des Jardins, 2010, pp. 200–201). Both Irène and her sister, Eve, were frustrated at the posthumous stories about their mother and tried to silence them. Although Irène's first impulse was to destroy all personal papers and letters of Marie, "Eve knew that unofficial accounts would be written anyway. She took control by writing a definitive biography and entering into an agreement with Universal Studies to make her [Marie's] work the basis of a screenplay" (Des Jardins, 2010, p. 201). MGM ended up releasing the movie, *Madame Curie*, in 1943, staring Greer Garson and Walter Pidgeon (Madame Curie (film), 1943).[3] Eve Curie's titled her book, *Madame Curie: A Biography by Eve Curie* (1937).

IRÈNE'S POLITICAL CAREER

After receiving the Nobel Prize in 1935, Irène and Fred decided to work separately. Fred was offered the position of director of research at the Caisse Nationale de la Recherche Scientifique. He became involved in transforming the old Ampère plant at Ivry into the Atomic Synthesis Laboratory, where they synthesized artificial radioelements. Meanwhile, Irène continued her research at the Institute, became a professor at the University of Paris, Sorbonne from 1932–1956, and became the research director at the Radium Institute in 1946. Fred also became the chair in nuclear physics and chemistry at the College de France. With these new positions, they basically "controlled every piece of serious nuclear work in France" (Crossfield, 1997, p. 115).

Irène's newfound fame as a Nobel laureate also propelled her into politics although she remained the scientific director of the Radium Institute until her death in 1956. She was part of the anti-Fascist coalition called the Popular Front in France in 1936. She also became one of the first cabinet ministers as an under secretary of state for scientific research. McGrayne (1998) explains,

> She took the job, calling it 'a sacrifice for the feminist cause in France.' She wanted to advance 'the most precious right of women…to exercise under the same conditions as men the professions for which they're qualified by education and experience' (p. 137).

It was ironic, however, that even though she was a cabinet minister, she was not permitted to vote, as women did not get that right in France until 1945. After three months, she resigned her cabinet position by prearrangement and turned over the job to Jean Perrin,[4] a 1926 Nobel laureate in Physics, her chemistry teacher in the cooperative school Irène had as an adolescent, and a good friend of the Curie family. She had quickly discovered that she did not have the patience or the diplomacy for politics. Around the same time, Irène began suffering from poor health.

Years earlier, Irène had contracted tuberculosis when she was pregnant with her first child, Hélène, in 1927. Despite this, Irène had a second child, her son Pierre, even though the doctors told her it would not to be wise to get pregnant again. By the late 1930s her tuberculosis worsened, and even weeks or months away in the Alps for a cure did not always restore her energy. She had been weakened by exposure to the high-energy radiation from X-rays during World War I while working with her mother. Later her immune system was further weakened by her work with radioelements, especially with polonium, and hindered her fighting the tuberculosis.

ONE MORE CHANCE AT A SECOND NOBEL PRIZE

Even with her health in decline, Irène had one more chance at a second Nobel Prize. She had begun conducting research with Pavel Savitch on uranium (atomic number 92). During the experiment, they thought they saw release of a neutron and a new radioisotope with a half-life of 3.5 hours that had properties similar to lanthanum (atomic number 57). However, two competitors from Germany, Otto Hahn and Lise Meitner, thought this was not correct. Hahn even belittled Irène's published research to Fred at a conference they both attended, perhaps trying to discourage her from continuing research on the subject. Irène and Savitch repeated their own experiment and saw the same result, so they republished their research. "They were within a hair's breadth of discovering nuclear fission, but did not rule out the possibility that it could be some unknown transuranium isotope, with $Z >$ 92" (Vujic, 2009), meaning that an isotope of some new element larger in atomic number than uranium's of 92 had formed.

Meanwhile Hahn and F. Strassman repeated the Curie-Savitch experiment and observed some lanthanum, but they also saw barium (atomic number 56). Both of these elements have a smaller atomic number than uranium. They published their results in January 1939. Scientists had expected to see an increase in the atomic number when bombarding with a neutron (as they saw with lighter elements), so this decrease in atomic number in the product was a great surprise.

Lise Meitner stayed in Germany until 1938, but with her Austrian passport and with the annexation of Austria by Germany, she essentially became a German national. Her professional associates and friends, because she was Jewish helped to smuggle Meitner out of Germany, initially into Holland, then to Denmark briefly, and finally to Sweden to be part of the newly founded nuclear institute at the University of Lund (Sime, 1996). This was an extremely difficult and stressful time for Meitner, and she wrote to the professional friend, Dirk Coster, who had helped her the most with her escape, "One dare not look back...one cannot look forward" (quoted in Sime, 1996, p. 209).

Once in Sweden Meitner was in almost daily contact with Hahn through letters. Meitner is the one who told Hahn that he had made the uranium atom undergo nuclear fission, a breaking apart of the element. Some mass is lost in this type of nuclear reaction, resulting in great releases of energy, much more than chemical reactions. Two authors, Meitner and her nephew, Otto Frisch, with whom she had worked with Otto Hahn at the Wilhelm Kaiser Institute for Chemistry in Berlin and who then was a refugee in Copenhagen, published a one-page note in *Nature* on February 11, 1939 entitled, "Disintegration of uranium by neutrons; A new type of nuclear reaction." Goldsmith (2005) writes, "It was clear that Meitner had succeeded while others failed in solving the mystery of nuclear fission" (p. 225).

However, Lise Meitner was not included in the 1944 Nobel Prize in Chemistry, with the sole recipient being Otto Hahn for their discovery of fission of heavy nuclei. In Germany, many scientists celebrated the news of Hahn's award, but "Lise's friends were furious. They viewed her exclusion as neither omission nor oversight but deliberate person rejection" (Sime, 1996, p. 326). Meitner in a letter she wrote on November 20, 1945 to Birgit Aminoff, a scientist herself and wife of a member of the Nobel Foundation, said that she felt, "[Otto] Frisch and I contributed something not insignificant to the clarification of the process of uranium fission—how it originates and that it produces so much energy, and that was something very remote from Hahn" (quoted in Sime, 1996, p. 327). Interestingly, "after the war [World War II] the Nobel chemistry committee voted to reconsider the 1944 award to Hahn—an unprecedented move, and evidence that the original decision was flawed" (Sime, 1996, p. 327).

Interestingly, in a private letter to Hahn in 1938 (which University of California, Berkeley, nuclear engineering professor Jasmina Vujic published) Meitner wrote on Irène and Savitch's research, published in *Comptes Rendus*:

In one of their C[omptes] R[endus] articles they emphasized strongly that their 3.5 h substance had very remarkable chemical properties and emphasized the similarity to lanthanum. The fact that they tried to place it among the transuranes doesn't change their experimental findings. And these findings led you to begin your experiments. And again you have not stated that quite clearly. One must not take people's words so literally. Curie obviously saw that something remarkable was going on, even if she did not think of fission. In November [1938] [George de] Hevesy heard her say in a lecture that entire periodic system arises from U + n bombardment. (Vujic, 2009, para. 10)

The letter shows that Meitner thought that Hahn should have cited Irène and Savitch's research. He did not, however, and Irène received only the one Nobel Prize, the one that she shared with her husband, Fred.

Once Fred was elected to the Academy of Science in 1943, Irène applied but was never elected, even though she had her name considered more than once. In the end, neither Irène nor her mother was ever elected to the French Academy of Science. Though both mother and daughter enjoyed great successes within the fields of chemistry and physics, they both found doors open to men with lesser credentials shut when they attempted entry. Finally, in 1962, one of Marie Curie's original research assistants, Marguerite Perey, discoverer of the radioactive element francium, was the first woman ever elected to the French Academy of Sciences (Bibliopolis, 1998–2011).

Irène received other awards, including the Matteucci Medal from the Italian Society for Sciences in 1932, Henri Wilde Prize in France in 1933, Marquet Prize from the Academy of Sciences in Paris in 1934, and the Bernard Gold Medal at Columbia University in New York City in 1940 (Callahan, 1997). She was elected an officer of the Legion of Honor in 1939.

Irène's health continued to decline but like her mother, she continued her research as much as she could. During World War II, Fred was part of the Resistance movement and had to go underground. His absence left Irène to do her best in taking care of their two children. After Hélène finished her baccalaureate examinations, she, her mother and brother, Pierre, secretly left France and hiked through the mountains into Switzerland on June 6, 1944. That day happened to be D-day, the day the Allied troops landed on the heavily guarded French coastline to fight the German army. The German guards were likely preoccupied and were not as engaged in looking for those fleeing France at that time.

In 1946, Fred became head of the French Atomic Energy Commission and helped France develop its first controlled nuclear reactor, which became active in 1948. Fred envisioned that France would only develop nuclear energy for peaceful purposes but after the end of World War II, the US and France wanted to develop the hydrogen bomb (McGrayne, 1998). During this period, Fred was the co-founder of the World Peace Council and was forced out of his scientific position due to his peace and socialist activism.

Antibiotics were developed during World War II. After the war, Missy Meloney, the woman who had brought Marie Curie to the US twice to raise funds from American women to purchase radium, sent the antibiotic streptomycin to Irène. This treatment cured her tuberculosis.[5] With improved health, Irène participated in international meetings for bans on atomic weapons, on peace, and for women's rights. However, due to their communist political leanings Irène and Fred lost favor especially in the US because of the McCarthyism era with its anti-Communist hysteria. Also on her third trip to the US in 1948 she was interned on Ellis Island for one night until the French embassy intervened on her behalf (Irène Joliot-Curie, n.d.). Travel to international conferences became much more difficult for both of them. For instance, in 1951 when Irène planned to attend a physics conference in Stockholm, the hotels would not give her a room (McGrayne, 1998). The American Chemical Society would not even offer Irène a membership (McGrayne, 1998). In 1956, Irène's health took a nosedive with the start of leukemia, and she died on March 17, 1956, at age of 58. Fred too was sick with radiation-induced hepatitis, and he died two years later. The French government gave both national funerals.

AFTERWORD

The Sorbonne University has commemorated Irène by inaugurating the Irène Joliot-Curie Prize, awarded annually to a "Woman Scientist of the Year." The winner of the 2010 Irène Joliot-Curie prize was Alessandra Carbone (Fondation d'Entreprise, 2010). This same foundation also offers the Young Woman Scientist Prize and the Corporate Woman Scientist Prize.

To date, the Nobel Committee has awarded a total of four Nobel Prizes in which five members of Curie family have been recognized (with Marie honored twice):

- Nobel Prize in Physics in 1903 (to Pierre Curie and Marie Curie, and jointly to Antoine Henri Becquerel)
- Nobel Prize in Chemistry in 1911 (to Marie Curie),
- Nobel Prize in Chemistry in 1935 (to Frédéric Joliot and Irène Joliot-Curie)
- Nobel Peace Prize in 1965 (to Henry Richardson Labouisse, Jr., Eve Curie's husband, on behalf of the United Nations UNICEF's efforts towards world peace) (The Nobel Prize in Peace, Acceptance speech, 1965).

An examination of Irène's biography demonstrates that because of her family's achievements, she gained fame before she could prove her own scientific worth. However, even after she had demonstrated her own scientific abilities, she lived and continued to live as a quasi-partner with considerable responsibility, with Marie until Marie's death in 1934, relying considerably on her. In 1946, Irène became the Director of the Radium Institute in Paris, which Marie had founded in 1914. Like her mother, Irène was often denied honors, likely because of her gender, even as her achievements surpassed many of her male counterparts who received such awards. This was the reality many women scientists faced during the 20th century. Irène benefited from being the daughter of a Nobel laureate and director of the Radium Institute, and thus was able to show what a woman, given a chance to conduct research, could do for scientific progress.

This chapter also describes the personal story of Irène, a woman driven by the expectations of greatness with two Nobel laureates as her parents, with her family name of Curie, and by her love for learning and for understanding the world through science.

NOTES

[1] Rutherford's gold foil experiment published in 1911 using α-particles bombarding gold foil showed that the nucleus of an atom contains all the positive charge and most of the mass in a very small volume relative to the size of the atom. The electrons that are negatively charged then must reside in the volume outside the nucleus.

[2] The Wilson cloud chamber detects particles of ionizing radiation by providing an environment of supersaturated water vapor in which an α-particle or a β-particle causes the water to become ionized along its trajectory. The ions condense the water vapor in the chamber into droplets, so one can see the particle tracks, like those of airline contrails in the sky.

[3] As a child, the author of this chapter saw this movie, *Madame Curie,* and after reading Eve Curie's biography of her mother, *Madame Curie: A Biography by Eve Curie* (Curie, 1937), she wanted to become a chemist and did so.

[4] Jean Perrin is considered the founder of the Centre National de la Recherché Scientifique (CNRS), the French National Science Foundation.

[5] When antibiotics were first discovered, they could cure tuberculosis, but with time, bacterial resistance to antibiotics developed, so penicillin and streptomycin were no longer so effective.

REFERENCES

Bensaude-Vincent, B. (1996). Star scientists in a Nobelist family: Irène and Frédéric Joliot-Curie. In H. M. Pycior, N. Slack, & P. Abir-AM (Eds.), *Creative couples in the sciences*. New Brunswick, NJ. Rutgers University Press.

Bibliopolis (1998–2011). Marguerite Perey. Retrieved from http://www.bibliopolis.com/main/books/hss_32971.html

Boudia, S. (2011). Marie Curie in the center of the atom and women in science. *Chemistry International*, 12–15 (January-February).

Brian, D. (2005). *The Curies: A biography of the most controversial family in science*. Hoboken, NJ: John Wiley & Sons, Inc.

Callahan, C. A. (1997). Irène Joliot-Curie (1907–1956) Physicist. In B. F. Shearer & B. S. Shearer (Eds.), *Notable women in the physical sciences: A biographical dictionary* (pp. 208–212). Westport, CT: Greenwood Press.

Crossfield, E. T. (1997). Irène-Curie following in her mother's footsteps. In M. F. Rayner-Canham & G. W. Rayner-Canham (Eds.), *A devotion to their science: Pioneer women of radioactivity* (pp. 97–123). Philadelphia, PA: Chemical Heritage Foundation.

Curie, E. (1937). *Madame Curie: A biography by Eve Curie*. New York: Doubleday, Doran & Co., Inc.

Curie, M. (1923). *Pierre Curie*. New York, NY: The Macmillan Company.

Des Jardins, J. (2010). *The Madame Curie complex: The hidden history of women in science*. New York: The Feminist Press.

Fondation d'Entreprise (2010). 2010 Irène Joliot-Curie Prize winners. Retrieved from http://www.fondation.eads.net/en/2010-Irène-joliot-curie-prize-winners

Gajendiran, N., Jayachandran, N., Rao, B. S., Unny, V. K. P., & Thyagarajan, S. (1994). Biotechnological production of high specific activity L-^{35}S-cysteine and L-^{35}S-methionine by using a diploid yeast Saccharomyces cerevisiae. *Journal of Labeled Compounds and Radiopharmaceuticals, 34*(3), 571–576.

Gilmer, P. J. (1982). Physical separation and biochemical characterization of H-2^b-encoded proteins on target cell plasma membranes and endoplasmic reticulum. *Journal of Biological Chemistry, 257*, 7839–7846.

Goldsmith, B. (2005). *Obsessive genius: The inner world of Marie Curie*. New York: W. W. Norton & Co.

Ham, D. (Winter 2002–03). Marie Sklodowska Curie: The woman who opened the nuclear age. *21st Century*, 30–68.

International Atomic Energy Association (2011). Retrieved from http://www.iaea.org/Publications/Factsheets/ English/polonium210.html

Irene Joliot-Curie (n. d.). Thoughts of research. Retrieved from http://Irène-curie.livejournal.com/

Joliot, F. (1935). Chemical evidence of the transmutation of elements: Nobel lecture. Retrieved from the Nobel Prize website: http://nobelprize.org/nobel_prizes/chemistry/laureates/1935/joliot-fred-lecture.pdf

Joliot-Curie, I. (1935). Artificial production of radioactive elements: Nobel lecture. Retrieved from http://nobelprize.org/nobel_prizes/chemistry/laureates/1935/joliot-curie-lecture.html

Langevin-Joliot, H., & Radvanyi, P. (2006). Irène Joliot-Curie (1897–1956). In N. Byers & G. Williams (Eds.), *Out of the shadows: Contributions of twentieth-century women to physics* (pp. 137–148). New York: Cambridge University Press.

Madame Curie (film) (1943). Retrieved from the Wikipedia website: http://en.wikipedia.org/wiki/Madame_Curie_%28film%29

McGrayne, S. B. (1998). *Nobel Prize women in science: Their lives, struggles, and momentous discoveries* (2nd ed.). Secaucus, NJ: Carol Publishing Group.

Nobelprize.org (1926). Jean Perrin. Nobel Prize in Physics. Retrieved from http://nobelprize.org/nobel_prizes/physics/laureates/1926/perrin-lecture.html

Nobelprize.org (1935a). Frédéric Joliot and Irène Joliot-Curie. Nobel Prize in Chemistry. Retrieved from http://nobelprize.org/nobel_prizes/chemistry/laureates/1935/joliot-curie-bio.html

Nobelprize.org (1935b). James Chadwick. Nobel Prize in Physics. Retrieved from http://nobelprize.org/nobel_prizes/physics/laureates/1935/chadwick-bio.html#

Nobelprize.org (1936). Victor F. Hess and Carl D. Anderson. The Nobel Prize in Physics. Retrieved from http://nobelprize.org/nobel_prizes/physics/laureates/1936/anderson-bio.html

Nobelprize.org (1977). Rosalyn Yalow. The Nobel Prize in Physiology or Medicine. Retrieved from http://nobelprize.org/nobel_prizes/medicine/laureates/1977/yalow-autobio.html

Pflaum, R. (1989). *Grand obsession: Madame Curie and her world*. New York: Doubleday.

Physicist of the week (2011). Retrieved from http://www.larrymusa.com/Physicists/Curie.aspx

Pycior, H. (1989). Marie Curie's "anti-natural path": Time only for science and family. In P. G. Abir-Am & D. Outram (Eds.), *Uneasy careers and intimate lives: Women in science, 1789–1979* (pp. 191–214). New Brunswick, NJ: Rutgers University Press.

Quinn, S. (1995). *Marie Curie: A life*. New York: Simon & Schuster.

Rutherford, E. (1919). Collisions of α-particles with light atoms. IV. An anomalous effect in nitrogen. The *London, Edinburgh and Dublin Philosophical Magazine and Journal of Science*, 6th series, 37, 581 [Retrieved from http://web.lemoyne.edu/~giunta/RUTHERFORD.HTMl]

Sime, R. L. (1996). *Lise Meitner: A life in physics*. Berkeley, CA: University of California Press.

The Nobel Prize in Peace, 1965, Acceptance speech (1965). Retrieved from http://nobelprize.org/nobel_prizes/peace/laureates/1965/unicef-acceptance.html?print=1

Vujic, J. (2009). Lise Meitner and nuclear fission. Retrieved from http://www.k-grayengineeringeducation.com/blog/index.php/2009/02/11/engineering-education-blog-lise-meitner-and-nuclear-fission-2/

Weart, S. R. (1979). *Scientists in power*. Cambridge, MA: Harvard University Press.

Penny J. Gilmer
Professor Emerita
Department of Chemistry and Biochemistry,
Florida State University
gilmer@chem.fsu.edu

JULIE DES JARDINS

3. AMERICAN MEMORIES OF MADAME CURIE

Prisms on the Gendered Culture of Science

INTRODUCTION

In January 2005, Lawrence Summers, then the president of Harvard University, opened a Pandora's box at a conference of the National Bureau of Economic Research. He posited that "issues of intrinsic aptitude" might be to blame for women's disproportionately poor standing in American science. Scientists and non-scientists were astounded at his audacity when news first broke of his comments, though transcripts later made public revealed more ambiguity in them. As it turned out, Summers cited more than biological rationales for the dearth of women in science--differences in socialization and patterns of discrimination were also possible culprits. But his suggestion that biology could be involved seemed to tear off the scab of a festering wound; the nurture/nature debate in science had been reopened in a very public forum.[1]

Until then, there were reasons to think that the charged debate over the "women's problem" in science was diminishing, even becoming a relic of the past. Though women still obtain science doctorates and fulltime science employment to a lesser degree than men, the trend in all science and engineering fields, aside from computer science, has been women's increasing numerical presence. In 1958, women earned 7.9% of doctorate degrees in all science, engineering, and health fields; by 2006 women represented 40.2% of the whole. In 1973 women were 4.3% of all full professors in science and engineering fields; in 2006 they were 19.4%, by no means a majority, but increasingly a force with which to contend.[2]

There is no reason to think that the numbers of women in science won't continue to rise, but are the numbers necessarily a gauge of the questions asked in science institutions or of the social ramifications of the work performed in them? One still has to wonder if the culture of science has changed, if women's qualitative experience of science empowers them, and if they truly enrich science with what they bring to the table. The highly charged reaction to Lawrence Summers in 2005 suggests to me that while many people think women can be competent scientists, they haven't shirked the ingrained notion that the concept of scienticity is masculine to the core. Despite women's growing numbers in science, the *culture* of science—its procedures, ideologies, and social organization—is fraught with bias that prevents women from working and succeeding on their terms.

M.-H. Chiu, P. J. Gilmer, and D. F. Treagust (Eds.), Celebrating the 100th Anniversary of Madame Marie Sklodowska Curie's Nobel Prize in Chemistry. 59–85.

And thus, while Summers may have inadvertently reopened debates about women and science that we hoped had been closed, he may also have done women and science a favor. He has allowed those of us observing science as culture to call for a collective refocusing of attention, to shift the crux of contentious feeling away from the classic argument of nurture or nature, to nurture or nurture: Is good science performed in the *culturally* feminine or masculine mode? Is there a feminine or feminist approach to scientific practice? And if there is, should there be?

Though it would be foolhardy to think in essentialist terms, we cannot deny that women scientists have brought unique perspective to scientific work and the natural world. Their biology does not orient them differently; women's perspectives of nature are often gained through the maternal, domestic, and *culturally* feminine work society assigns them. The converse is also true and stigmatizing: We often believe that women's presumed femininity gives them a certain relationship to nature, a relationship deemed too close and charged to promote disinterested science. A historical look at science as culture is the only way to assess the extent to which women have been scientists on empowering terms and can be in the future.

HISTORICAL PERSPECTIVES ON MARIE CURIE

The legendary Marie Curie is a woman whose story has been summoned to offer historical perspective on women scientists, though not typically the perspective of cultural context asked for here. She wasn't American, yet the sheer number of American books, films, and articles about her makes her the single best figure through which to analyze cultural constructions of women in American science. No doubt, her scientific discoveries help to make the case that science is not inherently manly. And yet Margaret Rossiter noted that when Curie came to the United States in the 1920s, her influence did less to inspire women into science than to create a strange inferiority complex in them that has not gone away. In the twenty-first century, it serves us well to be mindful of Curie's appropriation and remaking as an icon in American life, for only then can women scientists infuse her legacy with meaning that empowers.[3]

Curie did little to change the masculine cast of physical science with her American tours in the 1920s, but she might have had the publicity surrounding them been different. The tours had been the brainchild of Marie Mattingly (Missy) Meloney, a New York socialite and editor-in-chief of the women's publication, *The Delineator*. She had sought an interview with Curie in 1920, convinced that female readers of her magazine would want to hear from the reclusive scientist. Americans had been following Curie since *Vanity Fair* presented her and her husband Pierre to readers in 1904, months after they together with Henri Becquerel had shared the Nobel Prize in physics for radioactivity. In print, Marie Curie appeared to be a puzzling contradiction: Though she was the co-discoverer of radium, she was also the person responsible for family domesticity, and hence, a seemingly appropriate woman. The first American women with science degrees were presumably too domestic to be competent scientists in the professional, academic milieu; their ties to the home, real or not, were thought to make them too scattered and sentimental to achieve the intense focus professional science required. And yet for a time domesticity seemed not to tarnish Curie's reputation as a competent scientist. Only after Pierre Curie's death in 1906 did men use Curie's alleged domesticity, along with her non-marital sexuality, against her. Here we will explore why opinions of her changed, and to what extent Curie's early acceptance was largely perception in the first place. Her story sheds light on the ways women scientists continue to be conjured in the American mind.[4]

Early in the twentieth century Curie, like Lise Meitner, Ida Noddack, Harriet Brooks, and others, had enjoyed relative success in the "hard" (read masculine)[5] field of physics, but their success was largely in Europe, and, as we will see, made to appear to be success of another kind than what men achieved. By the 1920s and 1930s students at American women's colleges followed the lead of European standouts and majored in physical science in proportions equal to men. But their numbers tapered off in the graduate ranks, suggesting that there was a limit to the extent to which American women believed they could successfully combine high-level science and domesticity without social repercussions. Four times more women received doctorate degrees in the seemingly "softer" biological and social sciences in the 1930s than in Curie's field of physics, a field in which men earned 97 percent of the doctorates and won an even greater percentage of research posts afterward. Administrators cited women's lack of experience in prestigious research institutions as one factor, their tendency to marry and leave the profession as another. And there, too, was the problem of perception: few people could imagine women as physicists. This cultural factor cannot be minimized, since it has led to the historical obscurity of women who became physicists, despite the challenges, and to other women's internalization of the belief that they could never be monastic, cerebral, or masculine enough to enter the field.[6]

It's no wonder that Curie's tours did little to shake the virile image of physicists: women scientists were almost nowhere to be found in the publicity and events that accompanied them, and Curie herself was rarely presented to the American public in ways that altered preconceived notions about the gender and women scientists. Here I mine the work of Margaret Wertheim, Daniel Kevles, Bert Hansen, Marcel LaFollette, and others who have analyzed the making of science icons, and I engage Margaret Rossiter's assessments of the effects of Curie's tours on practicing women scientists in America.[7] But I also tease out the various Curies imagined by American women, medical men, industrial scientists, and the popular media over decades to assess the *cultural* effects of Curie and her tours. The incarnations of Curie—literary, filmic, and feminist—tell us about Americans' collective thoughts on women scientists in the twentieth century.

CURIE'S RADIUM CAMPAIGN, 1920–1929: CREATING AN ACCEPTABLE IMAGE
OF A WOMAN IN SCIENCE

Curie's First Trip to the United States

When Marie Curie granted Missy Meloney the interview that led to her American
tours, she had been a widow for nearly 15 years and the recipient of yet another
Nobel Prize, this time in the field of chemistry. American women, meanwhile,
were in the midst of winning suffrage and had come to comprise nearly half of the
undergraduate population on American college campuses. Modest numbers of
women had entered scientific institutions when the demands of World War I
expanded research opportunities in photographic, communications, and ballistic
technologies. Many who might have been shunted into home economics were
producing gas and projectile weapons, explosives, instrumentation, and other war
materials. Curie herself had left her laboratory in Paris for the battle front in 1916
to bring X-ray equipment to makeshift medical facilities on the frontlines, proving
that women, too, could contribute to the male realms of science and war.[8]

The opportunities the war created for American women also had their limits,
however. Though more and more women earned academic credentials in science
fields, they were hard-pressed to receive titles and salaries as scientists after
wartime contingency plans subsided. If they were lucky to find employment in
laboratories after college, they were typically segregated from men within and
across fields, congregating at the lowest rungs of prestigious fields or on higher
rungs in fields with little prestige at all. At women's colleges like Mount Holyoke,
Wellesley, and Vassar, women conducted research that rivaled that performed in
male institutions. And yet scientists at women's colleges couldn't shed their
identities as casual experimenters, pedagogues, and assistants, by virtue of their sex
and segregation.[9]

Prestige in professional science continued to rely on its masculine cast. And thus
women were ejected from physical sciences deemed "hard" in the name of higher
standards. At some universities, including Yale, NYU, Cornell, MIT, and the
University of Chicago, women instructors filled niches of expertise in hygiene,
nutrition, "social," "domestic," and generally "softer" science. Older generations of
women didn't complain, since these fields allowed them still to appear to be doing
appropriately feminine work in the professional sphere. Younger women, however,
increasingly tried to combine college, marriage, and work in science, and they
worried that they would never be seen as competent scientists if they didn't
compete directly with men in men's fields.

American women scientists felt like second-class citizens in the laboratory, and
yet there was Madame Curie, a woman who seemed to have defied the odds, to
succeed as a properly feminine woman and competent scientist at the same time.
She held a doctorate degree and won the highest of professional honors—even
while raising children. She was a single mother and a world-class scientist--an
everyday woman who made greatness look reachable. Missy Meloney thought

American women would see her as an icon for achieving it all--marriage, family, and career—without compromising her endearing femininity.

Curie's successes could be a positive influence on American women, Meloney figured, and perhaps there was something American women could do for Curie in return. Over the course of their conversations, Meloney discovered that the legendary scientist could no longer afford the radium she had discovered. She never patented the process for making it, and in fact shared all she knew so that others could make it readily. American chemical producers sold it to well-funded labs and medical facilities in milligram increments for $120 apiece. Curie wanted an entire gram of it, to keep at her institute in Paris, but she had largely resigned herself to watching others build on her methods for extracting it. As Curie described her predicament to Meloney, the American publicist envisioned a mutually beneficial situation in the offing: If American women raised money for Curie's radium, perhaps the French scientist would let them exploit her celebrity to advance their humanitarian causes and professional designs. Meloney figured that American women could use Curie's image just as chemical companies were exploiting Albert Einstein's image to raise funds for themselves and his educational initiatives overseas.[10]

But Meloney's iconic figure was a woman; any coverage of Curie in the American press would be more conspicuous by the paucity of coverage on women scientists as a whole. Taking into account scientists both as authors and biographical subjects, male scientists were fifteen times more visible than their female counterparts in mainstream American magazines. Moreover, journalists described science as an endeavor requiring culturally virile attributes--emotional detachment, intellectual objectivity, even physical strength at times. A good female scientist was, discursively speaking, an inept woman; as an exemplar of true womanhood was, by definition, an inept scientist. Meloney would have to find a way to subvert these contradictions in her publicity campaign. Rather than appear a walking contradiction, Curie would have to appear all things to all people to appeal to Americans as a cause worth funding.[11]

Women were presumably not natural scientists because professional-caliber science, as defined by its male practitioners, was not possible to achieve in women's emotionally charged domestic sphere. They were, however, deemed natural healers in their roles as nurturers of children and caretakers for the ill and aged. Women involved in professional medicine—clinical fields in particular-- appeared not to have transgressed their domestic roles to the same extent as those who occupied the sterile space of the laboratory. Sensing this, Meloney conjured an image of Curie not in the laboratory but in the sickroom; hers would not look like abstract science, but applied science, humanitarian science--the kind of science mothers could and should carry out in an expanded conception of the domestic sphere. Meloney made Curie appear less a science hero than a science martyr, a woman who, by happenstance, used science to perform the womanly work of healing.[12]

Meloney was taking a page from the books of other American women who had succeeded as scientists by appearing to be something else. Since the late nineteenth century Alice Hamilton and Ellen Swallow Richards had researched in laboratories at Harvard and MIT, but the direct domestic applications of their work in the fields of nutrition and sanitation made their trespass into male bastions of science permissible; the healing applications of their work made them domestic women in scientific contexts, forces of medical benevolence, integrators of the "hard" and "soft" sides of science in ways that made them appear scientists of another stripe, if scientists at all. Meloney understood that American women were emulating scientific healers like Richards and Hamilton as they entered the fields of nursing and clinical medicine in larger numbers than ever before. Presumably, they studied organic material rather than the lifeless stuff of physical science.

Initiatives underway to increase cancer education and press coverage of radium research seemed to affirm Meloney's strategy to reinvent Curie's physics, turning inanimate radium into a regenerative force for healing. The American Society for the Control of Cancer (ASCC) was soon to launch its first national "Cancer Week" and to release its first motion picture to educate the public and raise funds for cancer research. No doubt the society would welcome the chance to attach its cause to a recognizable celebrity like Curie, one who ostensibly represented humanitarian sacrifice to cure the disease. The martyrdom of cancer researchers was an image already established when Meloney transferred it on to Curie in the 1920s, for the press habitually reported on deaths considered linked to cancer and radium research. As more of the world's radium experts succumbed to mysterious illness, Curie's physical frailties appeared all the more saintly in Meloney's hands.[13]

Meloney called on her literary connections to get dozens of articles about Curie into print in 1920. In major publications throughout the States, Curie's story contained all the elements of an American legend in the making: It was a tale of travesty about a woman—a mother--who had sacrificed for the world but had received nothing in return. She had endured abject poverty and physical discomfort to discover the element that was the leading cure for cancer, but she had refused to patent its production so that the researchers of the world could begin using it to heal. Rather than be heralded a saint, Curie paid a price for her altruism. She needed money—not for her own creature comforts, but to pay for the radium she needed to perform research that would end human suffering. Articles emphasized Curie's importance to the field of cancer research and painted images of her as appealingly maternal and sacrificing. Meloney herself praised Curie in print for "minister[ing] to an agonized people." Curie's face, she wrote, "had suffering and patience in it," as did "every line of her slender body." In its totality, hers was "the mother look" epitomized.[14]

Meloney's iconic Curie was saint-like to some; but to younger, ambitious others, she could look to have achieved the American dream, even if not on American soil. Too poor to pursue science formally, Curie journalists reminded readers, had borrowed books from a factory library in her homeland of Poland and earned money to purchase a fourth-class ticket to Paris. The twenty-four-year-old had arrived in the Latin Quarter, where she studied by candlelight and exercised the frugality of legend.[15] American publicists made much of Curie's courtship with the only person who allegedly caught her attention during her monastic years at the

Sorbonne. Pierre Curie, a thirty-five-year-old physics professor, was a man of equal but different intensity when he met Marie in 1894. He believed that their single-minded devotion to science should be their gift to humanity, and Marie eventually agreed. To Meloney, Curie described the path she and Pierre walked together as an "*anti-natural*" one: they pared down all distractions outside their immediate family, ate and dressed plainly, and rarely entertained guests in their three-room apartment--all to live and breathe their research.[16]

The American press romanticized the Curies' austerity and their conducting of experiments side-by-side in their freezing, dilapidated shed in Paris. While Pierre studied the properties of radium, Marie extracted pure radium salts, dissolving pitchblende, a uranium ore, in acid before chemically separating its elements. Amid the hauling, stirring, measuring, and recording of data, Marie also managed to give birth to her daughter Irene. Only biographers in recent decades have considered childbirth--a private, domestic affair--an event integral in the life story of Curie the public scientist. Earlier in the twentieth century biographers were reluctant to reveal her as a mother and scientist at the same time, choosing one storyline or the other and thus sidestepping the fact that, at times, she thought the baby an unwanted distraction. Desperate for domestic help that she could afford, she searched for wet nurses, housekeepers, and nannies and was frustrated by the amount of time this took away from research, as did the additional teaching hours she had to take on to cover the cost of her helpers. Curie's father-in-law came to her aid and helped to care for Irene as his own. But sentimentalized accounts of a doting mother served Meloney's public relations campaign better, since they supported the image of Curie as a medical martyr.[17]

The American press often referred to the fact that Curie had been a widow since Pierre suffered fatal head injuries in a traffic accident in the Rue de Dauphine in Paris. Her widow status seemed to solidify further her image as altruistic, and her science as purely motivated. At the same time it also reminded readers that Curie had not transgressed the expectations that all women, even scientists, become wives. In referring to Curie as "Pierre Curie's widow," journalists reminded readers that Curie had once worked alongside a man who, they liked to think, was the mind behind her experiments. This early coverage of Curie set the tone for what has followed: biographers have since spent as much time writing about her husband as her, treating the couple as utter complements, despite the many more years of her conducting research alone. Pierre has been passed down to posterity as the thinker, and Marie as the doer, "the muscle" of the pair. The characterization is inaccurate, but it persists. Only in the context of a scientific relationship is the 'doer' deemed a role of lesser status.[18]

Though journalists spoke of the gory details of Pierre's accident, they left out any detail relating to the sexism Curie experienced in its aftermath. Of course this sexism has only been construed as such in recent decades, since men of the science establishment believed that their stigmatization of her was wholly deserved at the time. Curie had refused a widow's pension when Pierre died, choosing instead to take over his academic appointment at the Sorbonne. But when the period of mourning was over, reaction to her university appointment turned negative, as colleagues and the press looked critically at the woman propelled professionally by her husband's death. Pierre had been elected into the *Académie des Sciences* in 1905, but his colleagues took less kindly to his wife when she applied for admission six years later. Curie's detractors built their case against her when the wife of physicist Paul Langevin, Pierre's former student, alleged publicly that he and Curie were lovers and released supposed love letters to the tabloids, creating a publicity nightmare from which Curie never recovered.[19]

The internationally venerated Albert Einstein committed adultery without ill effect in the press, but Curie was different. Although she wasn't an adulteress, another man's wife revealed her as a sexual being, making the fiction of her saintly science more difficult to hold up for the public. Lenard Berlanstein notes that at the fin-de-siècle, the French press cast a flattering light on women who accomplished in the professional sphere, including Curie, but only when they could be portrayed as appropriate helpmeets fulfilling their wifely and maternal duties at home. Before the Langevin scandal journalists rarely broached the topic of Curie's scientific accolades without also reminding readers of the doting mother she continued to be despite them.[20] But once the Langevin letters were published, everything changed. In the daily newspaper *L'Excelsior,* a handwriting expert examined the alleged love letters and determined Curie unfit for membership in the *Academie.* A prominent French editor wrote of her in scathing terms: she was no longer the "Vestal Virgin of Radium" but a Polish interloper with inappropriate ambitions.[21]

In Europe Curie quietly endured the smear campaign, but in America, Meloney believed it possible to reinstate Curie's maternal image among Americans willing to forgive her faults. Meloney had the word of newspaper editors that they would make no mention of the love affair during her radium campaign. And thus the woman scientist who Meloney introduced to Americans appeared as the Virgin Mary in black—saint-like, and in no way sexual. Her refusal to patent her method for extracting radium was presented as an absolute sign of her altruism, and her tragic circumstances as a widow only buttressed the image. Curie appreciated Meloney's intentions, but had reservations. To base a campaign on her sentimental motivations was to make her look emotional, subjective, and hence defective to male scientists. The maternalism that American women evoked to win access to college and the vote on moralistic grounds was antithetical to the idea of science that Curie had come to revere as a scientist trained in the Western positivist tradition. She had abstained from ideological movements her whole life to work in the spirit of "pure science" and wanted nothing to do with developing medical applications for radium or advancing the cause of women. But for the sake of obtaining her radium, she reticently deferred to Meloney.[22]

There was no doubt of Meloney's instincts once the donations to Curie's cause poured in. When newspaper editor Arthur Brisbane wrote a check for $100 to the Radium Fund, he dedicated it not to a woman scientist, but to Julia Ward Howe, the patriot who wrote the Battle Hymn of the Republic. Carrie Chapman Catt, the pacifist and suffrage organizer, wrote a piece in support of the radium campaign in *Woman Citizen* called "Helping Madame Curie to Help the World," suggesting that she had embraced Curie as Meloney had hoped: as an expedient face of her maternalist politics.[23]

If Curie was uncomfortable representing these causes, she found Meloney's next request excruciating. Once she raised more than $100,000 to purchase the gram of radium, Meloney asked the French scientist to accept her gift in person, among her American admirers. In gratitude, Curie agreed to six weeks of grueling touring around the United States. For the summer of 1921, Meloney planned lunches with the ladies of the Radium Fund committee and visits with students at women's colleges before attending a massive reception of the American Association of University Women (AAUW) at Carnegie Hall. Standard Chemical and the Department of Mines also hosted events where Curie would receive specimens of precious ores. She would dedicate the mining bureau's low-temperature laboratory, pushing the button setting its machinery in motion. Curie's daughters Irene and Eve, now twenty-three and sixteen years of age, agreed to accompany their mother, serving as her companions and occasional stand-ins.[24]

Meloney was heartened that men from the University of Pennsylvania, Yale, Pittsburgh, Chicago, Northwestern, and Columbia bestowed Curie with honorary degrees, though the men of Harvard decided that Curie was undeserving of honors from their institution. Meloney's reaction was yet again to hold up Curie's maternity as something to behold. To Harvard president Charles Eliot she wrote: "The outstanding virtue of these years lies in the fact that having discovered radium and come into prominence [Curie] turned to her home as a normal mother and gave the intimate minute attention to her children which motherhood should impose."[25] Eliot and his colleagues were unmoved, for the prestige of Harvard science was at stake. Though they could admire her from afar, in America, Curie, the seeming philanthropist, threatened their identities as the most elite of professional scientists.

The snub was of no consequence to Curie, who traveled to venues grudgingly, but graciously smiling and shaking hands. Almost never were women scientists in her midst; nor was there talk of science for "science's sake." At Carnegie Hall, college women interpreted her work with radium as a gesture of humanitarianism rather than scientific acumen. Bryn Mawr College president M. Carey Thomas urged her collegiate audience to pursue science if so inclined, but more importantly, to use science to exert influence on politics and pacifist diplomacy. American women had won suffrage months before, and Thomas hoped Curie would inspire them to form a voting bloc to bring about military disarmament—"human legislation" as she called it.[26]

A ceremony at the White House had come to signify more than Curie ever hoped to represent. President Harding handed her a key that opened a box in which her radium would be placed once retrieved from the Bureau of Standards. Cabinet officers, military men, Supreme Court judges, and foreign diplomats convened before her, as representatives of women's societies welcomed her as their new "adopted daughter." Harding declared her radium a symbol of the "convergence of intellectual and social sympathies" between Curie and the American people: "We lay at your feet the testimony of that love which all the generations of men have been wont to bestow upon the noble woman, the unselfish wife, the devoted mother…[T]he zeal, ambition and unswerving purpose of a lofty career could not bar you from splendidly doing all the plain but worthy tasks which fall to every woman's lot."[27]

Curie bristled at her iconic martyrdom privately to Meloney. From thereafter she asked to have newspaper editors retract statements proclaiming her a saint of science, Mother of the Year, or the curer of cancer. During a speech at Vassar College Curie reminded her audience that her discovery of radium was the work "of pure science…done for itself" rather than with "direct usefulness" in mind. But, thanks to Meloney, her legendary altruism had already been established and fixed in the popular mind.[28]

Before long, publicists could no longer conceal that the awe Curie inspired wasn't necessarily returned. By the time the tour reached its third week, her irritation with American hospitality had become a topic for print. "Mme. Curie is 'completely tired out,'" The New York Times reported. "Questions and the 'small talk' of American women and men also have fagged her brain." The following day a journalist reported that the customary handshaking was "beginning to bore the French scientist"; she wore a sling to avoid the grips of admirers. The American press excused her behavior, supposing her aloofness to be an unfortunate symptom of radium illness. On the other hand, journalists also didn't know what to make of the woman. Did her "severely plain" dress suggest that she was masculine--too stuck in her head to be concerned with fashion; or feminine--too saintly to succumb to vanity?[29] Observers couldn't make up their minds. In the summer of 1921, Marie Curie stood squarely at the center of conflicting thoughts about women and science.

Curie's Second Trip to the United States

In 1928 Meloney convinced Curie to come to the United States once again, this time to accept a gram of radium her committee secured for the Curie Institute in Warsaw. Remembering how draining the first visit had been, the sixty-year-old Curie agreed to come stateside only if she could avoid interviews and situations in which she was obligated to meet the public. American women obliged, yet this final U.S. tour, like the last, was hardly about them at all. At Thomas Edison's Golden Jubilee, an event Curie attended grudgingly, one prominent male inventor paid homage to another, and at General Electric she was led on a tour of facilities occupied exclusively by men. Though a woman donated a statue of Curie to go alongside the chemistry building she dedicated at St. Lawrence College, men flanked Curie at the dedication ceremonies. Physicist George Pegram spoke: "We, with the rest of the world, honor Mme. Curie for her very life, for her steadfast devotion to science, her patriotic service, her modesty. We honor her as a wife and mother. The nobility of her life is such that our admiration for her character almost turns our attention from her scientific rank." In this tour, like the last, Curie's science--and the science of American women—virtually had been erased from view, as her maternity remained in the forefront of all the coverage.[30]

It didn't help that Curie's scientific legend had already lost luster to the more endearing Albert Einstein's in the eyes of the American public. The *New York Times* reported that at a meeting of the League of Nations' Committee on Intellectual Cooperation, Curie declined all social invitations, while Einstein was congenial and engaging. No doubt, his popularity could be attributed to the heightened prestige of theoretical physics following the development of quantum mechanics. He represented "pure science," that theorized in the mind, rather than the applied science that cured cancer--and that Americans had decided to associate with the female Curie. He had become an icon of a brand of genius—a form of Platonic transcendence—that was decidedly male. Women's role in this genius was to tend to the bodily needs of the men who embodied it, since they were presumably too distracted by the dailyness of domesticity to achieve it on their own. In the case of the younger Einstein, that caretaker was his wife Mileva Maric, who gave up her own science career to cater to Einstein and his children. He went on to leave Maric for another woman, but the exploits in his personal life did nothing to tarnish his scientific reputation. While scientists in Paris accused Curie of being neglectful of her children as she focused intently on her science, they revered male colleagues for the same single-minded devotion; it was irrelevant that such devotion wasn't in evidence at home.[31]

When Curie left New York the second time, check in hand, the fallout of the stock market crash on Wall Street was just setting in. Her departure coincided with the fiscal unraveling that led to the Great Depression and that devastated many sectors of the American economy, not the least of which was the chemical industry her discoveries and image had propped up and that American women had hoped to enter. Women scientists who had found jobs in laboratories after Curie's first tour relinquished them to men after the second tour. Their professional aspirations appeared inappropriate amid pressures to contribute to shrinking family wages, and thus many of them chose to forego science for pink-collar employment. For almost all women, Curie's path seemed an impossible dream, and Curie a superhuman anomaly.

Meloney had created a Curie that was extraordinarily competent, but also reassuringly maternal. She hoped to appeal to newly emerging professional women and traditionalists at the same time, without conceding that she was working at cross-purposes. In the end, her iconic Curie was Janus-faced: a maternal martyr and a prototypical superwoman--too smart, too dedicated, too focused, and talented to be emulated by ordinary mortals. Meloney's schizophrenic figure could not combat the institutional sexism in American science. The numbers tell the story: Fewer than 1000 women earned science doctorates in the decade of Curie's tours-- an increase from the previous decade, but not the sea change many women hoped for when they first heard Curie was coming to America. This was, in fact, only 5 percent of all science degrees conferred. More pathetically, in Curie's field of physics, women averaged less than three doctorates a year. If Meloney had succeeded in making physics look accessible and appropriate as a field of endeavor, she apparently only demystified it for Curie's sake, not for the collectivity of American women who quietly longed to pursue hard science.[32]

Of course by 1930 fewer young women were even wishing to make Curie's personal and professional choices for themselves. Though they may have still admired her scientific accomplishments, by her second tour they viewed her austerity and asexual persona as relics of a bygone Victorian era. A sociological study confirmed that Curie's name had little resonance for girls of the flapper age. When 347 teenagers were asked to name a heroine, real or literary, who inspired them, only three girls chose Curie. Respondents who desired careers preferred social science over physical science and artistic careers above all (46 percent), further underscoring how impractical and unfeminine girls perceived Curie's choices for their own lives. It would be another 40 years before Curie's story was invoked again to inspire careerism in young American women.[33]

CURIE'S MATERNAL MYTH: A LEGACY FOR AMERICAN WOMEN SCIENTISTS

Marie Curie finally succumbed to the effects of radium poisoning in 1934. For the next several weeks, newspapers across the world and in American cities likened her death to the ultimate maternal sacrifice to humanity. The *New York Times* declared Curie a "martyr to science" and declared, "few persons contributed more to the general welfare of mankind and to the advancement of science than the modest, self-effacing woman." On the day of her death the physicist Robert Millikan, President of the California Institute of Technology, was compelled to issue a public statement: "[Marie Curie] has been an entirely effective scientist and intensely interested in public welfare and various progressive movements. In spite of her continuous absorption in her scientific work, she has devoted much time to the cause of peace... She embodied in her person all the simpler, homelier and yet most perfect virtues of womanhood."[34]

It was not only male scientists who used her death to reinstate sacrificial forms of womanhood and increase their own visibility. Within the year, New York Mayor Fiorello La Guardia dedicated "Marie Curie Avenue" on the city's East Side and then campaigned with 5,000 onlookers in attendance. Her life clearly held meaning for Americans, but in 1934 most continued to emphasize her feminine benevolence over her masculine science. Curie's wish not to be linked to cancer research had fallen on deaf ears when she lived; and in death, she remained virtually synonymous with the cause. It was not coincidence that the ASCC released major motion pictures on cancer education in 1921, the year Curie first came to the States, and in 1937, the year that Doubleday released the American version of the classic biography of Curie written by her daughter Eve. Cancer researchers indirectly seized on and perpetuated Curie's celebrity and martyr status as they showed their films in schools, churches, and women's club functions across the country.[35]

The same year Eve Curie's book was published in the United States, Congress also passed the National Cancer Act to support all activities related to the prevention, diagnosis, and treatment of cancer. Meanwhile, President Franklin Delano Roosevelt authorized the appropriation of funds to build a national cancer research center in Maryland. The press coverage of cancer surged on radio programs and on the pages of mainstream magazines *Life* and *Good Housekeeping*. In the late 1930s, Americans became familiar with even more forms of the disease, including the rare brain cancer suffered by the character Judith Traheme in *Dark Victory*, an Oscar-nominated film starring the legendary Bette Davis. The press divulged details about the cancer-related death of composer George Gershwin and covered the rise of "glioma babies" born in American hospitals. Popular campaigns continued to extol the benefits of radium treatments for cancer, much as they had when Curie came to the States in the 1920s. Hollywood directors counteracted much of the panic stirred by the increased media coverage with portrayals of laboratory researchers unlocking the mysteries of the disease. Curie was depicted as the most devoted of them all.[36]

When the ASCC collaborated with women's clubs to form the Women's Field Army, spreading cancer education at the grassroots level, Curie, again, was the organization's natural choice of a symbolic figurehead. In 1938 the Metropolitan Life Insurance Company named Curie one of its "Health Heroes" in a popular literary series for children. Author Grace T. Hallock heralded Curie's discovery of radium as the reason why physicians could "save the lives of people suffering from the dreaded disease." As did all the literary and popular pieces that treated Curie as a medical martyr, Hallock's chronicled Curie's Spartan years at the Sorbonne and her decision to live in poverty to make radium available to the world. Yet again, Curie also appeared acceptably maternal and sacrificing, without sacrificing family for research: "The thought never occurred to Marie, that she might have to choose between family life and a scientific career," wrote Hallock. "She had them both and cheated neither."[37]

That Curie's maternal myth persisted was never the intention of Curie herself. In her lifetime she had written only one brief autobiographical piece,[38] which Missy Meloney asked her to write in the aftermath of her first American tour. Upon viewing the drafts, editors asked her to humanize her self-portrait, perhaps even emphasize her affection toward her children. Curie refused, insisting that the work was in tribute to her husband and to clarify their science, not to aggrandize herself. Meloney contemplated writing a more revealing portrait of a wife and mother, but Curie begged her not to write on her behalf, even asking her friend to destroy all letters she had written her over the years.[39]

Yet even with all the precautions, Curie could not stem the popular makeovers to come. Any number of Americans attempted to fill the voids she left, interpreting her life as they saw fit. Curie's daughters knew that their mother would have scoffed at posthumous treatments of her. They tried to suppress them, but publishers and Hollywood scriptwriters had agendas of their own.[40] Eve Curie wrote *Marie Curie* in an attempt to have the last definitive word, but even *her* portrait deviated little from the others:

> [Curie] belonged to an oppressed nation; she was poor; she was beautiful. A powerful vocation summoned her from her motherland, Poland, to study in Paris, where she lived through years of poverty and solitude. There she met a man whose genius was akin to hers. She married him; their happiness was unique. By the most desperate and arid effort they discovered a magic

element, radium. This discovery not only gave birth to a new science and a new philosophy: it provided mankind with the means of treating a dreadful disease.

At the moment when the fame of the two scientists and benefactors was spreading through the world, grief overtook Marie: her husband, her wonderful companion, was taken from her by death in an instant. But in spite of distress and physical illness, she continued alone the work that had been begun with him and brilliantly developed the science they had created together.

The rest of her life resolved itself into a kind of perpetual giving. To the war wounded she gave her devotion and her health. Later on she gave her advice, her wisdom and all the hours of her time to her pupils, to future scientists who came to her from all parts of the world.

When her mission was accomplished she died exhausted, having refused wealth and endured her honors with indifference.[41]

Eve Curie's picture of an altruistic, single-minded scientist and devoted wife inspired women for generations to come, but it also tormented readers hampered by family distractions, sexual urges, and human frailties that seemed not to cross her mother's 'anti-natural path.' Her heroine was still a medical martyr who did little to quash the image of female science formed in the American mind.

Marie Curie was a bestseller in decades which historian Bert Hansen characterizes as a high tide for popularized medical science generally. By the 1940s the *True Comics* franchise featured "Wonder Women of History" and included Curie in its coterie of medical, nursing, and public health pioneers. In the hands of popularizers, Curie identified with nurses Clara Barton and Florence Nightingale more readily than her colleague Albert Einstein. Americans also witnessed the rise of the "science biopic," (or, more specifically, the "medical researcher biopic") the most epic of them being William Dieterle's *The Story of Louis Pasteur* (1936), a film about the French chemist, once revered by Curie herself. Films about Alexander Graham Bell (1939) and Thomas Edison (1939, 1940) made science look heroic, while others about female figures like Florence Nightingale (1936) and Sister Kenny (1946) depicted their subjects as compassionate healers and martyrs.[42] In 1943 MGM released Mervyn LeRoy's *Madame Curie*, a film in which Meloney's image of Curie persisted: female science looked to be a benevolent enterprise, engaged strictly for altruistic purposes.

LeRoy's film was strangely schizophrenic in its messages about gender and science. Watched by troops overseas and housewives in hometown theaters, it served as both patriotic propaganda and prescriptive love story during World War II. As the government summoned living, breathing researchers to radar laboratories, ballistics testing grounds, and Manhattan Project sites, the film celebrated scientific progress as the best defense against Axis aggression. The final scene was a brief tableau of Curie 25 years after Pierre's death, espousing the nobility of science.

There were no depictions of her longer solo career, since they did not serve the purpose of promoting romantic marriage or masculine science—both preoccupations of the wartime propaganda machine.[43]

T. Hugh Crawford has since characterized *Madame Curie* as a potentially feminist film steeped in patriarchal discourse. Curie looked to be a masculine observer of natural phenomena, but she, as played by the attractive Greer Garson, was simultaneously the object of the film viewer's gaze, objectified as masculine scientists objectify the nature they study. Curie and her radium were both objects to be enamored with and mastered. In the film Pierre pursued Marie as doggedly as he did his science, only to prove that women, like nature, reveal themselves fully to man in the end. Crawford laments that there was no way to account for a more complex Curie in the viewing conventions of film or in the social order of wartime America. As a competent scientist and altruistic woman—though not an explicitly maternal one in this case--she only could be seen as a walking contradiction.[44]

As *Madame Curie* played in American theaters, a shift was taking place in university science programs and industrial laboratories. Wartime necessity caused university administrators temporarily to rescind anti-nepotism policies that, more often than not, barred female job applicants over male ones. Women taught in 12 percent of science classrooms in 1942 and nearly 40 percent by 1946; in chemistry and biology, women on college faculties increased nearly 230 percent. Women also made temporary inroads in weapons, radar, and other industries once restricted to men. Female meteorologists, geologists, and oceanographers joined the Navy's Hydrographic Office, the Geologic Survey, the Weather Bureau, and the Bureau of Standards. Women found masculine fields porous during the war, while those working in traditionally female niches of expertise became culturally more relevant than ever before. Members of the National Research Council's Food and Nutrition Committee, for instance, created guidelines for wartime diets and rationing, and women of the Office of Scientific Research and Development (OSRD) found new uses for penicillin and anti-malarial drugs.[45]

Had popular images of Marie Curie changed male employers' views about women scientists? It's likely that the exigencies of war were more responsible for the new opportunities. Historically, such states of emergency relax gender roles to make temporary openings in masculine fields once closed to women. Margaret Rossiter concludes that while women enjoyed unprecedented access to science research and teaching during the war, World War II didn't create a lasting or qualitative sea change for women scientists, much like the first world war and Curie's tours hadn't earlier. The percentage of female to male scientists on the National Roster was virtually unchanged in these years (4 percent in 1941 versus 4.1 percent five years later), and most women in these years occupied low-level, temporary, and untenured positions, overqualified for their jobs. Many women with science PhDs worked for the OSRD as librarians and technical aides, not in the laboratory or as researchers. Again, Curie's visibility may have stirred the pot, without actually pushing it over.[46]

Americans heard little during or after the war about Leona Woods Marshall, Kay Way, Joan Hinton, or the hundreds of other women who had followed Curie's path in science and helped to develop the atom bomb.[47] Their obscurity was odd given the increasing social stature of scientists generally caused by the war. Nuclear physicists, in particular, had garnered the most prestige of all. In 1947 Americans ranked them 18th out of 90 in terms of perceived professional prestige. By 1963 they ranked 3rd, just behind high-level politicians and diplomats. That Americans imagined nuclear physicists—or any scientists—of the postwar era as inherently male was born out in a study conducted by anthropologists Margaret Mead and Rhoda Metreaux in 1956: When they asked American high school students to draw a scientist, the vast majority drew figures with lab coats, glasses, and beards.[48]

In this postwar era a writer for *Life* magazine perpetuated the hero-worship of male atomic physicists, describing them as donning the "tunic of Superman." Robert Oppenheimer, Enrico Fermi, and Edward Teller of Los Alamos fame graced magazine covers, popular and scientific, and their connections to the Atomic Energy Commission, the National Institutes of Health, and the National Science Foundation propelled them further into the limelight as authorities on national policy. Americans viewed their scientific genius as the ultimate defense against Red Spread in the Cold War era, and viewed their genius as inherently male. Ironically, Curie's work in atomic science led to their heightened cultural authority, as she remained an icon of feminine benevolence—an image antithetical to disinterested, high-level, professional science as Americans imagined it.[49]

When Curie came to the States, one out of every 12 American doctorate degrees in mathematics and physical science and one out of every six in biological science belonged to women. During the 1940s and 50s the ratios of women to men in mathematics and physical science plummeted to 1 in 25, and in life science 1 in 11. In the 1960s *actual numbers* of women in science fields rose, but their *proportion* to men decreased or barely changed. Only in biological science did women maintain a significant presence (27%), but even here, as in all science fields, women were fewer up the promotional ladder. One could count on one hand the number of women among over 700 members of the National Academy of Science. Men of similar rank still had an easier time finding jobs in the 1960s, and made about $1.50 to every dollar made by female colleagues. While four out of five male scientists were married and living with spouses, only two out of five women could say the same. Marriage status was not an obstacle for men at any level, but the proportion of married women plummeted in science ranks beyond the bachelor degree.[50]

Though numbers of women in science fields remained low in the early 1960s, 1962–1963 proved to be as transformative a moment in feminist politics as it was in the conception of scientific epistemology. Maria Goeppert Mayer received a Nobel Prize in the virile field of atomic physics at the same time Betty Friedan demystified the dissatisfaction of suburban housewives in *The Feminine Mystique*. President Kennedy's Commission on the Status of Women and the National Research Council confirmed that at no other time in the nation's history had women been so committed to the fulltime raising of children *and* professional endeavors, despite the culturally pervasive image of the happy American housewife.

Such findings were integral to Congress passing the Civil Rights Act of 1964, which made it illegal to discriminate on the grounds of gender in any job sector, including science.

Equality between male and female scientists had never been the reality, yet more women scientists began to think it a goal worth pursuing in the 1960s and 1970s. One of the first consciousness-raising events organized after 1964 took place at MIT, a symposium on "American Women in Science and Engineering," followed by the organization of a wave of women's caucuses within professional science organizations to police hiring and promotional practices. This heightened activity of practicing women scientists coincided with the passing of Title IX of the Education Act Amendments and the Equal Opportunity Employment Act of 1972 and a national thrust towards affirmative action and female recruitment in the sciences, which led to several prominent appointments of women scientists in Washington and the passing of Edward Kennedy's bill to promote women in science in 1978.[51]

As feminists of the Women's Liberation Movement took up the problem of women in science with renewed interest, the time seemed right for biographers to make Marie Curie over yet again, transforming her into a modern role model for young women considering careers in science. Often Curie featured in biographical series about "female greats" who were exceptional in traditionally feminine ways. Alongside figures like Anne Frank, Mother Theresa, Amelia Earhart, and the Princess of Wales, for instance, she continued to be summoned to demonstrate traditional forms of altruistic, sacrificial womanhood. Often she appeared perfect in both feminine and masculine spheres, if described as operating in both spheres at all. Few authors radically questioned the sexist underpinnings of scientific institutions, which expected women to be like men in the laboratory and proper ladies in the home. It was too disruptive to the status quo to question the expectations of professional and domestic culture in the process of celebrating Curie's femininity.

This form of biography perpetuated the complex that had plagued women since Curie first stepped on American soil—but masculine narratives did too. Biographers in the service of liberal feminism included Curie in series about "Great Men of Science," in which they lumped her in with the likes of Thomas Alva Edison, Albert Einstein, and Galileo. In this context her life story was compensatory in tone, as authors inserted the female Curie in the man's world of the laboratory and measured her success by the extent to which she operated in this world imperceptibly as 'one of them.' These works often highlighted her heroism by detaching the exceptional woman from her earthly context, her greatness stemming from her ability to perform science above the fray of emotion and sentimentality associated with a mere mortal's personal, daily life. To fit Curie in this mold, biographers provided little information about the private, interior woman. They mentioned the births of her daughters in passing, with no honest assessment of how Curie accommodated work and family at once.[52]

If the work/family balance was neglected in works about Curie, it warranted no discussion at all in treatments of her husband and other male colleagues who biographers held to different standards. They described these "great men" often as absent-minded professors, too wrapped in thought to be expected to plan meals or take children to school. In their hands, Pierre Curie's absent-mindedness led to the traffic accident that killed him, but it was also the trait that propelled him into the ranks of science legend with the likes of Einstein and other male eccentrics who have been lauded for their single-minded intensity. Biographers have viewed Leo Szilard's refusal to flush toilets with amusement, while Richard Feynman's acts of "active irresponsibility" have made him famous; one biographer referred to Feynman admiringly as "All Genius and All Buffoon." Images of nonconformity should liberate all scientists from stereotypical molds, but invariably they have stigmatized one sex while elevating another. Marie Curie, like any woman scientist, rarely appeared as intense and likable, unless her intensity was maternally motivated.[53]

But that doesn't mean American women accepted these depictions absolutely. Publicists and authors have created an iconic Curie with plenty of contradictions, but they do not necessarily account for all the ways female scientists have chosen to interpret her intensity or find inspiration in her. Take the Nobel Prize-winning scientist Rosalyn Yalow. She was flattered when a journalist dubbed her "Madame Curie from the Bronx" in 1978, but not for the reasons one would expect. Yalow was a girl who, back in the 1930s, was inspired by Eve Curie's biography. "For me," she reflected, "the most important part of the book was that, in spite of early rejection, [Curie] succeeded. It was in common with my background, with my being aggressive." Yalow proclaimed herself a mother, a physicist, and a come-from-behind figure that, as a woman, had to work harder and longer to come out ahead. In her mind, Curie, too, was this "girl who came from nothing" to make good, a girl with masculine determination to prove everyone wrong. In graduate school Yalow took inspiration yet again from Curie's story, this time in the form of LeRoy's film adaptation. It strengthened her resolve to finish her doctoral studies in the Physics department at the University of Illinois, despite the hostility she experienced as a woman and a Jew.[54]

Curie was a model of masculine achievement for Yalow, and yet the characterization of Curie's science as nurturing was one that Yalow also internalized. The 1977 Nobelist won her prize for developing the medicinal tool radioimmunoassay (RIA), used to diagnose illnesses and save lives. Curie taught Yalow that she could be appropriately maternal, even as she burned the midnight oil, donned a laboratory coat, and called herself a scientist. If Curie gave radium to the world in the name of benevolence, then Yalow, too, would choose not to patent her discovery and work 100-hour weeks, thus achieving Curie's same altruism and anti-natural path. Yalow saw Curie as Missy Meloney had hoped American women would, not as a walking contradiction but as a woman who had it all—maternal instincts and masculine drive; a nurturing heart and objective methodology; a marriage and a science career; children and prize-winning discoveries.

Yalow liked to think that she had succeeded in passing Curie's torch with her own accomplishments. Yet more disconcertingly, she may also have perpetuated the same inferiority complex in women who worried that they could never be all things to all people, successful mothers and scientists, with no perceptible struggle. In the end, Yalow was downright hostile to the organized feminist movement, thinking that women should stop complaining and work twice as hard as men for success in the laboratory.[55]

Yalow thought that she and Curie served American women best by being role models of perfection. Liberal feminists liked that she appeared nurturing at home and ambitious in the laboratory. But radical feminists cautioned against the idea that women could turn appropriately masculine or feminine with the turn of a switch—or even if they'd want to, since the male scientist, as idealized in American culture, was not worth emulating after all. The most vocal among them, feminist Shulamith Firestone warned that "the public image of the white-coated Dr. Jekyll with no feelings" was dangerous: In this idealized type, emotions became an occupational hazard solved "by separating his professional from his personal self, by compartmentalizing his emotions," thus leaving him unnaturally divided between private and public selves. Did women really want to perpetuate male fantasies of unnatural divides, radical feminists asked, especially when they stigmatized women in the end?[56]

While few women scientists looked at their male peers or Western science in such sinister light, more of them came around to Firestone's critiques of the literal man-madeness of science. Women's awakening occurred in American culture generally, as they convened to discuss their oppression in the bedroom and the workplace, the kitchen and the laboratory and discovered that their complaints were more than individual hang-ups, but collective crosses to bear. Women developed a consciousness as an oppressed class, and they saw that the radical mantra "the personal is political" operated in many contexts. The private and the public, domestic and professional, emotional and objective, feminine and masculine were not in fact inherently opposed but imagined that way to create hierarchies of power.

In the 1980s organized women scientists still sought strategies for placing women in male-dominated institutions, but they were also critical of the leaking of women from the science pipeline after being socialized like men. They began to question if women's alleged lack of science ability had been imagined in the first place, and then nurtured by a culture that told women that this was a natural state of affairs. They viewed gender inequality as a theoretical and systemic phenomenon, the "woman in science problem" as culturally contingent. Helen Longino, Evelyn Fox Keller, and other feminist philosophers of science, too, wrote prolifically about science as gendered culture. Sandra Harding concluded that "the epistemologies, metaphysics, ethics, and politics of the dominant forms of science are androcentric and mutually supportive." Indeed, there were *cultural* reasons for the dearth of women in science.[57]

The most recent Curie biographies generally have accepted this radical premise. Intentionally or not, they have revealed science as gendered culture by casting Curie, the once infallible heroine, as a victim of science's patriarchal forces, including those that made her love affair with Paul Langevin the seeds of her public demise in ways Einstein's trysts were not for him. In a corrective mode they have attempted to reveal a more multifaceted woman, a Curie that had her likeable and unlikable moments; who was intense in the laboratory, occasionally domestic, and sometimes offensive to people in both realms; who loved her children but didn't feel compelled to live and breathe motherhood every waking moment. The most updated Curie is no longer larger than life, but reduced down to identifiable and reassuringly human size. Like real women, she defies easy classification as a perfect mother or scientist; in her revised world, scienticity and domesticity, objectivity and subjectivity, professionalism and sexuality do not have such distinctive boundaries.

Eve Curie and earlier biographers would have never considered unveiling the sordid details of Curie's love affair, and yet her sexual life is at the heart of a biography Susan Quinn wrote of Curie in 1995 called *Marie Curie: A Life*. Indeed the affair is titillating to a readership now conditioned to expect personal disclosures in tell-all fashion, but Quinn also used Curie's affair as a lens into her vulnerable human psyche. The private details of scientists' lives "reveal much about the way they work," a reviewer reflected of Quinn's portrait; any good biography must examine the "passions among the pipettes."[58] In 2004 Barbara Goldsmith authored yet another makeover of Curie called *Obsessive Genius*. This portrait, too, is unlike those Americans created of Curie in the 1920s and which women idolized on the movie screen in 1943. Like Quinn, Goldsmith claimed to portray the most authentic Curie by mining personal documents other biographers could or would not use, gaining access to diaries and workbooks that had been sealed until they could be decontaminated of radium.

Goldsmith needed a medical release to handle Curie's papers, suggesting that the heroic quality of biography has to a degree been transferred from the subject to author in recent years, as she goes to superhuman lengths to make her own discoveries of authenticity. Quinn set out to debunk Curie's maternal myth by revealing her as a sexual woman; Goldsmith debunked the myth of Curie "having it all," revealing how obsessively attentive Curie was to her science, often at the expense of her daughters. She had mental breakdowns that took her away from them for months, Goldsmith divulged. After Pierre's death, Curie wouldn't let her children utter his name in her presence; she was, like her own mother, an emotionally unavailable parent.[59]

Goldsmith's Curie is a modern woman struggling to balance work and family while fending off depression, doubt, and debilitating chauvinism. She does not rise above the obstacles in front of her as "great men of science" have long been said to do. She is a heroine with undeniable foibles. Rosalyn Yalow wouldn't have recognized this Curie, and it's likely she would have thought this portrait as unattractive as the one painted by French journalists in turn-of-the-century Paris. But Goldsmith wasn't out to create a hero that intimidated; hers is unusually focused, but also everywoman who longs to be understood. The "balance" Goldsmith's Curie strikes between home life and science is not glamorized, but real women likely understand it. If Goldsmith's portrayals are distorted, they wouldn't be the first; they may tell us most accurately about what we need Curie to do for us in the here and now as we relate her story yet again.

Goldsmith's Curie is one with whom women identify, but can she inspire younger impressionable girls into science? The children's biographies written about Curie over the years have been enlightening cultural texts. To some extent, their purpose has been to make her larger than life so that young readers will set their sights high. Their reduced plots and simplified characters fulfill an unabashedly prescriptive function, making them all the easier to mine for shifting ideals of gender.[60] As one would expect in literature for children, most of these texts have lacked details that would in any way mar a pristine image of Curie. Few have complicated her persona with elaborate details of the Langevin scandal or suggested that she was difficult, brash, or anything less than attentive to her daughters, if her home life has been mentioned at all. For young readers, authors have spent more time describing Curie in girlhood; more often than not, she has been a pretty daughter and sister, devoted to her family and country, and freakishly good at mathematics.[61]

In 2005 Carl Rollyson exhibited a new approach in his children's biography of Curie. He wrote it as a contribution to a series in which famous figures represented some admirable virtue for children to emulate. And Curie, he decided, would stand as the embodiment of honesty—a trait that has been coded as both masculine and feminine in different contexts: Scientific men have been perceived as honest insofar as they seek pure truths, unadulterated by subjective emotions. Women have been perceived as honest insofar as they occupy and embody the politically uncorrupted domestic sphere. Rollyson decided that Curie's decision to lay bare her methods for producing radium made her honest, but so did her meticulous experimental method. He turned the prickly personality which biographers had revealed in Curie in recent years into something positive and endearing: the result of her brute honesty when men expected her to exhibit a less severe form of feminine tact. Only the most virtuous (and by extension, feminine) of women would be willing to become unbecomingly mannish in the name of higher truth. Rollyson's Curie is one of them. In his portrait, she is masculine and feminine at the same time.[62]

Rollyson studied Curie because another of his biographical subjects, the late Susan Sontag, had been enamored with the French scientist since reading Eve Curie's biography as a child. Rollyson decided that Sontag--a model of modern, intellectual, independent, sexually explicit, single-motherhood—lived a life parallel to Curie's: "It is not just that Sontag wanted to be like Marie Curie, or that she built a backyard chemistry laboratory," he writes. "More important is Eve [Curie]'s evocation of a selfless career—so selfless that Marie Curie resembled a mythic goddess, a figure of such austere purity that she seemed invulnerable."[63] Rather than fixate on each woman's sense of balance between home life and work, Rollyson emphasized how both women were fixed on work for work's sake. In this, he freed Curie from the maternal mold, if not entirely from the altruism associated with it.

CONCLUSION: REMAKING CURIE FOR THE FUTURE

Marie Curie remains the best recognized of woman scientists, living or dead. More than any other, she has transcended her science to become any-woman's matron saint. She stands out as exceptional, and yet paradoxically almost everyone sees herself in some part of her legend as it has morphed over the twentieth century. The exposure to radioactive materials that made legends of her male peers turned her into a martyr in some circles, yet cast her in others as an irresponsible woman who endangered her unborn children for scientific exploit. Some thought her admirable in her suffering, but she *always* appeared to be suffering—necessarily and inherently suffering--since Americans viewed her as a woman trying to do things incommensurate with culturally pervasive definitions of womanhood. As a consequence, historian Naomi Oreskes thinks that the narrative conventions of heroism came out all wrong in Curie's constructed persona: "Her biographers generally cast her as a drudge rather than an Achilles, her physical exertions closer to those of a charwoman than a superman."[64]

In recent decades liberal feminists have enlisted Curie as a model of competence in making their case for equality in the workplace, while radical feminists have found it useful to cast her as an eccentric who thumbed her nose at male-dominated science as usual. If she has appeared a superhuman figure, she has also looked to be a fragmented personality. The appearances tell us little about the living, breathing Curie, but much more about our changing ideas about the work/family balance (presumably a woman's problem) and gender in American science. Modern makeovers of Curie reveal her other sides, as well as our growing appreciation of the fact that the private, domestic facets of scientists' lives impact their science. To separate the science from the rest is to erect walls that glorify a masculine brand of disinterested objectivity that simply doesn't exist. It is also to stigmatize female scientists who, we still wrongly presume, have personal and domestic attachments that male scientists do not.

The real Curie, like any woman, was mired in complexity, as is her historical legacy. We must grapple with this complexity as we summon her yet again in the twenty-first century. Only then can we have the perspective to change scientific culture in profound ways. Those who still refute the existence of a "cultural" problem in science likely think that the growing numbers of women in science fields since the 1970s will one day add up to a critical mass that will make feminist change inevitable. Maybe, but it hasn't happened yet. As late as 2007, the report *Beyond Bias and Barriers* confirmed that parity between male and female scientists had still not been achieved by any empirical measure. In 2008 the membership of the National Academy of Science was still disproportionately male: 2464 men to 232 women. "The glass ceiling has been raised," Vivian Gornick reported in 2009, "but it is still in place."[65]

The persistent presumption that women must be more devoted, more myopic, more talented than men is a sign that the "women in science" problem remains a deeply embedded problem of culture. We balk at the comments of Lawrence Summers, and yet still presume that competent women scientists must perform outside their female skins. Until we create new meanings around Curie—and women and science generally--the scientist conjured in the American mind will be male, and the woman scientist an oxymoron who suffers conspicuousness and invisibility at once.

Portions of this essay have been adapted from *The Madame Curie Complex: The Hidden History of Women in Science* (New York: The Feminist Press, 2010).

NOTES

[1] Zachary M. Seward, "Summers Releases Transcript of Remarks on Women in Science," *The Harvard Crimson*, February 17, 2005 (http://www.thecrimson.com/article.aspx?ref=505787).

[2] Joan Burrell, "Thirty-Three Years of Women in S&E Faculty Positions," National Science Foundation 08–308 (June 2008) [http://www.nsf.gov/statistics/inbrief/nsf8303].

[3] Margaret Rossiter, *Women Scientists in America: Struggles and Strategies to 1940* (Baltimore: The Johns Hopkins Press, 1982), 126–27, 130, 216.

[4] *Vanity Fair*, December 22, 1904; Emily Crawford, "The Curies at Home," *The World To-Day*, 6 (1904), 490. See also "Women and Scientific Research," *Science* 32 (December 23, 1910), 919–20; "Sex and Scientific Recognition," *Scientific American* 104 (January 21, 1911), 58.

[5] Several meanings have been implicit in the metaphorical use of "hard" and "soft" in the scientific lexicon: Hard science has been understood as intellectually and physically rigorous, fortified by airtight, indestructible positivist methodology. Subjects of "hard" research have been described as physically inanimate, not squishy, oozing, or alive; results of "hard" research have been consequently "hard and fast," versus the ambiguous findings of social scientists or other increasingly female investigators. Hardness and softness have long been assigned gendered connotations (the penetrating mind and hard muscles of men and the sentimental thinking and soft curves of women). For a theoretical discussion of "hard" and "soft" science, see Londa Schiebinger, *Has Feminism Changed Science?* (Cambridge: Harvard University Press, 1999), 160–64.

[6] Daniel Kevles, *The Physicists: The History of a Scientific Community in Modern America* (Cambridge: Harvard University Press, 1987), 275–77; Margaret Wertheim, *Pythagoras' Trousers: God, Physics, and the Gender Wars* (New York: W. W. Norton, 1997), 12.

[7] Margaret Wertheim, *Pythagoras' Trousers*; Kevles, *The Physicists*; Bert Hansen, *Picturing Medical Progress from Pasteur to Polio: A History of Mass Media Images and Popular Attitudes in America* (New Brunswick: Rutgers University Press, 2009); Marcel C. LaFollette, *Making Science Our Own: Public Images of Science, 1910–1955* (Chicago: University of Chicago Press, 1990); Rossiter, *Women Scientists in America*.

[8] Rossiter, *Women Scientists in America*, 116–118.

[9] Sandra Harding, *The Science Question in Feminism* (Ithaca: Cornell University Press, 1986), 62; Rossiter, *Women Scientists in America*, xvi, 29–72, 98–99, 107; Miriam Levin, *Defining Women's Scientific Enterprise: Mount Holyoke Faculty and the Rise of American Science* (Lebanon, NH: University Press of New England, 2005); Kevles, *The Physicists*, 202–203.

[10] Marie Mattingly Meloney, "Introduction," in Marie Curie, *Pierre Curie* (New York: The Macmillan Company, 1923), 12–17; "The Story of Radium," *New York Times*, (*NYT*) May 15, 1921, 84; Robert Reid, *Marie Curie* (London: Collins, 1974), 160, 247; Naomi Pasachoff, *Marie Curie and the Science of Radioactivity* (New York: Oxford University Press, 1996), 65. Einstein came to the States to raise money for the Hebrew University in Jerusalem. See Don Arnald, "Einstein on Irrelevancies," *NYT* (May 1, 1921), 50; Kevles, *The Physicists*, 212.

[11] LaFollette, *Making Science Our Own*, 79–80.

[12] Regina Morantz-Sanchez, *Sympathy and Science: Women Physicians in American Science* (New York: Oxford University Press, 1985); Beth Linker, "Strength and Science: Gender, Physiotherapy,

and Medicine in Early Twentieth-Century America," *Journal of Women's History*, vol. 17, no. 3 (September 2005), 105–32.

[13] David Cantor, "Uncertain Enthusiasm: The American Cancer Society, Public Education, and the Problem of the Movie, 1921–1960," *Bulletin of the History of Medicine*, 81 (2007), 39–69; Kevles, *The Physicists*, 206; "Roll of Martyrs to Science is Increasing," *NYT* (January 11, 1925), XX5.

[14] Meloney, "Introduction," 15–16; Thomas C. Jeffries, "The Story of Radium in America," *Current History Magazine*, 14 (June 1921), 2; William J. Mayo, "Do You Fear Cancer?" *Delineator*, 98 (April 1921), 35; G. Frank, "A Jeanne D'Arc of the Laboratory," *Century*, 102 (May 1921), 160; "Madame Curie: The Most Famous Woman in the World," *Current Opinion*, 70 (June 1921), 760–62; Marie Mattingly Meloney, "The Greatest Woman in the World," *Delineator* 98 (April 1921), 15–17; Nell Ray Clarke, "Radium—the Metal of Mystery: How Madame Curie Found It," *American Review of Reviews* 63 (June 1921), 606–610; "Mme. Curie, Widow of Prof. Pierre Curie, and with Him Co-Discoverer of Radium with her Two Daughters," *American Review of Reviews* 63 (June 1921), 562; "Curing Cancer with Radium," *Current History Magazine* 13 (October 1920), 34–36; "Madame Curie's Own Account of the Radioactive Elements," *Current Opinion* 70 (May 1921), 656–658; "She Discovered Radium, But Hasn't a Gram of It," *Literary Digest* 69 (April 2, 1921), 36–40; "Her Discoveries Made Others Rich," *Mentor*, 9 (May 1921), 36; "The Discoverer of Radium," *The Outlook* (May 25, 1921), 145; "Madame Curie's Visit to America," *Science* (April 8, 1921), 327–28. See also Judith Magee, "Marie Curie: A Study of Americans' Use of Marie Curie as a Devoted Wife and Mother, Saintly Scientist, and Healer of Humanity," Master's thesis, Department of Women's History, Sarah Lawrence College, 1989, 2–23, 3–11.

[15] Meloney, "Introduction," 23; "Madame Curie's Genius," *NYT* (May 1, 1921), 103; Marie Curie, "Autobiographical Notes," in *Pierre Curie*, 170–72; Benjamin Harrow, *Eminent Chemists of Our Time* (New York: D. Van Nostrand Company, 1920), 156; Bernard Jaffe, *Crucibles: The Lives and Achievements of the Great Chemists* (New York: Simon and Schuster, 1930), 246; Eleanor Doorly, *The Radium Woman: A Youth Edition of the Life of Madame Curie* (Hammondsworth, Middlesex, England: Puffin Story Books, 1953), 78–85 (original edition, Puffin Story Books, 1939); Reid, *Marie Curie*, 48–49; Rosalynd Pflaum, *Grand Obsession: Madame Curie and Her World* (New York: Doubleday, 1989), 18–30.

[16] For analysis of the Curies' "anti-natural path," see Helena M. Pycior, "Marie Curie's 'Anti-natural Path': Time Only for Science and Family," in Pnina G. Abir-Am and Dorinda Outram, eds., *Uneasy Careers and Intimate Lives: Women in Science, 1789–1979* (New Brunswick: Rutgers University Press, 1987), 191–214. "Love Story of Famous Mme. Curie Recalls Romance of School Days," *NYT* (May 27, 1923), XX5; Curie, *Pierre Curie*, 74–90; Jaffe, *Crucibles*, 247–48; Doorly, *Radium Woman*, 88, 95, 102–103; Reid, *Marie Curie*, 56–65, 68–73; Pflaum, *Grand Obsession*, 56.

[17] "Autobiographical Notes," 180–189; Harold Callender Paris, "Mme. Curie Works on with Her Pupils," *NYT* (December 23, 1928), 11, 15; James Kendall, *Young Chemists and Great Discoveries* (New York: D. Appleton-Century Co., 1940), 214; Curie, *Pierre Curie*, 96–104; Jaffe, *Crucibles*, 251–52; Doorly, *Radium Woman*, 116; Reid, *Marie Curie*, 85, 96–97, 106; Pflaum, *Grand Obsession*, 66–69.

[18] Curie, "Autobiographical Notes," 176–79, 193–94; Harrow, *Eminent Chemists*, 174–75; Doorly, *Radium Woman*, 127; Reid, *Marie Curie*, 84–85, 92, 131, 170; Pflaum, *Grand Obsession*, 62, 78, 82, 150, 270; Pasachoff, *Marie Curie*, 82.

[19] Curie, *Pierre Curie*, 113; Curie, "Autobiographical Notes," 192; Reid, *Marie Curie*, 74; Harrow, *Eminent Chemists*, 169.

[20] Lenard R. Berlanstein, "Historicizing and Gendering Celebrity Culture: Famous Women in Nineteenth-Century France," *Journal of Women's History* 16, no. 4 (2004), 65–91; "Madame Curie," *Femina*, 1 (January 1904), 6.

[21] "L'Académie des Sciences examine aujourd'hui la candidature de Mme Curie," *L'Excelsior*, January 9, 1911, cover; Reid, *Marie Curie*, 179–205; Pflaum, *Grand Obsession*, 156–174; Pasachoff, *Marie Curie*, 67–73.

[22] Magee, "Marie Curie," 3–7–3–8; Reid, *Marie Curie*, 53–54, 256; Marie Curie to Missy Meloney, November 7, 1920; September 15, 1921, Box 1, Mrs. William B. Meloney-Marie Curie Special Manuscript Collections, Columbia University Libraries, New York, New York, (MCC).

[23] Arthur Brisbane to Gentlemen, March 14, 1921, Box 1, MCC; Carrie Chapman Catt, "Helping Madame Curie to Help the World," *Women Citizen*, 5 (March 12, 1921), 1062.

[24] Meloney, "Introduction," 20–21; Marie Curie, "Impressions of America," Box 3, MCC; "Mme. Curie at Dedication," *NYT* (May 22, 1921), 2.

[25] "Mme. Curie in Boston," *NYT* (June 19, 1921), 25; Charles W. Eliot to Meloney, December 18, 1920, Marie Mattingly Meloney to Charles W. Eliot, December 24, 1920, Box 2, MCC.

[26] "Says Women Can and Must Stop War," *NYT* (May 19, 1921), 11.

[27] Curie, "Impressions of America"; Radium Presented to Madame Curie," *NYT* (May 21, 1921), 12; "President Harding's Speech to Madame Curie," *New York Herald*, European Edition (May 21, 1921), 1.

[28] "Radium Not a Cure for Every Cancer," *NYT* (May 13, 1921), 22; Magee, "Madame Curie," 3–12; "Honors for Mme. Curie Received by Daughter," *NYT* (May 24, 1921), 17; "Mme. Curie Again Honored," *NYT* (May 27, 1921), 16.

[29] "Mme. Curie's Brain Fagged by 'Small Talk' of Americans," *NYT* (May 28, 1921), 1; "Memorial Hospital Greets Mme. Curie," *NYT* (May 29, 1921), 16; Reid, *Marie Curie*, 169; Pflaum, *Grand Obsession*, 152; Mme. Curie Sails to Receive Radium Gift," *NYT* (May 5, 1921), 14; "Madame Curie's Genius"; "Mme. Curie to End All Cancers."

[30] Marie Curie to Meloney, August 21, 1928; July 28, 1929; n.d., 1929, Box 1, MCC; "Mme. Curie to Get Medal," *NYT* (October 21, 1929), 16; "Clubwomen Give Mme. Curie a Medal," *NYT* (November 6, 1929), 27; "Mme. Curie Speaks at St. Lawrence," *NYT* (October 27, 1929), 24.

[31] "Einstein Evolving Yet Another Theory," *NYT* (July 27, 1930), 1; Schiebinger, *Has Feminism Changed Science?* 72–74; Kevles, *The Physicists*, 175–77, 212, 269; Wertheim, *Pythagoras' Trousers*, 187; Jurgen Renn and Robert Schulmann, eds., *Albert Einstein/Mileva Maric: The Love Letters* (Princeton: Princeton University Press, 1992), xi–xxviii.

[32] Kevles, *The Physicists*, 204–206.

[33] Lorine Pruette, *Women and Leisure* (New York, 1924). More on Pruette's findings in William O'Neill, *Everyone Was Brave: A History of Feminism in America* (New York: Quadrangle, 1971), 322.

[34] "Madame Curie is Dead; Martyr to Science," *NYT* (July 5, 1934), 1; "Millikan Mourns Her," (July 5, 1935), 17.

[35] "Daughter Will Use Curie's Radium," *NYT* (July 20, 1934), 6; "Mayor Dedicates Marie Curie Av.," June 10, 1935, Amusement Section, 19; "Marie Curie Street," July 8, 1935, books section, 14; Cantor, "Uncertain Enthusiasm," 40–41.

[36] Susan E. Lederer, "Dark Victory: Cancer and Popular Hollywood Film," *Bulletin of the History of Medicine*, vol. 81 (2007), 100–107.

[37] Grace T. Hallock, *Health Heroes: Marie Curie* (New York: Metropolitan Life Insurance, 1938), 3, 10–11, 14, 22.

[38] This autobiographical piece follows Curie's biography of her husband in *Pierre Curie*.

[39] Marie Curie to Marie Meloney, July 8, 1921; September 15, 1921; August 28, 1932, Box 1, MCC.

[40] Eve Curie to Missy Meloney, November 20, 1936; February 9, 1937; July 27, 1934; February 12, 1938, Box 1, MCC.

[41] Eve Curie, *Marie Curie*, Vincent Sheean, trans. (Garden City: Doubleday, Doran and Company, 1937), ix–x.

[42] Bert Hansen, "Medical History for the Masses: How American Comic Books Celebrated Heroes of Medicine in the 1940s," *Bulletin of the History of Medicine*, vol. 78, no. 1 (Spring 2004), 149–53, 160; "True–Adventure Comic Books and American Popular Culture in the 1940s: An Annotated Research Bibliography of the Medical Heroes," *International Journal of Comic Art*, vol. 6, no. 1 (Spring 2004), 117–47; Alberto Elena, "Exemplary Lives: Biographies of Scientists on the Screen," *Public Understanding of Science*, vol. 2, no. 3 (July 1993), 205–223; Bruce Babington, "'To catch a

star on your fingertips': diagnosing the medical biopic from *The Story of Louis Pasteur* to *Freud*," *Signs of Life: Cinema and Medicine* (London: Wallflower Press, 2005), 120–131.

[43] Metro Goldwyn Mayer, *Madame Curie*, 1943.

[44] T. Hugh Crawford, "Glowing Dishes: Radium, Marie Curie, and Hollywood," *Biography* 23.1 (Winter 2000), 75–76, 71–89.

[45] Schiebinger, *Has Feminism Changed Science?* 30–31; Margaret Rossiter, *Women Scientists in America: Before Affirmative Action* (The Johns Hopkins University Press, 1995), 1–26.

[46] Rossiter, *Women Scientists in America*, 1–26.

[47] The best source for details on women physicists of the Manhattan Project is *Their Day in the Sun: Women of the Manhattan Project* (Philadelphia: Temple University Press, 1999) by Ruth Howes and Caroline Herzenberg.

[48] Harriet Zuckerman, *Scientific Elite: Nobel Laureates in the United States* (New York: The Free Press, 1977), 2; Margaret Mead and Rhoda Metreaux, "Image of the Scientist among High School Students," *Science* (August 20, 1957), 384–90. For other social science studies emphasizing the masculine image of the postwar scientist, see Walter Hirsch, "The Image of the Scientist in Science Fiction: A Content Analysis," *American Journal of Sociology* 63, no. 5 (1958); Anne Roe, *The Making of a Scientist* (New York: Dodd, Mead, 1953).

[49] Kevles, *The Physicists*, ix, 334; Ralph E. Lapp, *The New Priesthood: The Scientific Elite and the Uses of Power* (New York: Harper and Row, 1965), 4.

[50] Alice Rossi, "Barriers to the Career Choice of Engineering, Medicine, or Science Among American Women," in Jacquelyn A. Mattfeld and Carol G. Van Aken, eds., *Women and the Scientific Professions: the MIT Symposium on American Women in Science and Engineering* (Cambridge: MIT Press, 1965), 58–60, 66, 73–74.

[51] Mattfeld and Van Aken, eds., *Women and the Scientific Professions: the MIT Symposium on American Women in Science and Engineering*; Anne M. Briscoe, "Phenomenon of the Seventies: The Women's Caucuses," *Signs: Journal of Women in Culture and Society*, 1978, vol. 4, no. 1., 152–158.

[52] Some of the books in series of women and scientists include Keith Brandt, *Marie Curie, Brave Scientist* (Mahwah, NJ: Troll Associates, 1983); Louis Sabin, *Marie Curie* (Mahwah, NJ: Troll Associates, 1985); Angela Bull, *Marie Curie* (London: Hamish Hamilton, 1986); Tom McGowan, *Radioactivity: From the Curies to the Atomic Age* (New York: Franklin Watts, 1986); Richard Tames, *Marie Curie* (New York: Franklin Watts, 1989); Sean M. Grady, *Marie Curie* (San Diego: Lucent Books, 1992); Steve Parker, *Marie Curie and Radium* (New York: Chelsea House Publishers, 1992).

[53] Schiebinger, *Has Feminism Changed Science?* 73, 76; Richard P. Feynman, *"Surely You're Joking, Mr. Feynman,"* Edward Hutchings, ed. (New York: W. W. Norton, 1985); John Gribbin and Mary Gribbin, *Richard Feynman: A Life in Science* (New York: Dutton, 1997); George Greenstein, *Portraits of Discovery: Profiles in Scientific Genius* (New York: John Wiley and Sons, Inc., 1998), 122; Leona Marshall Libby, *The Uranium People* (New York: Charles Scribners' Sons, 1979), 63–65.

[54] Elizabeth Stone, "A Mme. Curie from the Bronx," *New York Times Magazine* (April 9, 1978), 29; Sharon Bertsch McGrayne, *Nobel Prize Women in Science: Their Lives, Struggles, and Momentous Discoveries*, second edition (Washington, DC: Joseph Henry Press, 1998), 336.

[55] The most comprehensive published discussion of Yalow's personality, ambitions, and affinity for Curie is Eugene Straus' *Nobel Laureate Rosalyn Yalow: Her Life and Work in Medicine* (Cambridge: Perseus Books, 1998).

[56] Harding, *The Science Question in Feminism*, 79–80; Genevieve Lloyd, *The Man of Reason: Male and Female in Western Philosophy* (New York: Routledge, 1993 [original, 1984]); Shulamith Firestone, *The Dialectic of Sex: The Case for Feminist Revolution* (New York: Bantam, 1970), 182–83.

[57] Harding, *The Science Questions in Feminism*, preface, 224.

[58] Susan Quinn, *Marie Curie: A Life* (Da Capo Press, 1996); Tom Wilkie, "The Secret Sex Life of Marie Curie," *The Independent* (June 13, 1995); "Sex and Lies Before Videotape: Writing and Rewriting Women's Lives," (a review of Susan Quinn's *Marie Curie: A Life*," *Los Angeles Times*, May 21, 1995, book review section, 2).

[59] Barbara Goldsmith, *Obsessive Genius: The Inner World of Marie Curie* (New York: W. W. Norton, 2005); Interview of Barbara Goldsmith on "Talk of the Nation," *National Public Radio*, December 12, 2004. For other recent treatments, see Marilyn Bailey Ogilvie, *Marie Curie: A Biography* (Greenwood Press, 2004); Rosalynd Pflaum, *Grand Obsession: Marie Curie and Her World* (New York: Doubleday, 1989).

[60] For a discussion on mining popular texts for prescriptions of gender and scienticity, see Judith Yaross Lee, "Scientists and Inventors as Literary Heroes," in Joseph W. Slade and Judith Yaross Lee, eds., *Beyond the Two Cultures: Essays on Science, Technology, and Literature* (Ames: Iowa State University Press, 1990), 255–57.

[61] Juvenile texts examined for this essay include the *Health Heroes* series of the Metropolitan Life Insurance Company, 1938; Eleanor Doorly, *The Radium Woman; A Youth Edition of the Life of Madame Curie* (Hammondsworth, Middlesex Great Britain: Puffin Story Books, 1939); Bertha Morris Parker, *The Scientist and His Tools* (Evanston, IL: Row, Peterson and Company, 1944); Keith Brandt, *Marie Curie, Brave Scientist* (Mahwah, NJ: Troll Associates, 1983); Louis Sabin, *Marie Curie* (Mahwah, NJ: Troll Associates, 1985); Angela Bull, *Marie Curie* (London: Hamish Hamilton, 1986); Tom McGowan, *Radioactivity: From the Curies to the Atomic Age* (New York: Franklin Watts, 1986); Richard Tames, *Marie Curie* (New York: Franklin Watts, 1989); Sean M. Grady, *Marie Curie* (San Diego: Lucent Books, 1992); Steve Parker, *Marie Curie and Radium* (New York: Chelsea House Publishers, 1992); Naomi Pasachoff, *Marie Curie and the Science of Radioactivity* (New York: Oxford University Press, 1996).

[62] Email correspondence between Julie Des Jardins and Carl Rollyson, August 26, 2009; Carl Rollyson, *Marie Curie: Honesty in Science* (New York: iUniverse, Inc., 2005).

[63] Carl Rollyson and Lisa Paddock, *Susan Sontag: The Making of an Icon* (New York: W. W. Norton, 2000), 10–11.

[64] Naomi Oreskes, "Objectivity or Heroism? On the Invisibility of Women in Science," *Osiris*, 11, second series, 1996, 110.

[65] Michele L. Aldrich, "Women in Science," *Signs*, vol. 4, no. 1 (Autumn 1978), 126–35; Betty M. Vetter, "Changing Patterns of Recruitment and Employment," in Violet B. Haas and Carolyn C. Perrucci, eds., *Women in the Scientific and Engineering Professions* (Ann Arbor: University of Michigan Press, 1984), 61; "Women in the Natural Sciences," *Signs* vol. 1, no. 3 (Spring 1976), 718; Lilli Hornig, "Professional Women in Transition," in *Women in the Scientific and Engineering Professions*," 53; Schiebinger, *Has Feminism Changed Science?* 35, 61; Vivian Gornick, *Women in Science: Then and Now* (New York: The Feminist Press, 2009), 103–104.

Julie Des Jardins
Baruch College, Department of History
City University of New York
jdesjardins@mac.com

4. MARIE CURIE, ETHICS AND RESEARCH

INTRODUCTION

Recently *Chemistry and Engineering News* (Bard, Prestwich, Wight, Heller, & Zimmerman, 2010) carried a series of commentaries on the culture of academic research in chemistry with a focus on the role of funding in research. Initially, Alan Bard decried how decisions about tenure seem more and more to focus on grant getting rather than consideration of the applicant's accomplishments generated because of access to this funding. Bard argued further that often this funding was based, not on the quality of the proposed research but on a researcher's ability to "hype their research" and damming truth in the process (Bard et al., 2010, p. 27). According to him, there was a disturbing trend in universities for researchers to be encouraged, almost expected, to generate patents and from there, even to be involved in initiating "start up" companies. Other researchers responded.

Glen Prestwich and Charles Wight (Bard et al., 2010) argue that if researchers were able to present a clear connection between "taxpayer dollars" and funded research, the public would realize the value that science delivers. Prestwich and Wight argue further that a new cadre of researchers is involved in identifying real world problems, translating basic research into applications, and creating products as well as publications. Moving from basic research to applications that address real world problems is called *translational research*, and Prestwich and Wight see this research as a positive development in chemistry. Adam Heller (Bard et al., 2010) weighs in claiming that the pursuit of "patent-protected, people-serving products" was not "a sad sign of our times but a reawakening of the proud history of academic chemistry and chemical engineering" (p. 29). I find it interesting that one of Heller's choices for historical examples of chemists that had transcended academic chemistry and chemical engineering was Fritz Haber. For me Haber is a challenging figure in chemistry research because although he won the 1918 Nobel Prize in Chemistry "for the synthesis of ammonia from its elements" (The Nobel Foundation, 2010), which allowed the Earth to support many more humans than before, he also played a significant role in the German development of poison gas during World War I. Heller's reference to Haber raised the issue of the role of ethics in research. Comments by Prestwick and Wight also led me to reflect on reports of how Marie and Pierre Curie conducted research and disseminated their findings in the identification of two new elements, polonium and radium, and their exploration of the phenomenon Marie Curie called *radioactivity*. Historian of science, Helena Pycior (1993) notes that Marie Curie made sure readers were made

M.-H. Chiu, P. J. Gilmer, and D. F. Treagust (Eds.), Celebrating the 100th Anniversary of Madame Marie Sklodowska Curie's Nobel Prize in Chemistry. 87–102.

aware of the fact that Marie proposed this term in her biography of Pierre Curie (Curie, 1923). Unlike Haber, whose role in developing chemical weapons in World War I makes him in some respects a more challenging scientific figure to endorse wholeheartedly, Marie Curie has no such problems. In her own writing and that of her biographers, Curie is presented as espousing very clearly ideas about the nature of scientific endeavor that take on an almost fantastical quality in our cybermodern era, but values that were heartfelt, and consistent with the modernist era in which she lived and worked. As I hope to show in this chapter, Marie Curie was no shrinking violet when it came to supporting and endorsing industry, especially if it allowed her to further develop and maintain the field of radioactivity, and her approach was entirely consistent with ethical theories that are part of modernist philosophy.

Both these contemporary examples and Marie Curie's history as a researcher raise for me questions of what role ethics play in scientific research, whether success in science is really only about patenting a new process or product, and the possible role of existing ideologies in the way researchers frame ethics associated with the practice and outcomes of their research. In the following sections I will try to explore these questions.

SO WHAT ARE ETHICS?

Applied ethics is an attempt to "apply moral principles to a concrete world of practice" (May, 1980, p. 358). Marie Curie is a good case study to examine research and ethics even though her writings and those of her biographers sometimes do not let us see behind the heroic façade. In this chapter, I seek to explore Curie's evolving ethical stance in the scientific enterprise, in particular her desire to ensure the longevity of research associated with the chemistry, physics, and biomedical applications of radium. Her research provides a context for considering the nature and role of ethics in scientific and chemical research.

From a universal perspective, research ethics can be thought of as a set of principles about how researchers should conduct themselves when they are engaged in research (Shrader-Frechette, 1994). Historically, these consisted of philosophical recommendations that became accepted as "communal codes of behavior" (p. 2). For example, philosopher Francis Bacon (1620/1968) when proposing a new sense-based philosophy for generating new knowledge via experiment recommended the use of witnesses that could verify the observations or 'matters of fact' claimed by an experimental philosopher like Robert Boyle. In her book, *Ethics of Scientific Research*, Kristin Shrader-Frechette (1994) notes historic interest in what should constitute the norms of experimental research; however, calls for a code of ethics typically are associated with the professionalization of various science disciplines, suggesting that codes constitute agreed communal practices to which individual members are expected to conform.

Today much research is conducted in universities or industries rather than private laboratories in people's homes or in laboratories maintained by professional organizations, such as the Royal Society of London. University research generates many more patent applications than does research conducted in other contexts, including private research laboratories. University research involvement is attractive to outside companies making such scientific research into a commodity (Shrader-Frechette, 1994). The development of science as an enterprise raises questions implicit in the commentaries from Bard, Prestwich and Heller (Bard et al., 2010) including whether there exists specific universal ethical rules about benefit and risk of research and how these rules might be applied. Such a view of ethics has developed historically through cultural ideologies that afford space for chemistry and physics to be acknowledged as disciplines or fields with associated symbolic and cultural capital that derive maximum benefit for participants (Bourdieu, 1984).

Aristotle saw ethical knowledge as practical knowledge, separate from theoretical knowledge, and that working skillfully in your chosen profession could be part of a good life, which was the purpose of being virtuous. Aristotle's argument that theoretical knowledge was more valuable than productive practical knowledge held sway in Europe with universities being the sites of theoretical knowledge production up until the 16th and 17th centuries. As experimental philosophy began to coalesce into a discipline in the 17th century, it brought together the practical and the theoretical. In 1620, Francis Bacon published his inductive philosophy in which he made an argument for the value of experience and the practical knowledge of craftsmen such as metallurgists, tanners, ceramicists, navigators and so forth, which could make contributions to his new science.

Jeffery Kovac (2000) argues that chemistry is a good place to examine scientific ethics because chemistry has a long history of defining itself as a profession through a process of self-definition. Early chemists such as Antoine Lavoisier saw themselves as leaders in the need to rationalize the language and practice of chemistry, laying out new nomenclature that was directly associated with analytical practice (Milne, 2011). In 1787 Lavoisier, in collaboration with Antoine Fourcroy, Claude-Louis Berthollet and Guyton de Morveau, set out to create terminology for the New French Chemistry. Lavoisier presented his arguments to the elitist Academy of the Sciences, the society established in 1666 by Jean Baptiste Colbert, French Finance Minister under the reign of King Louis XIV, to support and protect French experimental and natural philosophy. The Academy was a government organization that was designed to produce professional scientists (Hahn, 1971). Consistent with other professional organizations set up in the 17th century to support and promote experimental and natural philosophy, women were not admitted.

Kovac (2000) raises the question of what constitutes a code of practice, that is a code of ethics for chemistry. He introduces the issue of how researchers reading about research they do not know in depth, depend on the integrity of the researchers actually reporting the research to have conducted the research as they described. In a specific field of research, researchers that are seen as leaders possess, or are assigned, intellectual authority that the observable facts they report are true. This situation was clearly described by Michael Polanyi (1962) who was critical of the view that new scientific knowledge was generated by a separate observer observing a subject to collect objective data that formed the basis of testable generalizations. Instead he took a phenomenological approach to argue that scientific discovery was based on a dedicated community of practitioners, which understood that facts could not be separated from the values of the inquirer. Polanyi also believed that a free society could recognize the truth of a reality that was independent of, but revealed by, individuals seeking the truth, reporting their findings openly so that open discussion within a community could determine the quality of specific knowledge claims. However, in *Meaning* (co-authored with Harry Prosch, 1975) he acknowledges exactly the issue raised by Kovac in appraising our knowledge claims, that is expertise, the establishment of truth depends on the personal characteristics of the researcher making the claims. Because often we are unable to observe directly the process of data development and attendant claims about knowledge, we must feel comfortable accepting the truthfulness of the person making those claims and that they actually produced the data and conducted the analysis in the manner they describe. Thus, being ethical becomes conflated with communal attributions of expertise and truthfulness.

Thinking about the research of Marie Curie and those writing of her work (e.g. Françoise Giroud, 1986, Pycior, 1993) I am reminded that her claims for expertise were often obscured by the fact that she was a woman working in an area of expertise dominated by men. Indeed, the French Academy of Sciences did not elect a woman until 1979.

TRUST, EXPERTISE, AND ETHICS

The role of trust and the intellectual authority of 'experts' seems critical to an examination of professional and personal ethics. According to philosopher, John Hardwig (1991) trust plays a key role in knowledge claims. He argues, "Although epistemologists debate various theories of knowledge, almost all seem united in the supposition that knowledge rests on evidence, not trust" (p. 693). He claims further "those who do not trust cannot know; and those who do not trust cannot have the best evidence for their beliefs," (pp. 639-640) and that for members of epistemic communities, such as chemists, trust is a central component of knowledge construction. In order for a researcher like a chemist to have good reasons to accept another researcher's claims of truthfulness, the researcher must convince the research community and individual researchers of their *expertise*, they must keep up-to-date in the field; their *conscientiousness*, they must be thorough and careful in their procedures; their ability to be *self-critical*, that is, they must possess "adequate epistemic self-assessment" (p. 700) so that they are critical of their own practice with respect to its reliability and applicability to the knowledge claims under consideration. Thus, a chemist's acceptance of a researcher depends as much on how truthfulness is seen as an aspect of their moral character as on the findings the researcher presents. On the other hand, scientists tend to accept published findings when they do not have time themselves to vet the strategies used to develop these data and such when findings are presented by recognized experts in the field.

Both expert and the less expert have ethical responsibilities in a research context. The expert must fulfill the requirements of being conscientious, expert, and self-critical and the layperson must exercise care in critically evaluating the information she is presented. These are social, public, ethical constructs that the community expects members to endorse. Trust is in a sense "blind trust" because it is based on our confidence in the moral rightness of the actions of a system or an individual (Giddens, 1990). It is also associated with the ideology of *modernity*, a belief in stories of progress that are based on the acceptance of universal human values. Giddens argues:

> In conditions of modernity, trust exists in the context of (a) the general awareness that human activity – including within this phrase the impact of technology upon the material world – is socially created, rather than given in the nature of things or by divine influence; (b) the vastly increased transformative scope of human action, brought about by the dynamic character of modern social institutions. (p. 34)

Human moral imperatives become one of the bases upon which humans rely in order to determine whether or not they will accept knowledge claims made by others. I think we can agree that Marie Curie who began her public research agenda with a study of the magnetic properties of steel in 1894 and continued being a researcher until to her death from anemia in 1934, conducted research during the modernist era. However, modernism is not static. Within a modernist framework, practices are constantly reevaluated, so practices are constantly changing. This dynamism applies also to value systems, so knowledge and values mutually influence each other. Within modernity, science and chemistry are seen as objective knowledge and the growth of science is understood to be the result of human activities on nature, which is an inert object of study. *Humanity,* as a term is also a product of modernism, seen as a representation of abstracted individuals as subjects (Rouse, 1991). Researchers can talk of humanity without having to consider the individual humans that might be affected by their research. Within modernity, science is constituted by a formal method that provides instrumental success in the service of humanity for the detection and elimination of error. At the same time, one is expected to be skeptical and tolerant when examining claims for truthfulness. Steven Shapin notes "modernity guarantees knowledge not by reference to virtue but by reference to expertise" (1994, p. 412). In this context, knowledge and ethics are interrelated as they are in the research of Marie Curie who has become a modernist icon.

MODERNISM AND ETHICAL THEORIES

Modernist philosophy is well served by a number of ethical theories: teleological, consequentialist (utilitarian), and deontological.

Teleological Ethics

Teleological ethics take their name from the Greek, *teleos*, which is associated with teleology, a type of explanation in which the nature of an object is related to its purpose or goal. In teleological ethics, research that is directed towards finding the truth that is, discovering and disseminating new knowledge, is fundamentally ethical (May, 1980). Any research, which may involve compromising the truth, would be inappropriate from a teleological perspective regardless of any positive social outcomes that might emerge from such a study. What is problematic from a teleological ethics perspective is support, usually financial, of research that is conducted because of the interests of a funder. However, the application of teleological ethics to research can be problematic because the social and cultural implications of the study are often ignored, if only the pursuit of knowledge is seen as a fundamental good.

Consequentialist Ethics

A variation of teleological ethics, and one that plays a significant role in any research "involving human subjects" conducted in universities in the United States, is *consequentialist ethics*. The form of consequentialist ethics of interest is *ultilitarianism*. Utilitarian ethics takes the position that research should produce the greatest good for the greatest number. Utilitarians are less interested in the purity of the researcher's or the research approach they use to achieve a result. For utilitarians, the morality of an action is determined by its consequences. It is from utilitarianism that we have the imperatives of informed consent, and confidentiality. These concepts are engendered from an ethical and philosophical stance that the knowledge generated by research is intrinsically good, or at least value neutral, so truthful means must be used in the conduct of research that will generate this knowledge (May, 1980). Under the umbrella of this ethical approach, researchers are expected to explore risk-benefit analysis of proposed research and evaluate the cost of the research against the benefits of that research. It is the assessment of cost and benefits, which can lead researchers to decide whether the benefits might outweigh the need for informed consent. Utilitarianism has informed laws and policies associated with research involving human subjects in the United States as defined by the Belmont Report, which outlines the ethical principles that should be followed in research involving "human subjects". According to May, utilitarian ethics are results-oriented and less interested in the researcher's motives. Also, utilitarian ethics is appealing to some groups because it allows for the quantification of moral questions.

But for many people utilitarian ethics is unappealing for a number of reasons. First, one person's benefit can be another's detriment and second, often the benefit is held in the hands of the powerful. Third, we are left with the question, how could we decide the harm that can be tolerated? Fourth, utilitarian ethics is ethics for the individual or collections of individuals but not for the communal.

Deontological Ethics

Many people feel there are fundamental principles such as honesty, truthfulness, integrity and respect for living things that should not be reduced to a rule. For them, *deontological* (derived from the Greek word for duty or that which is binding) *ethics* offers an ethical theory that, based on reason, endorses categories of universal moral laws. These laws are to be abided by all humans. For example, lying would not be acceptable under any circumstances. This form of ethics particularly applies to humans because, according to deontological ethics, they are carriers of reason. Immanuel Kant originally proposed this ethical approach as he "sought to locate duty in the very structure of human reason" (May, 1980, p. 363). Researchers who accept the notion of universal moral laws and ground their research in these laws may operate from within a deontological ethical framework.

However, as one might recognize, one of the challenges of deontological ethics is that it leaves no room for context. One is expected to apply the same ethical principles universally. Like utilitarian ethics it is also an individualistic form of ethics leaving no space for a dialogic or communal considerations. Critical theorist, Jürgen Habermas (1972), argues these forms of ethics are based on the myth of disinterested knowledge and perhaps all humans would be more ethical if we acknowledged and revealed our interests (if we are aware of them) behind claims for pure knowledge. Making our interests explicit is not the only aspect of moral behavior that Habermas addressed. As I have argued already, modernism typically is associated with notions that there are universal norms, which include teleological, deontological, and consequential ethics. In response to modernist universal claims, the philosophy of post-modernism rejected all such claims arguing that no such universal ethical stances existed. However for Habermas, associated with such rejection there is a risk that authoritarian regimes would become powerful in a way that he had seen Nazism become powerful. He argued for a critical stance to all forms of interests making the argument that a strong universal form of ethics such as that associated with deontological ethics provided a basis for critically examining any norms and stances that contradicted these ethics (see Habermas, 1990). Critical theory tries to understand why the world is the way it is and then, through critique, strives to know how it should be (Ewart, 1991). From my perspective, critical theory accepts the dignity and autonomy of a rational subject but recognizes that this develops over time and is culturally and historically situated (Benhabib, 1986). The twin aspects of development and situation are missing from modernist perspectives of ethics. Laying out these ethical theories, I am reminded of Marie Curie and her drive to find out why mineral sources of uranium, such as pitchblende, were hundreds of times more radioactive than expected and how this could be explained by the existence of new elements. In the next section, I examine some of the available evidence about Marie Curie, which suggests that her ethics were more consistent with the modernist ethics of teleological and utilitarian ethics, which provided her with a moral basis for making decisions about her practice with respect to advocating for the field of radioactivity.

MARIE CURIE AND ETHICS

Thinking about Marie Curie's relationship to ethics, I am left with questions. What was Marie Curie's standpoint and how was it influenced by cultural, historical, epistemological, and ontological presuppositions? What interests drove Marie Curie to her quest for knowledge about the nature of radioactivity and the isolation of pure samples of these highly reactive and dangerous elements? Historian of science, Dominique Pestre (1997), argues that there exist two contrasting images of Marie Curie, one has her as the pure scientist, a disinterested researcher working in poor ill-equipped conditions for the love of science, while the other acknowledges her links to industry and her activity in the social and political milieu of the early twentieth century. He argues further that she belonged to a group of intellectuals in Paris that distinguished themselves from others based on how they described and justified their actions, how they decided to structure their collaborations, and what they considered to be legitimate. In her own published narratives such as *Pierre Curie,* initially released only in the United States and Canada and only published in English, Curie does not provide much insight into what drove her to learn except her love of learning and the support of her family, which might have been enough!

In her late teens, she was attracted to the positivist philosophy of August Comte as interpreted by Polish nationals. Positivism, a philosophy of modernism, was based on empirical study, valuing of sense-observations, and applying a specific method to create new knowledge. Under this philosophy, the mathematical sciences were elevated forms of knowledge. For Poles, positivism provided them with non-violent methods for asserting nationalism while they were under the control of foreign powers (Goldsmith, 2005). Perhaps this philosophy was also important in Curie's approach to her research. Her dream was to attend the Sorbonne in Paris, and she entered into a pact with her sister, Bronya, to financially support each other's education, which they did. In 1891, Marie was in Paris enrolling to complete a degree in physics. Giroud (1986) notes that although towards the end of the 19th century French science was in a bit of a mess, as a well brought up young Polish woman, Marie Curie was completely oriented towards France, which educated Poles saw as the epitome of culture. Also, as an additional bonus, Curie's lowly level of scholarship would not inhibit her admission to the Sorbonne when she would have been hard-pressed to gain admission to the university in countries, such as Germany and England, where cutting-edge physics research was being conducted. Curie was driven to be successful. She moved out of her sister's Paris apartment so that she could focus more of her efforts on her studies. After two years, and the award of a degree in physical sciences, Curie felt she needed more mathematics and, as the recipient of a generous scholarship awarded by the Polish government for outstanding students to study abroad, she was able to achieve that goal. When she started employment, she paid back the value of the scholarship to her funders.

Marie Curie as Ethical Expert

In 1894, Curie received her degree in mathematics and first met Pierre Curie. I think they recognized in each other shared passions, even though their personalities were completely different. As Giroud notes, "there is no evidence she [Curie] would have been able to live with a fighter for very long. That would have been one too many" (p. 54). At the time Curie was studying science and mathematics in France there was contempt in French scientific circles for inventors. In France, the goal for a scientist would be to be involved in 'pure' research, that is the type of research that would be ethically appropriate from a teleological perspective (Giroud, 1986). Of course, the same could be said for English science.

This type of pure science was appealing to Curie. In her autobiographical notes (Curie, 1923), she remarks that her:

> ... attention had been drawn to the interesting experiments of Henri Becquerel on the salts of the rare metal uranium. Becquerel had shown that by placing some uranium salt on a photographic plate, covered with black paper, the plate would be affected as if light had fallen on it. The effect is produced by special rays which are emitted by uranium salt and are different from ordinary luminous rays as they can pass through black paper...

> My husband and I were much excited by this new phenomenon, and I resolved to undertake a special study of it. (p. 180)

Pierre Curie and his brother had developed an electroscope that could measure minute electrical currents and this had been modified to measure ionization current of gamma rays from a sample emitted in an ionization chamber against electricity produced by a quartz strip (Boudia, 1997). Marie was to use this instrument to measure the ionization effects of rays emitted by uranium salts. This was a finicky machine requiring skill and patience to use. Pierre had to step in to refine the machine and to coach Marie with its use in order for her to be able to use the electrometer to get useful results in her search for elements and minerals that produced rays (Goldsmith, 2005). In fact, the use of the electroscope was so tricky that other researchers needed to trust the data that Marie Curie produced, which is where expertise becomes an issue.

The original research data from this process is on display in the Curies' notebooks. In these notebooks, one can observe through their writing the interaction between Marie and Pierre Curie from the beginning of 1898. In the notebooks, Marie records her initial failure to obtain useful data. Following this note, Pierre notes the adjustments he made to the instrument and then Marie records the data she is generating (Goldsmith, 2005). Curie (1923) writes:

> ... I examined all the elements then known, either in their pure state or in compounds. I found that among these bodies, thorium compounds are the only ones which emit rays similar to those of uranium. The radiation of thorium has an intensity of the same order as that of uranium, and is, as in the case of uranium, an atomic property of the element.

> It was necessary at this point to find a new term to define this new property of matter manifested by the elements of uranium and thorium. I proposed the word radioactivity which has since become generally adopted. (p. 96)

Curie notes further that of the minerals she examined, only those with thorium or uranium showed radioactivity but, interestingly, the radioactivity of these minerals was higher than would have been expected based on her measurements of the radioactivity of pure samples of uranium and thorium. She confirmed this abnormality was not due to experimental error and so it required an explanation (Curie, 1923). She and Pierre decided to work on this problem together and for their investigations they chose the now almost mythic mineral, pitchblende, which was a source of uranium. They worked on separating out various chemical fractions and determining each fraction's level of radioactivity, discovering two fractions similar to, but different from, bismuth and barium, which they called respectively polonium and radium. The Curies published their claims for the discovery first of polonium (named by Marie for her home country) July 1898, and then in December of the same year, radium. The claims were made prior to the development of unique spectra because the samples they obtained were not pure enough to generate such spectra but on December 19, 1898 Eugène Demarçay, an expert spectroscopist, was able to obtain a spectrum for radium.

In any papers they published, Marie and Pierre Curie were meticulous in acknowledging each other's expertise and contribution to the data and analysis they conducted (Pycior, 1993). Marie Curie began her doctoral studies with the support of an already established researcher who shared her desire and willingness to be meticulous in acknowledging each other's contributions. How this account stands in contrast with Penny Gilmer's (2007) account of a research experience she had as an assistant professor at Florida State University. As a biochemist, she agreed to collaborate with a colleague in biological sciences and taught one of his graduate students how to spin label membrane samples and analyze the spectra of "the complex, slow motion of the spin label inserted in the membrane" (p. 138). However, when a manuscript on the research was developed for publication the 'colleague' refused to include Gilmer as coauthor. She notes that he most likely would not have done that had she been male. Authorship is one avenue open to researchers that allows the truth of their claims to be presented and their expertise acknowledged. No wonder Gilmer was left with a sense of betrayal when her just claims were ignored.

However, although physicists might be willing to admit spectral lines as acceptable evidence of a new element, chemists were much more demanding expecting a pure sample as evidence of a new element and they would remain skeptical until such a sample was produced (Goldsmith, 2005). In confirmation of this claim, Curie (1923) wrote, "In our opinion, there could be no doubt of the existence of these new elements, but to make chemists admit their existence, it was necessary to isolate them" (p. 99). Although the work was challenging, Curie's initial studies indicated that radium would be easier to extract from pitchblende than polonium. Thus began the focus of her studies for the rest of her life.

In 1903, Marie Curie and Pierre Curie shared with Henri Becquerel the Nobel Prize in Physics for the discovery of radioactivity and in 1911 she was awarded the Nobel Prize in Chemistry, which acknowledged her role in producing pure samples of polonium and radium. It is interesting to note that she might not have been included in the 1903 award if Pierre had not made an argument to the committee for her role in their research, making her the first women to be so acknowledged. In

1911 an affair with physicist, Paul Langevin, which became the fodder of gossip and right-wing newspapers in France, also was used to discredit her. She observed that she generated far more criticism than Frenchman Langevin, suggesting that being a foreigner and a woman were the main causes for such criticism. She was asked by a member of the Nobel Committee not to come to accept the award but she replied, "the Prize has been awarded for Radium and Polonium. I believe there is no connection between my scientific work and the facts of private life" (Quinn, 1995, p. 328).

Curie demonstrated a greater capacity for self-criticism than did Pierre Curie but perhaps she was just more willing to take risks associated with making claims for knowledge priority than Pierre Curie was. In contrast to Pierre, Marie Curie's discussions in her papers were often highly speculative (Malley, 1979). For example, when the Curies detected two types of rays, one more penetrating ray that was deflected by magnetism and one less penetrating that was not deflected, Marie Curie speculated on the particulate nature of the rays but ever the positivist, Pierre Curie was not willing to make such speculations (Pycior, 1993). She more readily accepted than did Pierre the explanatory power of the material nature of the rays proposed by Ernest Rutherford and Fredrick Soddy, which was at odds with the model of the atom and the nature of radioactivity originally proposed by the Curies (Malley, 1979).

Curie (1923) writes of their ethos:

> Our investigations had started a general scientific movement, and similar work was being undertaken in other countries. Toward these efforts Pierre Curie maintained a most disinterested and liberal attitude. With my agreement he refused to draw any material profit from our discovery. We took no copyright, and published without reserve all the results of our research, as well as the exact processes of the preparation of radium. In addition, we gave to those interested whatever information they asked of us. This was of great benefit to the radium industry, which would thus develop in full freedom, first in France, then in foreign countries and furnish to scientists and to physicians the products which they needed. (p. 111)

Their research was disinterested in that their goals were to further aspects of the radium industry without seeking personal financial gain. Such a position is consistent with teleological ethics, disseminating new truthful knowledge with the goal of furthering their field of study. Curie acknowledges that as she and Pierre were making their processes available to other scientists, they also initiated collaboration with the company, Société Centrale des Produits Chimiques, the same company that marketed the instruments Pierre developed. While the Curie's assistant, André Debierne, scaled up the Curie's laboratory procedures into industrial methods, the Curies negotiated a proportion of the produced radium salts that they could use for their experiments exploring the nature of radioactivity (Pestre, 1997).

A Lasting Legacy, Standpoint, and Ethics

Curie operated in a field of cultural production composed of physicists and chemists and so she was aware of sources of symbolic capital that were important to the field, at the same time she had a goal to ensure the ongoing success of the program of study that she and Pierre initiated. Making money would be considered impure but she sought to have radioactivity identified as a central element of a network of endeavors that would make production an integral part of the process, which also supported medical applications and reinforced the control of humans over nature for the betterment of humankind. Xavier Roqué (1997) argues that Marie Curie "regarded scientists as disinterested searchers for truth, whose work benefited humanity in many unexpected ways. Money should not be a concern for them. A well-organized society, then, should see to it that these workers are well equipped and supported" (p. 277). This ethos of purity and disinterestedness was consistent with the ethos of the French scientific community at the time (Curie, 1937). After the first world war, Curie wrote a report on the radium industry for the French government in which she proposed the creation of a state-run factory that would carry out industrial functions for the Radium Institute, which she had set up and ran for the French government, and carry out other functions for the radioactivity field. In her proposal, she clearly saw that scientists should have a leadership role because they had the expertise but also disinterest to do what was best for science and for society (Pestre, 1997).

In many respects it seems that Curie wanted to have control over the development of this field. Marie Curie was heavily involved in the emerging field of metrology for radium, that is establishing standards and controls over purity in numerous applications including industry, manufacturing, commercial, and medical applications (Boudia, 1997). Curie's expertise in purification and identification of radium and the ability of her laboratory to produce quality radium salts made her an obvious choice. For example, the free sample of radium salts that the Curies gave Ernest Rutherford, which allowed him to explore his theory of transmutation, was "three hundred times more active than a German sample he had purchased" (Goldsmith, 2005, p. 124).

Curie went so far as to offer her own laboratory as a site for a national measuring service. For this, the Rector of the University of Paris criticized Curie. He wrote a disapproving letter to the Dean a year after the service had started claiming that Curie offered the service to benefit old industrialist friends (Boudia, 1997). She responded vigorously arguing, "the trust granted to the measurements was only based on our scientific reputation and our professional competence and not at all on our professional status" (Curie [1913] quoted in Boudia, 1997, p. 260). Curie went on to say, "I have been led to think that there is a public service to be organized (measurements) which I cannot ignore, and that it could not have been properly established without myself, and my laboratory's participation" (from Boudia, 1997, p. 260).

For Marie Curie working on the metrology of radium and on industrial applications of radioactivity were entirely consistent with her image of integrity as a scientist and truthfulness of her claims as an expert in their field of radioactivity but by doing so, she was looking after the good of the *collective*, performing a societally important task (Pestre, 1997). She accepted that she had a pedagogical responsibility.

> You cannot hope to build a better world without improving the individuals. To that end each of us must work for his own improvement, and at the same time share a general responsibility for all humanity, our particular duty being to aid those to whom we think we can be most useful. (Curie, 1923, p. 168)

This was sentiment that she would return to in other contexts including her work on international committees (Curie, 1937). The evidence presented suggests to me that Marie Curie located herself in a modernist world and she saw herself as a scientist and an intellectual and with that attribution she had a responsibility for transforming social order through science and social political action. Her participation in both scientific meetings, she participated regularly in the Solvay conferences where discussions of metrology took place, and in industrial and social activities provide evidence of how she constructed this responsibility. She was a member, and became chair, of the International Committee on International Cooperation, which was set up as an advisory board for the League of Nations following World War I (Giroud, 1986).

Curie's ethics were tied up with her interactions with others, even when she found this to be a strain at times. For example, in 1929 she was a guest of the American Society for the Control of Cancer. When she first extracted pure samples of radium she had high hopes for its use in medicine to control specific forms of cancer and promoted its use for those purposes. In her speech, which was read to the four hundred attendees, she stated that, "radium is dangerous in untrained hands" (New York Times, 1929). She also commented on the plight of the Radium Girls (see Clark, 1997), women that had been employed to paint dials on watches using a mixture of glue, water, and radium powder who had started to suffer the ill effects of radium toxicity including serious bone decay (radium displaces calcium in bones) and cancers and were suing their employer, the Radium Luminous Materials Corporation. Curie was reported as saying she had not seen anything in French factories or institutions like that reported for the Radium Girls, "not even in wartime when countless factories were employed in work dealing with radium" suggesting that necessary safety procedures had not been used. She also commented that she would be happy to give any aid she could but that once radium had entered the body there was no way of destroying the substance or reducing its effects on the body (reported in Neuzil & Kovarik, 1996, p. 43). Note the modernist elements in this case. From Curie's perspective as reported here, it was not the science that was open to criticism, radium is radium, but the practices used in the factories that had exposed these young women to potentially dangerous doses of radium that had been absorbed internally.

CURIE, MODERNISM, AND ETHICS: FINAL THOUGHTS

The work of Habermas (1972) encouraged me to look for, and try to understand, the interests that drove Marie Curie but I also wanted to consider ethics beyond the general moral obligations of individualist ethics to consider her engagement with others and with the contexts in which she conducted her research. I think for Curie trust was key as both a process and as a product because trust cannot exist without others. In science, as I have argued, trust is a key element in any interaction. I think Curie recognized a responsibility; perhaps we could call it a covenant, between her and society in which she lived, but it was always couched in her recognition of herself as a scientist in the modernist perspective with all that that entailed. From that perspective, her ethics could be described as deontological, accepting that there are some ethical stances that are universal. In the time in which she lived, modernism was the prevailing ideology. People believed that science was an elevated form of knowledge and scientists like Curie were asked to comment, not just on science, but on aspects of society. In the lingua franca of the day, the New York Times referred to Marie Curie and other scientists of her ilk like Albert Einstein as savants, "French woman savant devotes every odd moment at Geneva to Scientific Treatise" (Streit, 1930, p. 1). While she felt driven to rush to publication so that the Curie's discovery of radioactivity, polonium and radium would be acknowledged, she also endorsed a commitment to contributing to what she saw as the well being of society. I think she also wanted to ensure that the field she and Pierre had established should continue not just for personal recognition but also for collective betterment. As seen through the critical lens of Habermas, I think Curie's experiences, especially as she sought to build the discipline of radioactivity, finding applications in industry and health that would support humanity, suggest how professional organizations might consider critically evaluating their approach to professional ethics. I think there is value in more conversations, such as those of Bard et al. (2010), because they make explicit the interests of professional members, an important step for looking critically at professional ethical stances.

When institutions propose a code of ethics they do so from a position of power and authority seeking to organize a rational and moral community for the members of that institution by proposing a set of universal ethical stances. Taking a critical perspective, like that proposed by Habermas, I think institutions should be open about their interests, clear about their goals and motivations, so that they are not hidden behind universal moral principles, and develop a form of *situated ethics* based on the historical and cultural development of the institution and on communal discourse. They should also explore the context in which expertise within research studies is attributed and the relationship between attributed expertise and truth. In a critical world, values and knowledge are dynamically integrated and it would be of benefit to professional institutions if they were able to capture that integration in their code of ethics. We need to move beyond general moral principles that are necessarily external of the very participants and their everyday experiences that such codes are thought to address. However, if professional organizations elect to take a modernist approach to research ethics they should do so with structures in place, which support the self-reflective elements of modernism so that the code is dynamic. I think we can learn from Marie Curie how some of that could be done, or done better. In the postmodern era in which we live with its skepticism of transcendental universal perspectives and grand narratives, this approach might seem rather quaint but it is no less heartfelt for that.

REFERENCES

Bacon, F. (1620/1968). Paraceve/Novum organum. In J. Spedding, R. L. Ellis, & D. D. Heath (Eds.), *The works of Francis Bacon.* New York: Garrett Press. (Original publication 1620, facsimile reprint of 1870 publication).

Bard, A. J., Prestwich, G. D., Wight, C. A., Heller, A., & Zimmerman, H., E. (2010). Academic chemical research. *Chemistry and Engineering News, 88*(3), 26–29.

Benhabib, S. (1986). *Critique, norm and utopia: A study of the foundations of critical theory.* New York: Columbia University Press.

Boudia, S. (1997). The Curie laboratory: Radioactivity and metrology. *History and Technology, 13,* 249–265.

Bourdieu, P. (1984). *Distinction: A social critique of the judgement of taste.* R. Nice (trans.). Cambridge, MA: Harvard University Press.

Clark, C. (1997). *Radium girls: Women and industrial health reform, 1910–1935.* Chapel Hill, NC: University of North Carolina Press.

Curie, E. (1937). *Madame Curie: A biography.* Vincent Sheean (trans.). New York: Da Capo Press.

Curie, M. (1923). *Pierre Curie.* C. & V. Kellogg (trans.). New York: Macmillan.

Ewart, G. D. (1991). Habermas and education: A comprehensive overview of the influence of Habermas in educational literature. *Review of Educational Research, 61,* 345–378.

Giddens, A. (1990). *The consequences of modernity.* Stanford, CA: Stanford University Press.

Gilmer, P. J. (2007). As a woman becoming a chemist, a biochemist, and a science educator. In K. Tobin & W-M. Roth (Eds.), *The culture of science education: A history in person* (pp. 133–145). Rotterdam: Sense Publishers.

Giroud, F. (1986). *Marie Curie: A life.* Lydia Davis (trans.). New York: Holmes & Meier.

Goldsmith, B. (2005). *Obsessive genius: The inner world of Marie Curie.* New York: Norton.

Habermas, J. (1972). *Knowledge and human interests.* London: Heinemann.

Habermas, J. (1990). *Moral consciousness and communicative action.* Cambridge, MA: MIT Press.

Hahn, R. (1971). *The anatomy of a scientific institution: The Paris Academy of Sciences 1666–1803.* Berkeley CA: University of California Press.

Hardwig, J. (1991). The role of trust in knowledge. *The Journal of Philosophy, 88,* 693–708.

Kovac, J. (2000). Professionalism and ethics in chemistry. *Foundations of Chemistry, 2,* 207–219.

Malley, M. (1979). The discovery of atomic transmutation: Scientific styles and philosophies in France and Britain. *Isis, 70,* 213–223.

May, W. F. (1980). Doing ethics: The bearing of ethical theories on fieldwork. *Social Problems, 27,* 358–370.

Milne, C. (2011). *The invention of science: Why history of science matters for the classroom.* Rotterdam: Sense Publishers.

Neuzil, M., & Kovarik, W. (1996). *Mass media and environmental conflict: America's green crusades.* Thousand Oaks, CA: Sage Publications.

New York Times (1929). Mme. Curie warns of perils in radium *New York Times (1923-Current file); Nov 1, 1929;* ProQuest Historical Newspapers New York Times (1851–2007) w/ Index (1851–1993) p. 23.

Pestre, D. (1997). The moral and political economy of French scientists in the first half of the XXth century. *History and Technology, 13,* 241–248.

Polanyi, M. (1962). *Personal knowledge: Towards a post-critical philosophy*. Chicago, IL: University of Chicago Press.

Polanyi, M., & Prosch, H. (1975). *Meaning*. Chicago: University of Chicago Press.

Pycior, H. M. (1993). Reaping the benefits of collaboration while avoiding its pitfalls: Marie Curie's rise to scientific prominence. *Social Studies of Science, 23*, 301–323.

Quinn, S. (1995). *Marie Curie: A Life*. New York: Simon & Schuster.

Roqué, X. (1997). Marie Curie and the radium industry: A preliminary sketch. *History and Technology, 13*, 267–291.

Rouse, J. (1991). Philosophy of science and the persistent narratives of modernity. *Studies in History and Philosophy of Science, 22*, 141–162.

Shapin, S. (1994). *A social history of truth: civility and science in seventeenth-century England*. Chicago, IL: University of Chicago Press.

Shrader-Frechette, K. S. (1994). *Ethics of scientific research*. Lanham, MD: Rowman & Littlefield.

Streit, C. K. (1930). Einstein evolving yet another theory. *New York Times (1923-Current file);* Jul 27, 1930. ProQuest Historical Newspapers New York Times (1851–2007) w/ Index (1851–1993) p. 1.

The Nobel Foundation (2010). *The Nobel Prize in Chemistry 1918*. Retrieved from http://nobelprize.org/nobel_prizes/chemistry/laureates/1918/

Catherine Milne
Department of Teaching and Learning
Steinhardt School of Culture, Education, and Human Development,
New York University
catherine.milne@nyu.edu

SECTION 2: WOMEN CHEMISTS IN THE PAST TWO CENTURIES

MARILYN BAILEY OGILVIE

5. MARIE CURIE, WOMEN, AND THE HISTORY OF CHEMISTRY

When in December 1911 Marie Curie stood on the platform in Stockholm, Sweden, to accept the Nobel Prize in Chemistry for isolating radium, she made history for the second time. In December 1903 she had become the first woman to be selected a Nobel Laureate. She shared the 1903 prize in physics with two physicists, her husband Pierre and Henri Becquerel. As a woman Nobel laureate, Marie Curie was an oddity in 1903 and 1911 as she still would be today. Women Nobel Prize winners in the sciences (physics, chemistry, and physiology/medicine) are still very scarce. From Marie Curie's 1903 prize in physics through 2009 when three women scientists were selected: Elizabeth Blackburn, Carol W. Greider (physiology or medicine) and Ada E. Yonath (chemistry) there have been only 16 (counting Marie Curie twice) women Nobel Prize winners in the sciences. In contrast, almost 520 men received the prize from 1901 when the first award was given through 2009. Marie Curie's second historical accomplishment was becoming the first person to receive more than one Nobel Prize. The awarding of the prize to her daughter, Irène Joliot-Curie, in 1935 made the two the only mother-daughter pair to win the Nobel Prize. The Sorbonne University in Paris also realized Marie Curie's talents when after Pierre Curie's death she was appointed the first female professor.[1]

PARTICIPATION OF WOMEN IN EARLY SCIENCE

The dearth of women Nobel Prize winners might cause people to assume that women did not participate in the scientific enterprise before the late nineteenth and early twentieth centuries.

Women of Antiquity

However, women have practiced some form of science since the beginning of recorded history. References to women are sparse in the chronicles of early science. Of those listed, almost all relegate women to the more practical and less theoretical aspects of science. One of the early women mentioned in the literature is the Theban Aglaonike who reputedly could "pluck the moon from the heavens."[2] Perhaps she had a means of predicting eclipses and that women in antiquity such as Agamede who used plants to cure a variety of ills had a general explanation for

M.-H. Chiu, P. J. Gilmer, and D. F. Treagust (Eds.), Celebrating the 100th Anniversary of Madame Marie Sklodowska Curie's Nobel Prize in Chemistry. 105–118.

their success, but there is no evidence that this was the case.[3] A more intriguing example is found in the work of alchemist Mary (or Maria or Miriam) the Jewess who purportedly moved in both the practical and theoretical spheres.[4] Queens, nuns, and saints from the Middle Ages and learned ladies of the Renaissance through the Enlightenment also participated in certain aspects of science.

Beginning in the eighteenth century an important group of women emerged who specialized in scientific illustration, ornithological observations, and plant collecting. Others observed the heavenly bodies, taught science and mathematics in girls' schools, served as science bibliographers, wrote popular books, and worked in museums. Some served as assistants to husbands, brothers or fathers who were scientists. Marie Lavoisier used this strategy as well as her skill as a scientific illustrator to enter science.

Marie Anne Pierrette Paulze Lavoisier (1758–1836)

Marie Anne Pierrette Paulze Lavoisier was the wife of chemist Antoine Laurent Lavoisier and who, after his death, married another scientist, Benjamin Thompson, Count Rumford. She was only 13 years old when she married Lavoisier. At the time of their marriage, he was 28 and had already achieved fame as a chemist and had been elected to the Academy of Sciences in 1768. Marie was both intelligent and interested in science and quickly became involved in her husband's scientific activities until he was executed during the last days of the Reign of Terror on May 8, 1794. Since Marie Lavoisier's work was so thoroughly interwoven with that of her famous husband it is difficult to assess its originality. But it is known that her artistic talent was very useful to her husband. She drew the diagrams for his treatise, *The Elements of Chemistry* (1789). Her husband's laboratory notebooks also included her contributions and numerous of her entries are scattered throughout the books. She also translated English scientific works into French including Richard Kirwan's 1787 *Essay on Phlogiston* with a commentary by Antoine Lavoisier and his associations. It is clear that through her drawings, translations, interpretations of notes, and skillful editing of Lavoisier's memoirs, she made important additions to the body of scientific knowledge.[5]

NINETEENTH AND EARLY TWENTIETH CENTURY STRATEGIES: ELLEN HENRIETTE SWALLOW RICHARDS (1842–1911)

Many of the same barriers to women's success in science continued throughout the nineteenth and early twentieth centuries. Although the political and educational systems in both the United States and Europe underwent upheavals during these years increasing the likelihood that women could be involved in science, it remained difficult for a woman to become a scientist. Suffrage movements throughout the western world and educational reforms that proceeded alongside the political changes reduced legal barriers to women becoming scientists, but subtle barriers remained. In fact as science became more professionalized criteria were developed that made it more difficult than previously for a woman to succeed in the scientific enterprise. Those who were fortunate enough to earn degrees still had a difficult time finding professional positions. Women interested in chemistry and physiology devised strategies to circumvent the obstacles to employment. They constructed places for themselves within "women's fields," areas that did not appeal to men. Chemist Ellen Swallow Richards founded home economics as a discipline and opened up this field to other nineteenth-century women who were interested in chemistry.

Ellen Henrietta Swallow Richards took advantage of the newly minted women's colleges to gain an education. In order to save enough money to attend college she worked at a number of menial jobs. The three hundred dollars she had earned and saved made it possible for her to enter Vassar College in 1868 where she received a bachelor's degree in 1870. Influenced by her astronomy teacher Maria Mitchell, she was interested in astronomy as an undergraduate. However, she decided to change to chemistry as she presumed that it would be more likely to have a useful application. She applied to the Massachusetts Institute of Technology (MIT) that, like Vassar, was a young institution. She was the first woman to be admitted to the "scientific school." Although she was admitted free it was not, as she had supposed, because of her financial need but because the president could deny that she was a student if confronted by complaining trustees or students. She received a bachelor's degree from MIT in 1873 as well as a master's degree from Vassar for a thesis she had submitted on the chemical analysis of iron ore. Although she remained at MIT for two additional years she was never awarded a doctorate because the department heads wanted to avoid having a woman receive the first such degree in chemistry. In 1875 Swallow married a professor of mining engineering and head of MIT's new metallurgy laboratory. This marriage hearkened back to strategies of the past making it possible for a wife to continue with her work under the "guidance" of a male relative.

Richards was now financially secure and had an understanding husband. She devoted her time to furthering the cause of scientific education for women. Her efforts resulted in the establishment of the Woman's Laboratory at MIT to provide training in chemical analysis, industrial chemistry, mineralogy, and biology. She also taught science to women at a correspondence school, the Society to Encourage Studies at Home, founded by Anna Ticknor in 1882. Richards not only taught women science at the correspondence school, but also stressed the importance of healthful foods, comfortable dress, and both physical and mental exercise. She was also the founder of the organization that later became the American Association of University Women.

Richards was discrete in her push for women's acceptance at MIT. This policy was successful, for the young women students at the Woman's Laboratory at MIT were soon admitted to regular courses, and by 1882 four women had received degrees. Chemistry as an academic field was a male bastion. However, Richards by establishing a woman's field, home economics where chemistry could be studied as a legitimate women's academic area and applied to the female sphere of the home, departments of home economics opened all over the United States providing employment for women chemists. In addition to providing a field in academia where women could be full professors or department heads, these new departments had a downside. They lacked the prestige possessed by regular chemistry departments and, in some cases, may have hindered the appointment of women in regular chemistry departments.[6]

MARIE CURIE (1867–1934): THE EARLY YEARS

By applying chemistry to the traditional woman's sphere of the home, Richards avoided the stigma attached to "scientific women" and provided jobs in academia and industry formerly open only to men. It also resulted in a segregated work place where women were seldom integrated into the mainstream of scientific employment. Marie Curie, for her part, did not attempt to make chemistry a woman's field. Science, to her, did not have a gender component. Nevertheless, her life was totally influenced by her sex.

As a girl, Marie was prevented from attending a university in her native Poland. Accepting a position as a governess away from her home in Warsaw, she attempted to earn enough money to attend the Sorbonne in Paris. To the displeasure of her employers, she fell in love (and it was reciprocated) with the eldest son of the family. Since her employers were horrified that their son might marry a mere governess, the love affair was a disaster, making her wary of any commitment in the future. Thus when she met Pierre Curie in Paris, she was reluctant to entrust her affections to another relationship. However, once she reluctantly decided to trust him, her loyalty was unswerving and one of the most important spousal collaborations resulted. They married in 1895 after Marie had earned a degree in physics (1893) and mathematics (1894).

Marie and Pierre lived under difficult circumstances in Paris. They were poor, worked very hard, and soon had a young child, Irène (b. 1897), to care for. Nevertheless Marie Curie was determined to obtain a doctorate. At this time, no woman in Europe had completed this degree, although a German woman, Elsa Neumann (1872–1902) was writing a thesis on electrochemistry and eventually would finish it. Neumann was unmarried and had no children. The challenges that Marie faced as wife, mother, and scientist appeared insurmountable. Equally daunting was the disapproval of her colleagues who were convinced that a married woman, and especially a woman with children, should never work for a doctorate.

Ignoring all of the reasons why she should not get a doctorate, Curie searched for a dissertation topic. Being familiar with the literature, she was aware of Wilhelm Roentgen's discovery of x-rays and Henri Poincaré's and Antoine Henri Becquerel's work on phosphorescence. Becquerel's new kind of ray that did not require exposure to light intrigued Marie Curie. She proposed to determine whether other substances besides uranium caused the air to conduct electricity. Together, she and Pierre developed a technique for determining this. They tested dozens of materials and found that thorium and its compounds caused the air to conduct electricity and produced rays similar to those from uranium.

The project that began as descriptive evolved into a theoretical one in which she speculated on a cause for the radiation. Marie Curie arrived at a unique postulate that was vital for understanding the phenomenon of radiation. She hypothesized that radiation was not an ordinary chemical reaction that occurred between molecules but that it issued from the atom itself, and that radiation was an atomic property proportional to the amount of the radioactive substance being measured. In her own words she wrote:

> My determinations showed that the emission of the rays is an atomic property of the uranium, whatever the physical or chemical conditions of the salt were. Any substance containing uranium is as much more active in emitting rays, as it contains more of this element.[7]

This theory had enormous implications both for her work and for subsequent work by others in the field. The Curies tested various elements using Pierre's delicate electrical apparatus to determine which substances emitted the rays. They obtained a large quantity of the uranium ore, pitchblende, from the Joachimsthal region on the German-Czech border. After analyzing the pitchblende, the Curies found that it produced a current much stronger than that produced by uranium alone. Using known chemical methods they broke the pitchblende down into its different components and measured the radioactivity of the products. They then used spectroscopy to identify the highly active elements. Marie used the tedious technique of fractional crystallization to separate out different substances from a solution of pitchblende. She repeated the technique many times, retaining the more radioactive fraction and discarding the less active crystals. She found with subsequent fractional crystallization the crystals became increasingly more radioactive.

Before beginning this monotonous project, Marie was already convinced that there was a new very radioactive element in the pitchblende. She and Pierre eventually came up with a substance that was 330 times more active than uranium. Even though they had not obtained a pure form, they were so sure that they had a new element that Marie wrote, "In July, 1898, we announced the existence of this new substance to which I gave the name of polonium, in memory of my native country."[8] In 1898 they became the first scientists to use the term "radioactive" to describe the behavior of those uranium-like materials that emitted rays.[9]

After removing the highly radioactive bismuth and polonium they discovered that the remaining liquid was still highly radioactive. They concluded that they had another new element (the other impurity in the liquid was barium known not to be radioactive). The new element was radium, 900 times more radioactive than uranium.

This discovery that earned Marie Curie the Nobel Prize for chemistry many years later, was not enough for Marie. In order to convince fellow chemists that their conclusions were correct she sought to produce a pure form of the new elements. This task required a large quantity of pitchblende. Using their own meager savings they bought the pitchblende and paid to have it delivered to Paris. In 1899 a large number of sacks of this radioactive material was dumped in the yard of the School of Physics. The story of the abandoned shed with its dirt floor that formerly was a medical school dissecting room that became Marie's laboratory is well know. She observed that

In summer, because of its skylights, it was a stifling as a hothouse. In winter one did not know whether to wish for rain or frost; if it rained, the water fell drop by drop, with a soft, nerve-racking noise, on the ground or on the worktables, in places where the physicists had to mark in order to avoid putting apparatus there. If it froze, one froze.[10]

It was Marie who carried out the exhausting and interminable task of attempting to isolate radium. To Pierre it was unnecessary to work so hard in order to demonstrate what they already knew. Possibly because of her gender, Marie needed to establish her scientific credentials in a different way than Pierre; she sensed it was necessary to obtain pure radium and to determine its atomic mass. The backbreaking labor was rewarded when she produced one-tenth of a gram of almost pure radium after treating over a ton of pitchblende residues. Marie defended her thesis on June 25, 1903, and was awarded the degree of Doctor of Physical Science at the University of Paris with the added honor of *très honorable*.

As Marie's fame grew throughout the early twentieth century women were able to see that people of their sex could be outstanding scientists. However, the scandal that erupted after Pierre's violent death postponed this influence. The end of the beautiful and fruitful collaboration between the two was cut short when Pierre slipped on a rain-slicked street and was dragged under a horse cart and brutally mangled. Marie was devastated, but was appointed to Pierre's Chair at the Sorbonne and carried on his lectures, though without joy. About five years after Pierre's death, Marie was accused of having an affair with the physicist Paul Langevin, transforming Marie from a grieving widow to a wicked home wrecker. Newspapers in Paris were full of reports. Duels were fought between her supporters and detractors. These reports had dire effects on Marie's physical and mental health. A campaign was even mounted to keep her from being awarded the Nobel Prize in Chemistry in 1911. Although it is often claimed that Parisian women saw Marie Curie as a role model for their chemistry, for many the memory of the scandal was still fresh. As time passed, this memory weakened, and Curie's reputation gradually was restored. Although Curie's success undoubtedly influenced other women chemists she, herself, was not involved in mentoring other women.

CURIE AND OTHER WOMEN SCIENTISTS

New scientific fields tend to be more woman-friendly than older established ones. Thus it is not surprising that radioactivity became one of the areas of chemistry where women, following Marie Curie's example, became prominent. Three well-known research groups, the French, British, and Austro-German group had more than their share of women researchers. After Pierre's death, Marie Curie was the acknowledged head of the French school with André Debierne serving as the research manager. Later, Irène Joliot-Curie took his place.[11]

Women chemists and physicists from many different countries migrated to Curie's laboratory resulting in a very cosmopolitan atmosphere. Whereas some women spent many years at the laboratory, others worked there for only a short amount of time. It seemed important to those whose primary work was with the British or the Austro-German group to have time in Curie's laboratory on their resumes. Others who worked only with Rutherford and Thomson in the British group or the Austro-German group did not have direct contact with Curie but were indirectly influenced by her larger than life persona and made important contributions to twentieth century chemistry and physics.

Even when they spent only a short time in the Curie laboratory many women made vital contributions to the new science of radioactivity. The following women, their countries of origin, and the years that they worked in Curie's laboratory illustrate the diversity found among these female scientists: Sybil Leslie (1909–1911), Swedish chemist Eva Ramstedt (1910–1911), Russian physicist Jadwiga Szmidt (summer of 1911), Hungarian scientist Irén Götz (1911–1913), Russian refuge scientist Catherine Chamié (1921–1950), Romanian chemist, Stefania Maracineanu (1922–1925), Polish chemist, Alicja Dorabialska (1925–1926), Hungarian chemist Elizabeth Róna (1926), and finally, Irène Joliot-Curie, Marie's daughter who inherited the Curie empire were among these women.[12] Although Lucie Blanquies (fl. 1908) had a promising start in Curie's laboratory where she worked from 1908–1910, she disappeared from the record. During her time in the laboratory Blanquies measured the range of α-particles from different radioactive substances, enabling her to compare the initial energies of the particles. However in analyzing the decay product of actinium, she arrived at results that other researchers were unable to duplicate.[13] The importance of women in the new science of radioactivity should not be judged by Blanquies, but is better illustrated in the lives and works of two women who worked in Curie's laboratory, Ellen Gleditsch and Harriet T. Brooks.

Ellen Gleditsch (1879–1968)

The Norwegian chemist, Ellen Gleditsch was one of the first women to work with Marie Curie for any significant length of time. Long before the hint of scandal began to tarnish Curie's reputation, Gleditsch arrived in Paris in 1907, and returned on many different occasions to work in the laboratory. The oldest of ten children in a caring and loving but poor family, Ellen struggled to continue her education. Influenced and encouraged by her mentor Eyvind Bodtker, a paper she had written was translated into French and published in the *Bulletin de la sociétète chimique de France* 35 (1907):1094–1097. Bodtker was able to convince a skeptical Marie Curie to allow Gleditsch to work for her. The experiment was a great success for both Gleditsch and Curie. Observing the difficulties that a woman scientist with a husband and children experienced, Gleditsch vowed never to marry in order to devote herself totally to chemistry. Hampered by a lack of equipment when she returned to Oslo, she sought other opportunities to study abroad. She planned to go to the United States to work with Bertram Boltwood of Yale University, notorious for his lack of sympathy for women scientists and especially for his disparaging remarks about Marie Curie, but was initially delayed by family responsibilities. Finally in 1913 with a scholarship from the American-Scandinavian Foundation she went to the United States to work with the reluctant Boltwood. Gleditsch determined the half-life of radium to be 1,686 years, later adjusted to the current value of 1,620 years.[14] During the year she spent at Yale, she earned the respect of the recalcitrant Boltwood who was appreciative of her work. After returning to Oslo, she continued to work with various radioactive materials and was one of the first individuals to use the ratio of lead to uranium in a mineral to determine its age, and determined the atomic mass of lead and chlorine isotopes from uranium materials.

During World War I, Gleditsch felt isolated from the world scientific community. However in 1916 her situation at the University of Oslo was greatly improved. As the importance of the new field of radiochemistry was recognized, she was appointed to a *dosentur*, a non-tenured lectureship at the University. From 1916–1929 she held this lectureship and then was appointed professor of organic chemistry, a position that she held from 1929–1946. Gleditsch received many honors including the Nansen Prize from the Norwegian Academy of Science and honorary doctorates from Smith College (1914), the University of Strasbourg (1948) and the University of Paris (1967).

Harriet Brooks (1876–1933)

Several of Curie's disciples only worked briefly in Paris but spent much of their career working with Ernest Rutherford and J.J. Thomson in England. The Canadian scientist, Harriet Brooks grew up in less than affluent circumstances but was able to attend college at McGill University after her family moved to Montreal in 1894. An excellent student, Brooks earned an honors BA in mathematics and natural philosophy as well as a teaching diploma. Upon completing her degree in 1898, Rutherford hired her as his first student researcher after he arrived at McGill from England. Rutherford assigned her a project related to his early interest on wireless transmission. This project, examining the effects that an electrical discharge conducted through steel needles had on their magnetization, earned her an M.A. degree in 1901. Her next project with Rutherford was to investigate a mysterious "emanation" from radium. They found that the emanation was chemically different from radium and concluded that it was a gas with a much lower molecular weight than radium. This discovery suggested a theory of atomic transmutation to Rutherford and Frederick Soddy. Brooks and Rutherford also studied the absorption behavior in a magnetic field and the decay of emissions from radioactive substances, to determine whether the different radioactive elements emitted the same kinds of radiations.

Intending to work on a Ph.D. degree at Bryn Mawr College, Brooks obtained leave from the Royal Victoria College (McGill) where she was teaching as well as doing research with Rutherford. Bryn Mawr awarded her a prestigious fellowship to study in Europe. In spite of the objections of her family, Brooks took her fellowship at the Cavendish Laboratory working under J.J. Thomson. She was disappointed both by the Cavendish Laboratory and what she considered her own research deficiencies, a view not shared by her mentors. Instead of returning to

Bryn Mawr, she went back to McGill as a non-resident tutor in physics and mathematics and a member of Rutherford's research group. During this time at McGill, she made an important discovery that was overlooked and rediscovered later by Otto Hahn/Lisa Meitner and Russ/Markower. Brooks published some of her work on radioactive decay based on the research that she did at the Cavendish Laboratory that laid the foundation for the concept of radioactive decay sequences.

Brooks found being a woman only a minor impediment in her early research years. As an undergraduate she had found it financially expedient to obtain a teaching diploma from the Normal School at McGill. By taking tuition-free night classes she was assured of a teaching position after she graduated, one of the few ways that a woman could be certain of making a living. By accepting this diploma, however, she agreed to commit herself to three years of teaching but was able to satisfy the requirement by tutoring at the Royal Victoria College. Although she attended Bryn Mawr College where intelligent women were appreciated where she received a Presidential Fellowship, her lack of self-esteem and her discomfort with different environments held her back, even when her mentors agreed that her work was excellent.

An unexpected gender problem occurred when Brooks accepted a position as a physics tutor at Barnard College, the women's part of Columbia University in New York City. At Barnard she became engaged to Columbia physics professor Bergen Davis whom she had met during her year at the Cavendish. After she informed Dean Laura Gill of the engagement, Gill replied that if the marriage actually occurred Brooks must end her official relationship with the college. Incensed by Gill's attitude, Brooks wrote that it "is a duty I owe to my profession and to my sex to show that a woman has a right to the practice of her profession and cannot be condemned to abandon it merely because she marries."[15] After breaking her engagement to Davis (to the delight of Dean Gill), she resigned from Barnard and spent the summer with social reformer, Prestonia Martin, in their collectivist community in upstate New York. In October, she accompanied several Fabian socialists, including the Russian writer, Maxim Gorky, to Europe. She spent part of 1906–1907 in Paris working in Marie Curie's laboratory. In Curie's laboratory, Brooks investigated radioactive recoil, radioactive gases, and the decay rate of actinium B.[16] Although Curie invited her to stay for the 1907–1908 years, Brooks decided to follow Rutherford to the University of Manchester where he was moving from McGill. While awaiting word on a fellowship at Manchester, she became engaged to Frank Henry Pitcher, a physicist whom she had met at McGill; the couple had three children, two of whom did not survive childhood. After her marriage, Brooks no longer worked in science. Harriet Brooks Pitcher died in 1933 from an unspecified blood disease, possibly caused by her early exposure to radiation.

Gleditsch and Brooks were representative of two women chemists who benefitted from Marie Curie's reputation—Gleditsch more directly and Brooks, indirectly. Although the new science of radioactivity may have been more hospitable to women than some of the older established fields, women still found it difficult to receive credit for their discoveries. Nevertheless, in spite of the fact that some male scientists continued to insist that Curie's success was an anomaly, others accepted women as capable of superior theoretical achievements. Although it remained difficult for women to succeed in areas of science outside the traditional "women's work" areas, it no longer seemed impossible as other women continued to make startling new contributions. The new science of radioactivity, however had unforeseen consequences for the health of both male and female practitioners.

MARIE CURIE, THE LATER YEARS

Harriet Brooks was one of a number of scientists, including Marie's daughter, Irène, who worked in the new science of radioactivity and who suffered from the effects of radiation. Although the proximate cause of Pierre Curie's death was a tragic accident, there is good evidence that he had experienced symptoms of radiation poisoning long before his accident. Marie herself did not have obvious symptoms of the harmful effects of radiation during the time when Pierre became ill, although it is possible that radiation caused her miscarriage in 1904. Radiation was responsible for Marie's increasingly fragile health, although she refused to admit that her "baby" radium could have harmful effects. She much preferred the evidence that it was useful in the treatment of cancer.

Eighteen days after Curie's acceptance speech for her second Nobel Prize, she was rushed to the hospital and diagnosed with an infection of the kidney and ureter that required surgery. Physically she was weak for many months, but her state of mind was even more devastated, reflecting the disgrace of the Langevin affair. She suffered from a serious psychological breakdown and hid from her colleagues and friends, even using her maiden name, Sklodowska. During the first part of December 1912, she returned to the laboratory but used that time to catch up with advances that had been made during her absence. By 1913 she seemed more comfortable with herself than before; she entertained more frequently, attended the Solvay Conference in Brussels, dedicated a radium institute in Warsaw built in her honor, and received an honorary degree in Birmingham, England.

During the academic year, 1912–1913, the Sorbonne (University of Paris) proposed at Marie's insistence to build an institute of radioactivity in honor of Pierre on a new street, the Rue Pierre Curie. Although the institute was completed on July 31, 1914, World War I intervened, and it was not used as a laboratory for over four years. Curie recognized the potential of x-rays to save lives of those injured in battle and approached French government officials with a plan to establish a fleet of x-ray cars, soliciting money from individuals and corporations for this purpose. With her daughter, Irène, she visited battlefields and established fixed radiological stations whenever possible. She also used the new Radium Institute as a school for training young women in x-ray techniques.

Pure research being impossible during the war, Curie's research took a practical turn. Once the radiology stations were set up, she became involved in the use of radium for medicinal purposes. Although she had long realized that radium could be used to treat cancer, she came to realize that it was useful in treating scar tissue from wartime injuries as well as arthritis and other ailments. However because radium itself had become extraordinarily expensive, she gave the Health Service the emanation (radon gas) that radium sporadically emitted rather than radium. Since she had no assistants, Curie herself would draw off the radon from its parent radium and seal it in thin glass tubes. Curie finally admitted that her radium could have harmful effects as well. She advised the technicians to take special precautions when working with the "emanation." In spite of her misgivings, she concluded the effects of working with radium were temporary and would disappear as soon as the work ceased.

During the war years, Curie was making plans for the future. Although the new Institute dedicated to the memory of Pierre was completed in 1915, she lacked both the money and help to develop the Institute into a first-class research facility, and she feared that a war-ravaged Paris would never be able to support the Institute. In her autobiographical notes she wrote

> I frequently ask myself whether, in spite of recent efforts of the government. I shall ever succeed in building up for those who will come after me an Institute of Radium, such as I wish to the memory of Pierre Curie and to the highest interest of humanity.[17]

Although a sparsely equipped laboratory would have satisfied Curie's wishes, she realized that in order to host a first-rate institute as a suitable testament to Pierre she must have the newest sophisticated equipment and a supply of radium. After a futile exhausting search for funds from French governmental agencies, she reluctantly succumbed to a request for an interview by Marie (Missy) Meloney, the editor of an American women's magazine the *Delineator*. As much as she dreaded interviews, Curie saw a potential source of funds from the United States, a country that had emerged relatively unscathed from the war. The two women got along well, and Meloney convinced Curie to come to the United States in 1921 to launch a huge fund-raising campaign among the women. Flamboyant Missy was able to raise not only enough money for a gram of radium but collected $50,000 to spare. In 1929, Marie made a second successful fund-raising trip to the United States.

These trips were both psychologically and physically difficult for Curie. She had always been a very private person, and dreaded public appearances. Although the ebullient Americans were generous with their money, they wanted to entertain their icon properly which meant days filled with speaking engagements and visits to national monuments. Exhausted physically, she was relieved when she was back in her own laboratory. She began to suffer from cataracts that she reluctantly admitted might be the result of radium exposure. Evidence poured in from other laboratories and industries indicating that radioactivity was the culprit in the appearance of various blood diseases in exposed workers. Even as she grew increasingly frail, Curie continued to go to the laboratory. She died on July 4, 1934, of aplastic anemia.

CURIE'S LEGACY FOR WOMEN IN SCIENCE

Marie Curie's legacy has been constructed differently to reflect varying ideas of an ideal woman scientist. To many, she represented the quintessential woman scientist—a one-dimensional woman whose total life was her science. She was not allowed to have human emotions or failings. When they appeared they were often swept under the carpet in order to maintain her reputation. Curie was a complex person, capable of love, doubt, and loyalty; she exhibited the same doggedness to these characteristics as she did toward her science. The image of Marie Curie inspired some talented women in subsequent generations to realize that they could be successful in science. Others found her a daunting role model. Not understanding that science was not Curie's entire life but only one aspect of it, they declined to make such a commitment.

As we have seen, Marie Curie had many female predecessors in chemistry. Looking back in time, we find women who may have made important additions to their field, but the culture denies us a record of their contributions. If they hoped to pursue a scientific career, they had to develop strategies that male scientists found acceptable. A favorite strategy involved pursuing fields that reflected women's place in the domestic sphere, so-called "women's work" which men did not care to pursue. As discussed previously, Ellen Swallow Richards' developed home economics as a discipline where women could practice chemistry, and apply it in jobs in academia, industry, and social fields. However, the downside of this practice was that as more women entered these fields they became devalued, and it became difficult for women to enter mainstream chemical positions.

A second popular strategy, collaboration with a spouse, has long been one that women used to enter the sciences. The contribution of the female collaborator is often difficult or sometimes impossible to ascertain. It has long been acceptable for women to work as scientific illustrators or translators (again women's work). We know that Marie Lavoisier illustrated her famous husband's work and provided translations. But while we may suspect, we do not know what other contributions Mme Lavoisier may have made. Even in the twentieth century it was much simpler for potential women scientists to have a male collaborator. The best-known husband-wife collaboration was between Marie and Pierre Curie. In spite of evidence to the contrary, many of their scientific contemporaries, including Ernest Rutherford and Bernard Boltwood, credited Pierre with the theoretical contributions, with Marie's involvement centered on the minutiae of laboratory analyses. To support this view they pointed to the fact that Marie's theoretical contributions were made mostly during Pierre's lifetime. Although it is true that her most scientifically creative years were those in which she and Pierre shared ideas, the basic hypotheses that guided the future course of the investigation of radioactivity were hers.

As the cultural climate has evolved, the need for women to collaborate with a male in order to succeed in science has decreased. Along with educational, political and cultural reforms, Marie Curie's success was a factor in this in bringing forth this attitudinal change. This is not to say it is as easy for a woman to become a successful scientist as it is for a man, but as the number of women scientists increases, impediments, while there, tend to decrease.

NOTES

[1] The Nobel Prize Internet Archive, Female Nobel Laureates (2011). Available from http://nobelprizes.com/nobel/women.html

[2] Apollonios of Rhodes, Horace, Plato, Plutarch, Plutarch, Morals, Virgil. See Ogilvie 1986, C1, C16, C21, C27,C33.

[3] Homer, Hyginus. See Ogilvie 1986, C29, C15, C17.

[4] Ogilvie, 1986, pp. 128–129.

[5] Ogilvie & Harvey, 2000, v. 1, pp. 752–753.

[6] Rossiter, 1982, pp. 30–31; Ogilvie & Harvey, 2000 , v. 2, 1095–1097.

[7] M. Curie, 1923, p. 180.

[8] M. Curie, 1923, p. 186.

[9] M. Curie and P. Curie, 1898.

[10] E. Curie, 1938, p. 169.

[11] M. Rayner-Canham and G. Rayner-Canham, 1997, pp. 4–5.

[12] M. Rayner-Canham and G, Rayner-Canham, 1997, pp. 29–30.

[13] M. Malley in Ogilvie & Harvey, 2000, v.1, p. 142.

[14] M. Rayner-Canham and G. Rayner-Canham, p. 57.

[15] M. Rayner-Canham and G. Rayner-Canham, p. 134.

[16] M. Malley, 2000, v. 1, p. 184.

[17] M. Curie, 1923, p. 221.

REFERENCES

Curie, E. (1938). *Madame Curie: A biography.* New York: Doubleday, Doran, and Co.

Curie, M. (1904). *Recherche sur les substances radioactives* (2d ed., rev. and corr.). Paris: Gauthier-Villars.

Curie, M. (1923). *Autobiographical notes. Pierre Curie.* (Trans. C. & V. Kellogg). New York: Macmillan.

Curie, P., & M. Curie (1898). On a new radio-active substance contained in pitchblende. *Comptes Rendus, 127,* 175–178.

Female Nobel Laureates. The Nobel Prize Internet archive. Available from http://nobelprizes.com/nobel/women.html

Malley, M. B., (2000). Harriet T. Brooks (1876–1933). In M. Ogilvie & J. Harvey (Eds.), *The biographical dictionary of women in science: Pioneering lives from ancient times to the mid-20th century,* (vol. 1) (pp. 184–185). New York: Routledge.

Ogilvie, M. (1986). *Women in science: Antiquity through the nineteenth century. A biographical dictionary with annotated bibliography.* Cambridge, MA: MIT Press.

Ogilvie, M. (2000). Marie Anne Pierrette Paulze (1758–1836). In M. Ogilvie & J. Harvey (Eds.), *The biographical dictionary of women in science: Pioneering lives from ancient times to the mid-20th century,* (vol. 2) (pp. 752–753). New York: Routledge.

Ogilvie, M. (2011). *Marie Curie. A biography.* Amherst, NY: Prometheus.

Pasachoff, N. (1996). *Marie Curie and the science of radioactivity.* New York: Oxford University Press.

Quinn, S. (1995). *Marie Curie: A life.* New York: Simon and Schuster.

Raynor-Canham, M., & Rayner-Canham, G. (1994). *Harriet Brooks: Pioneer nuclear scientist.* Montreal: McGill-Queens University Press.

Raynor-Canham, M., & Rayner-Canham, G. (1997). *A devotion to their science: Pioneer women of radioactivity.* Philadelphia: Chemical Heritage Foundation.

Reid, R. (1978). *Marie Curie.* New York: New American Library.

Rossiter, M. (1984). *Women scientists in America: Struggles and strategies to 1940* (Vol. 1). Baltimore: Johns Hopkins University Press.

Rosser, S. (Ed.). (2008). *Women, science, and myth: Gender beliefs from antiquity to the present.* Santa Barbara, CA: ABC-CLIO, Inc.

Marilyn Bailey Ogilvie
Professor Emerita
University of Oklahoma
mogilvie@ou.edu

RACHEL MAMLOK-NAAMAN, RON BLONDER, AND
YEHUDIT JUDY DORI

6. ONE HUNDRED YEARS OF WOMEN IN CHEMISTRY IN THE 20TH CENTURY

Sociocultural Developments of Women's Status

INTRODUCTION

The Scientific Revolution established science as a source for the growth of knowledge. During the 19th century, the practice of science became professionalized and institutionalized in ways that continued through the 20th century. As scientific knowledge rapidly increased in society, it was incorporated into many aspects of the characteristics and functions of nations and states. A chain of advances in knowledge, which have always complemented each other, has marked the history of science. Technological innovations bring about new discoveries, which lead to other innovations, which inspire new possibilities and innovative approaches to long-standing scientific issues and open questions.

However, women scientists often had difficulty in combating gender discrimination in their professional lives. For example, socialist women scientists who believed in Marxist principles regarding class as the dominant social force have long resisted the idea of struggling against gender bias because it would detract from the presumably more basic class struggle. Many other women scientists disliked attracting attention as women, as opposed to being acknowledged as just (presumably gender-neutral) scientists.

This chapter is devoted to the contribution of five women whose chemistry discoveries were part of the development of scientific and technological innovations from the beginning of the 20th century. We also discuss reasons for women's underrepresentation in the sciences.

BACKGROUND

The 20th century was characterized by a major shift in the way that vast numbers of people lived, as a result of changes in politics, ideology, economics, society, culture, science, technology, and medicine. Terms such as *ideology*, world war, *genocide*, and nuclear war became common. Scientific discoveries, such as the theory of relativity and quantum physics, drastically changed the scientific world as it was then known, and scientists realized that the universe was much more complex than previously believed (Read, 1995; Wolff, 1967). Hopes were dashed

M.-H. Chiu, P. J. Gilmer, and D. F. Treagust (Eds.), Celebrating the 100th Anniversary
of Madame Marie Sklodowska Curie's Nobel Prize in Chemistry. 119–139.

at the end of the 19th century that the last few details of scientific knowledge were about to be completed. Increased scientific understanding, more efficient communication, and faster transportation transformed the world in those hundred years more rapidly and widely than in any previous century. It was a century that began with horses, simple automobiles and airplanes and culminated with the space shuttle and the space station. These developments were made possible by large-scale exploitation of fossil fuel resources (especially petroleum), by which large amounts of energy were available in an easily portable form; however, this also caused widespread concerns about pollution and the long-term impact on the environment. Other new developments included humans exploring outer space for the first time, even taking their first footsteps on the Moon (Mamlok, 1996; Mamlok-Naaman, Ben-Zvi, Hofstein, Menis, & Erduran, 2005).

The media, telecommunication, and information technology (especially computers and the Internet) made the world's rapidly increasing knowledge more widely available to everyone. Many people's view of the world greatly changed as they became much more aware of the struggles of others and, as such, became increasingly concerned with human rights. Advancements in medical technology also improved the welfare of many people and the average life expectancy of humans increased from 35 years to 65 years in a short period of time during the 20th century (Brooks, 1996; McKeown, 1976).

Rapid technological advancements, however, also allowed warfare to achieve unprecedented levels of destruction. In World War II alone over 60 million people were killed and nuclear weapons gave humankind the means to annihilate or greatly harm itself in a very short period of time. The world also became more culturally homogeneous than ever with rapid developments in transportation and communications technology, popular music and other influences of Western culture, mass migration, and the rise of international corporations, and what was arguably a true global economy by the end of the century.

Scientific Discoveries

The beginning of the 20th century ushered in a revolution in physics. The long-held theories of Newton were shown to be sometimes incorrect. Beginning in 1900, Max Planck, Albert Einstein, Niels Bohr and others developed quantum theories to explain various anomalous experimental results by introducing discrete energy levels. Not only did quantum mechanics prove that the laws of motion did not hold on small scales but, even more disturbing, the theory of general relativity, proposed by Einstein in 1915, revealed that the fixed background of space-time, on which both Newtonian mechanics and special relativity depended, could not exist. In 1925, Werner Heisenberg and Erwin Schrödinger (Goldstein, 1995) formulated the quantum mechanics, which explained the preceding quantum theories. The observation by Edwin Hubble in 1929 that the speed at which galaxies recede correlates with their distance, led to our understanding that the universe is expanding, and to the formulation of the Big Bang theory by Georgios Lemaitre.

Note that currently, general relativity and quantum mechanics are inconsistent with each other and efforts are underway to reconcile the differences.

From the late 1920s to the present, the field of Signal Production-Reproduction for video acquisition and replay has rapidly developed. Dr. August Karolus at the University of Leipzig, Germany, first developed a television signal. His student and laboratory assistant, Dr. Erhard Kietz, researched frequency constancy of electric tuning forks for his dissertation in 1939; he later emigrated to the US where he developed several patents in the field of video signals for Ampex Corporation.

Further developments took place during World War II, which led to the practical application of radar and the development and use of the atomic bomb. Though the process had begun with the invention of the cyclotron by Ernest O. Lawrence in the 1930s, physics in the postwar period entered into a phase of what historians have called "Big Science", requiring massive machines, budgets, and laboratories in order to test physics theories and to move into new frontiers. The primary patron of physics became state governments, which recognized that the support of basic research could often lead to technologies useful for both military and industrial applications.

Women's Status

Women have been and still remain underrepresented in science and engineering. During the Scientific Revolution of the 17th century aristocratic women were active as both patrons and spokespeople of natural philosophers. In the 19th century, the ever-increasing professionalization of science and specialization of scientific domains, as well as its increasing location in the laboratory, caused science to depart from its traditional domestic base. This transition, however, further excluded women from science because social pressure kept them tied to their homes and children (Rayner-Canham & Rayner-Canham, 1997). Nevertheless, some women made important contributions: Mary Somerville and Jane Haldimand Marcet in England, through their informal textbooks, and Maria Mitchell, in the United States, who taught science to many women at Vassar College. The rise of women's colleges in the last third of the 19th century, as well as the willingness of some universities to allow foreign women to study or even graduate, created the first generation of formally educated women scientists. In the 20th century, the shortage of technical personnel during the two world wars temporarily opened up further opportunities for women in science.

Women's place in science tended to greatly vary by discipline. Women encountered substantial resistance in the laboratory sciences. However, they were more readily accepted in observational sciences such as botany and classical astronomy, where the need for large-scale collecting and observing encouraged the spreading of an amateur subculture for both men and women. In theoretical sciences—except for mathematics, in which there was an often-explicit bias against women—they also faced fewer barriers since the equipment and facilities required were minimal. Both observational and theoretical pursuits seemed tolerably compatible with women's primary familial responsibilities; observation also belonged to a socially acceptable tradition of amateur practice. During the 20th century an increasing number of women, many of them aided by enlightened male mentors, excelled in the experimental as well as the theoretical sciences. Among them were Marie Sklodowska Curie, a co-discoverer of radioactivity and radium, who worked in state-funded laboratories in Paris and won two Nobel Prizes; her elder daughter, Irène Joliot-Curie, who shared the 1935 Nobel Prize in Chemistry with her husband Frédéric Joliot for discovering artificial radioactivity; Hertha Ayrton who worked at the interface of physics and engineering with support from the feminist Langham Place Group and from her physicist husband William Ayrton and who became the first woman nominated for fellowship in the Royal Society of London; Lise Meitner, a protégée of Max Planck, who headed the physics division at the Kaiser Wilhelm Institute for Physical Chemistry in Germany between the wars and played a role in discovering nuclear fission; and Rita Levi-Montalcini who shared a Nobel Prize for her research in neurobiology.

However, women still continued to face discrimination in most fields of science, and many had difficulty reconciling the demands of research with those of the home and family. Some women scientists, believing that the demands of science were not compatible with the traditional role of women, remained single. Several well-known women scientists who did marry collaborated with their scientist husbands. Examples include 1) Marie and Pierre Curie, 2) Maria Goeppert-Mayer (Nobel Laureate in Physics) and her husband Joseph Mayer, 3) Gerty Theresa Cori and her husband Bernardo Houssay received together the Nobel Prize in Physiology or Medicine, and 4) Irène Joliot-Curie, the daughter of Marie and Pierre Curie, and her husband Frédéric Joliot were awarded the Nobel Prize for Chemistry (Gupta, 2011). Although a scientific marriage often facilitated a woman's acceptance into a broader scientific community, it often led colleagues to assume that the work of the wife was secondary to that of her husband.

British culture proved relatively conducive to some extent regarding the enrollment of women in science because the British Empire provided ample imagination, independence, and travel for women of the middle upper class. The biologist Dorothy M. Wrinch, born in the then British colony of Argentina, and who distinguished herself in mathematics at Cambridge, became the first woman to receive a doctorate in science from Oxford in 1929 and was a pioneer in researching protein structure and molecular biology.

Beginning in the 1960s, the civil rights movement and the women's movement combined to bring gender inequality in science to social, cultural, and legal scrutiny as well as public awareness. Overt discrimination became illegal. Shortages in scientific personnel in the late 1980s led to developing a gender-responsive science policy that would enable more women to become scientists and combine their professional careers with diverse family-oriented activities. Several innovative policies, initiated by the National Science Foundation, the National Institutes of Health, and other agencies, made significant headway regarding the problem of recruitment. Nevertheless, gender segregation continues to plague fields such as medicine, where most women are relegated to the specialties of pediatrics, obstetrics, and psychiatry. New fields in science and engineering also display a consistent pattern of gender hierarchy, inequality, and de facto segregation (Schiebinger, 1989).

Since 1966, the number of women receiving bachelor's degrees in science and engineering in the US has increased almost every year, reaching 227,273 in 2007 (National Science Foundation, 2011), approximately half of the total. Interestingly, the number awarded to men has not increased appreciably since 1976. In addition, the proportion of women graduate students in science and engineering has markedly risen since 1991, reaching 44% in 2007 in the US. However, there have been substantial differences regarding the subjects studied, with women accounting for more than 70% of those enrolled in psychology 2008 but only 18% in computer science and in engineering. Impressively, both the number and the proportion of doctoral degrees awarded to women have increased steadily since 1989, from 9% to 22% in engineering, and from 15% to 22% in computer sciences in 2008. In most fields women's participation has risen over the two decades that ended in 2008. The general increase in the share of degrees that women earn reflects rising numbers of degrees for women and level or declining numbers earned by men (National Science Foundation, 2011).

In January 2005, Harvard University President Lawrence Summers sparked controversy when, at an the National Bureau of Economic Research conference on Diversifying the Science & Engineering Workforce, he made indiscreet comments suggesting that the lower numbers of women in high-level science positions may be due to innate differences in abilities or subject preferences between men and women (Summers, 2005). This frustrated many who attended and who felt that these issues, or at least his presentation of them, had been thoroughly refuted during the conference and that, additionally, such statements were irresponsible coming from a university president. The resulting controversy was a factor in his later resignation.

FIVE DISTINGUISHED WOMEN IN CHEMISTRY

In this section we describe the four women who earned Nobel Prizes in Chemistry, and another one who is well known for her achievement in developing a medical drug used to battle multiple sclerosis. First, we would like to concisely describe X-ray radiation and its historical context to support the scientific parts of the chapter. X-rays are a form of electromagnetic radiation with wavelengths of approximately 0.1–100 Å, corresponding to energies ranging from 120 eV to 120 keV. X-rays can penetrate solid objects, and they are heavily used in diagnostic radiography and crystallography to take images of the inside of objects.

On Nov. 8, 1895, Wilhelm Conrad Röntgen (accidentally) discovered an image cast from his cathode ray generator projected far beyond the possible range of the cathode rays (now known as an electron beam). Further investigation showed that when electrons strike materials in a cathode tube they produce a type of radiation that induces fluorescence outside the tube. These rays, however, were not deflected by magnetic fields, and they penetrated many types of matter. A week after his discovery, Röntgen took an X-ray photograph of his wife's hand which clearly revealed her wedding ring and her bones. The photograph, utilizing the new form of radiation, caught the attention of the general public and aroused great scientific interest. Röntgen named the new form of radiation X-radiation, where X standing for the "Unknown" nature of the radiation.

At that time, no one knew that this radiation, with its unknown nature, would be the common theme that would link the four Nobel Prizes in chemistry earned by the following women: Marie Curie, Irène Joliot-Curie, Dorothy Crowfoot Hodgkin, and Ada Yonath. Becquerel, who heard about Roentgen's results, hypothesized that a phosphorescent substance could also produce X-rays and that the cathode ray tube used by Röntgen was unnecessary. In his experiments, he found that uranium emitted radiation without being exposed to sunlight. He actually discovered that uranium was radioactive, but at the time he thought the emitted radiation was invisible phosphorescence.

Marie Curie

Marie Sklodowska was born on November 7, 1867 in Warsaw, Poland, married Pierre Curie in July 1895, and died on July 4, 1934 in Sancellemoz, France. Becquerel's new kind of ray intrigued Marie Curie when she was searching for a subject for her doctoral thesis (Groliers Electronic Encyclopedia, 1995; Porter, 1994). In 1911 she began her Nobel lecture with a short description of the phenomena that earned her the first Nobel Prize in physics in 1903:

> Some 15 years ago the radiation of uranium was discovered by Henri Becquerel, and two years later the study of this phenomenon was extended to other substances, first by me, and then by Pierre Curie and myself. This study rapidly led us to the discovery of new elements, the radiation of which, while being analogous with that of uranium, was far more intense. All the elements emitting such radiation I have termed radioactive, and the new property of matter revealed in this emission has thus received the name radioactivity. (Curie, 1911, unnumbered)

Marie Curie was the first to stress, "radioactivity is an atomic property of matter*"* and not a result of interaction between light and matter. She realized that "the task of isolating radium is the corner-stone of the edifice of the science of radioactivity." Over the course of several years, Marie and Pierre processed tons of pitchblende, progressively concentrating the radioactive substances and eventually isolating the chloride salts: Radium chloride was isolated on April 20, 1902, as she described:

> Tons of material have to be treated in order to extract radium from the ore. The quantities of radium available in a laboratory are of the order of one milligram, or of a gram at the very most, this substance being worth 400,000 francs per gram. Very often material has been handled in which the presence of radium could not be detected by the balance, nor even by the spectroscope.

And yet we have methods of measuring so perfect and so sensitive that we are able to know very exactly the small quantities of radium we are using. (Curie, 1911, unnumbered)

In addition to isolating the radium salt, she also characterized its chemical and physical properties. First she detected a new line in the spectrum indicating the existence of a new element. She then determined the average atomic mass of the metal in the salt. In the next experiments she prepared pure radium salts.

Preparing pure radium salts and determining the atomic mass of radium proved that radium was a new element, which enabled a definite position to be assigned to it. Radium is the higher homologue of barium in the family of alkaline-earth metals; it appears in Mendeleev's table in the corresponding column—on the row containing uranium and thorium. The spectrum of radium is precisely known. These clear-cut results for radium have convinced chemists and justified establishing the new science of radioactive substances.

Marie and Pierre Curie discovered two new chemical elements. *Polonium* was named for Curie's native country, Poland, and *radium* was named for its intense radioactivity. Marie never forgot her Polish homeland because the French nationalist journalists kept reminding her about it. Even after she won the first Nobel Prize, the press in France published lies and false news about Curie. They kept mentioning her Polish background and described her as a Polish blond woman who broke the marriage of Paul Langevin, a French scientist. It became known that she was willing to be nominated for election to *l'Académie des Sciences*. Although examples of factors other than merit deciding an election did exist, Marie herself and her eminent, research colleagues thought that based on her exceptionally brilliant scientific merits, her election was self-evident, but she was rejected.

Despite these attacks, she felt part of the French nation and generously gave her knowledge to national efforts during the First World War. In 1914 she established units of mobile X-rays, to be sent to the front line of the battles. She trained young women in simple X-ray technology, she herself with her daughter, Irène, drove one of the vans and actively participated in locating metal bullets. Throughout the war she was intensively engaged in equipping more than 20 vans that acted as mobile field hospitals and also equipped about 200 fixed installations with an X-ray apparatus.

Irène Joliot-Curie

Irène Curie, born in Paris, September 12, 1897, was the daughter of Pierre and Marie Curie, and since 1926 the wife of Frédéric Joliot. She shared the Nobel Prize in Chemistry in 1935 with her husband, in recognition of their synthesis of new radioactive elements. In her Nobel lecture, she described the extraordinary development of radioactivity since Becquerel through her parents' discoveries and she presented her and Frédéric Joliot's achievements:

We have shown that it is possible to create a radioactivity characterized by the emission of positive or negative electrons in boron and magnesium, by bombardment with alpha rays. These artificial radio-elements behave in all respects like the natural radio-elements. (Joliot-Curie, 1935, unnumbered)

In 1938, her research on the action of neutrons on the heavy elements was an important step in the discovery of uranium fission. Appointed lecturer in 1932, she became Professor in the Faculty of Science in Paris in 1937 and afterwards Director of the Radium Institute in 1946. Being a Commissioner for Atomic Energy for six years, Irène took part in its creation and in the construction of the first French atomic pile in 1948. She took part in the inauguration of the large center for nuclear physics at Orsay for which she worked out the plans. This center was equipped with a synchrocyclotron of 160 MeV, and its construction was continued by Frédéric Joliot after her death in 1954 (Nobel Lectures, 1966).

Dorothy Crowfoot Hodgkin

Dorothy Crowfoot Hodgkin was born on May 10, 1910 in Cairo, Egypt. She received many awards and honors throughout her lifetime (Adams & Glusker, 1995; Vijayan, 1995). At age 37 she was inducted into the Royal Society in England. In 1965 she received the Order of Merit, the highest civilian honor in Britain—she was only the second woman after Florence Nightingale to receive this award.

Although Dorothy's work changed the face of modern biology, she also had many other interests. Her family was always important. Dorothy encouraged many science students from all over the world. She helped establish and support the Hodgkin Science Scholarship intended for a student from a third world country. Dorothy also was known in international circles as a tireless champion of disarmament and world peace.

Dorothy Crowfoot Hodgkin was a British biochemist and crystallographer. She used X-rays to determine the structural layouts of atoms and the overall molecular shape of over 100 molecules including penicillin, vitamin B-12, vitamin D, and insulin. Hodgkin's improvements using X-ray crystallography made the technique an important analytical tool. Dorothy Crowfoot Hodgkin won the 1964 Nobel Prize in Chemistry for her determination by X-ray techniques of the structures of biologically important molecules.

X-ray crystallography is a method of determining the arrangement of atoms within a crystal, in which a beam of X-rays strikes a crystal and diffracts into many specific directions. From the angles and intensities of these diffracted beams, a crystallographer can produce a three-dimensional picture of the density of electrons within the crystal. From this electron density, the mean positions of the atoms in the crystal can be determined, as well as their chemical bonds, their disorder, and various other information. As Hodgkin describes in her Nobel lecture:

The experimental data we have to employ are the X-ray diffraction spectra from the crystal to be studied, usually recorded photographically and their intensities estimated by eye. These spectra correspond with a series of harmonic terms which can be recombined to give us a representation of the X-ray scattering material in the crystal, the electron density. (Hodgkin, 1967, p. 71)

However, the X-ray diffraction spectra cannot be transferred directly to the 3D structure of the investigated molecule. Many cycles of calculation should be applied in order to obtain the electron density map of the molecule and the position of the atoms.

With most crystals, the conditions for direct electron-density calculation are not initially met and one's progress towards the final answer is stepwise; if some of the atoms can be placed, particularly the heavier atoms in the crystal, calculations, necessarily imperfect, of the electron density can be started from which new regions in the crystal may be identified; the calculation is then repeated until the whole atomic distribution is clear. (Hodgkin, 1967, p. 72)

Hodgkin correctly analyzed the structure of biochemically important molecules such as cholesterol iodide and vitamin B-12. Understanding the molecular structure of vitamin B-12 has helped scientists to better understand how the human body uses B-12 to build red blood cells and prevent some types of anemia. Her discovery of the molecular layout of penicillin motivated scientists to develop other antibiotics. Her discovery occurred during World War II, so this information aided scientists in developing the antibiotics necessary to treat war injuries.

In 1969, after more than 30 years studying molecules, Dorothy unlocked the key to the three-dimensional structure of insulin. This breakthrough has helped scientists control the disease, diabetes.

Ada Yonath

Ada Yonath was born in 1939 in the Geula quarter of Jerusalem. Her parents had immigrated to Israel from Poland and her father was a rabbi. They settled in Jerusalem and ran a grocery store but they had difficulty making ends meet.

"People called me a dreamer," says Ada Yonath of the Structural Biology Department of the Weizmann Institute, Rehovot, Israel, in recalling her decision to undertake research on the ribosome – the cell's protein factory. Solving the ribosome's structure would give scientists unprecedented insight into how the genetic code is translated into proteins. By the late 1970s, however, top scientific teams around the world had already tried and failed to enable these complex structures of protein and RNA to take on a crystalline form that could be easily studied. It was hard work that brought results: Yonath and colleagues made a staggering 25,000 attempts before they succeeded in creating the first ribosome crystals in 1980.

Ribosomes exist in all cells in all living organisms. Although central to the cell's functioning, they are anything but simple. Dozens of different proteins and strands of RNA form a complicated machine divided into two principal components. The smaller component, known as the 30S subunit, works mainly to decode the genetic code in messenger RNA. The larger 50S subunit then takes this information and uses it to combine the proper sequence of amino acids that make up the final protein. Early on, researchers struggled to map the atomic structure of even one of these subunits. Producing an X-ray structure requires first creating crystals of millions of copies of a ribosome aligned in near perfect order. If that ordering is precise enough, then a beam of X-rays can be fired at the crystal. The pattern in which those X-rays subsequently deflect off the crystal can then be used to map the arrangement of atoms in the molecule.

In the late 1970s, Yonath decided, when she was a young student at the Weizmann Institute in Israel, to take on the challenge of addressing one of the key questions concerning the activities of live cells, namely, to decipher the structure and mode of action of ribosomes—the cell's protein factories. This was the beginning of a long scientific journey that has lasted decades, and which required courage and devotion from the start. The journey began in a modest laboratory with a modest budget, and with the years, this operation increased to tens of researchers under the guidance of Yonath.

In 1980, Yonath managed to generate the first low-quality crystals of a ribosome. By 1990, she had improved the quality of her crystals but she still struggled to obtain a good quality structure because the X-ray destroyed the crystals as soon as the X-ray beam interacted with the crystal. At that time, it was widely assumed that, even if there were crystals, the ribosome structure might never be determined because it was clear that, alongside the improvement of the crystals, ribosome crystallography required the development of innovative methodologies. Yonath developed a new methodology called cryo-temperature X-ray diffraction, as she described in her Nobel lecture:

When more suitable synchrotron facilities became available, and several crystal forms were grown (see Figure 1), the radiation sensitivity of the ribosomal crystals caused extremely fast crystal decay. Hence, pioneering data collection at cryo temperature became crucial. (Yonath, 2009, p. 219)

Steitz, along with his longtime Yale colleague, Peter Moore, jumped into the fray in 1995, following Yonath's recipe for making ribosomal crystals. By 1998, they used additional insights gleaned from electron microscopy studies to help them acquire a low-resolution 9 Å structure of the ribosome. In August 2000, Steitz's group then published a higher 2.4 Å resolution structure of the large subunit. Meanwhile, the groups of Yonath and Ramakrishnan (the co-recipient of the Nobel Prize with Yonath) published slightly lower resolution structures of the smaller subunit the following month. Since then, the three groups, plus other teams, have used those structures and others to better understand in atomic detail how ribosomes translate genetic information into proteins.

1980   1984   1990

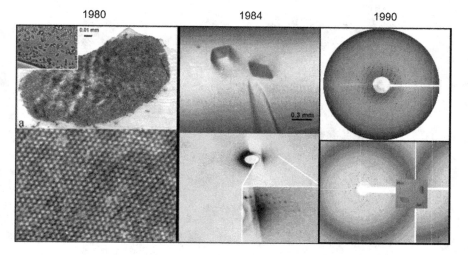

Figure 1. From a poor micro crystal to three-dimensional crystals yielding useful diffraction of ribosomal crystals: Left: Microcrystals of B50S, obtained in 1980 and a negatively stained section of them, viewed by electron microscopy. Middle: the tip of a ~2-μm long crystal of B50S and its diffraction pattern, obtained in 1984 at the EMBL beam line at DESY/Hamburg at 40°C. Note that the diffraction extends to 2.8 Å (top right), and the decay it underwent (bottom), even at cryo temperature, after collecting about 3% of the data. Diffraction patterns, from crystals of H50S obtained at ID13 ESRF at −1800°C (high-resolution photo was provided by Ada Yonath, as a pre-publication figure).

Yonath's basic research, which began in attempting to better understand one of the basic principles of nature, eventually led to understanding how a number of antibiotics function—something that is likely to aid in developing more advanced and effective antibiotics. This discovery will hopefully also help in the struggle against antibiotic-resistant bacteria, a problem now recognized as one of the most central medical challenges of the 21st century. Figure 2 shows Ada Yonath delivering her Nobel Prize lecture in Stockholm in 2009.

Figure 2. Ada Yonath delivering her Nobel Lecture in Stockholm in 2009. Her first slide of the presentation is on the screen behind her (Yonath, private communication).

Ruth Arnon

Ruth Arnon is one of Israel's leading chemical immunologists (Shalvi, 2009). Her academic work has spawned across several decades promoting scientific discoveries that have enabled people to live fuller lives. Her work has included the development of Copaxone (along with Professor Michael Sela and the late colleague Dr. Devorah Teitelbaum) which is a major medical drug used to battle multiple sclerosis, as well as the development of a synthetic influenza vaccine administered through the nasal cavity. Ruth Arnon has overcome several hurdles throughout her career and is a well-recognized and notable immunologist in Israel and worldwide with ~400 published articles, chapters and books in immunology and biochemistry.

Born in Tel Aviv in 1933, Ruth Arnon is a second generation "Sabra"[1] and attributes her scientific zeal to her father, Alexander Rosenberg, who was an electrical engineer. Upon graduating from the Herzlia Hebrew Gymnasia high school, Ruth Arnon commenced her undergraduate studies at the Hebrew University. She graduated with a M.Sc. degree in chemistry and proceeded to serve in the Israeli Defense Forces as an officer for two years. During this time, she met her husband, Uriel Arnon, who was studying to become an engineer at the Technion University in Haifa.

At a time when a young newly married woman's role was to be the caretaker of the family, Ruth Arnon sought out opportunities to continue her academic studies while simultaneously beginning her family. She gave birth to her eldest daughter in 1957, also the year that she commenced her doctoral studies under the supervision of Professor Michael Sela at the Weizmann Institute. Together, the pair published extensively and became prominent figures at the Institute. Throughout her tenure at the Weizmann Institute, Ruth Arnon worked as an Associate Professor, Professor, Head of the Department of Chemical Immunology, Director of the MacArthur Center for Parasitology, Dean of the Faculty of Biology, Vice-President and Vice-president for International Scientific Relations. In addition to her many roles and positions at the Weizmann Institute, Ruth Arnon has been a visiting scientist at universities worldwide, including the Rockefeller Institute in New York, Institute Pasteur in Paris and the Imperial Cancer Research Fund in London.

Outside the academic arena and the laboratory, Ruth Arnon has served as a member, Vice President and President of numerous scientific organizations in Israel and worldwide. Recently, she was elected to be the President of the Israel Academy of Sciences and the Humanities. This new position has crossed the gender line making Ruth Arnon the first woman to head the prestigious academy; through this new position, she aims to increase and strengthen relationships between the academy and similar organizations internationally.

CHALLENGES WOMEN FACE DURING THEIR SCIENTIFIC CAREERS

In an attempt to understand, predict and change human behaviors, Bandura (1986, 1997) put forth the Social Cognitive Theory (henceforth SCT). The SCT explains that there are interrelated factors that can be used to evaluate human behavior and development: i) cognitive, which refers to watching others and learning from them; ii) environmental aspect, which refers to the social and physical factors that affect human behavior, and iii) personal and social factors such as self-efficacy and role models.

In relating the SCT to the current topic, women have expressed different opinions and experiences pertaining to the sustainability in the sciences (e.g., Bebbington, 2003; Davis, 2001; Ellemers, van den Heuvel, de Glider, Maass, & Bonvini, 2004; Nolan, Buckner, Marzabadi, & Kuck, 2008; Toren, 2000; Wyer, 2003; Zeldin & Pajares, 2000), which may be attributed to any one of the factors of the SCT. However, intervention methods may alter the influence of one of the factors, which ultimately will affect the behavior of the individual. For example, gender equity policies will affect an individual's environment and increase his or her self-efficacy level (personal) which in return will affect his or her behavior and, overall, his or her attitude towards involvement in the sciences (Bandura, 1997).

The Social Cognitive Career Theory (henceforth SCCT) posited by Lent, Brown and Hackett (1994) expanded on Bandura's (1986, 1997) SGT by including academic performance associated to the development of career choice and the behaviors associated with careers. The SCCT emphasizes three factors relevant to academic development—self-efficacy, outcome, expectations and goals. The basic interlocking models comprising the theoretical framework are 1) interest, 2) choice, and 3) performance. In applying their theory to women, Lent et al. (1994) further acknowledged that women must also contend with social and contextual factors which influence their self-efficacy and ultimate career outcomes as well as with challenges such as balancing work and home.

Promotional Status and Staying in a Prestigious Career

Science is considered to be a field engraved in social networking due to the immense amount of collaboration required among researchers to effectively progress with their careers. More specifically, social networking is a key component within the academic profession because it allows individuals to collaborate together to further their research or gain new research ideas, assists with career choices and paths, and assists with broadening one's research direction. However, entrance into these communities may pose difficulties for women at all levels of their academic and professional careers (Davis, 2001) and may have a direct impact on their views of self-efficacy.

According to Bandura (1997), self-efficacy is formed by an individual's interpretation of four sources of information—mastery experience, vicarious experiences, verbal persuasions, and the psychological and affective states of an individual such as their stress levels, tension and strengths. Together, these four sources assist in developing an individual's view of his or her capabilities. Bandura (1997) posited that the most effective determining source is derived from the mastery experience because as an individual succeeds amongst his or her own adversities, his or her level of self-belief increases by understanding how he or she is able to turn a failure into a success. Although this source of information plays a valuable role in one's sense of self-efficacy, several factors have been found to equally influence, both positively and negatively, the self-efficacy views of women engaged in science careers.

Through observing and speaking with 15 women who work in careers emphasizing mathematics, Zeldin and Pajares (2000) found that the most beneficial factors in building self-efficacy beliefs in women's capabilities came from vicarious experiences and verbal persuasions. Both of these factors were most influenced by family members, teachers (at all levels of an individual's academic career), peers and supervisors and mentors in the workforce. On the other hand, as compared to their male colleagues, self-efficacy beliefs in men were derived from their own perceptions and interpretations of their continued achievements and successes

(Zeldin, Britner, & Parajes, 2008) which is in line with Bandura's (1997) hypothesis that the most valuable factor of self-efficacy is mastery experiences. In an effort to understand the impact that mentors have on women in chemistry during their undergraduate, graduate, and postdoctoral years, Nolan et al. (2008) noted that women perceived this relationship as being less effective and supportive than their male colleagues. Nolan et al. (2008) further concluded that this negative perception of mentoring acts as a barrier and affects the future career decisions of women in chemistry and ultimately, affects and dictates an individual's identity and self-efficacy.

In looking at how such groups benefit women, Davis (2001) observed a group of women in the United States comprising graduate (while studying) and postgraduate (at work) students and academics of all professional university rankings. The group provided participants with a safe place to be themselves, to collaborate with one another, to discuss issues which they faced, to ease their feelings of isolation, and to provide personal and professional support. She found that the women who participated in the group were able to establish a voice for themselves by collaborating with their colleagues in the group and, in return, this provided them with a social networking system that allowed them to progress with their careers and enter their own individual science communities. Generally speaking, women thrive in highly social stimulating environments, as compared to men, and therefore active participation in these groups is highly encouraged (Zeldin & Pajares, 2000).

In order to enter, sustain and progress in the science field, individuals not only need to have the support of others, but they also have to have the determination to meet the demands imposed by their career choice at the organizational level. Heavy emphasis is placed on the quantity and quality of publications in order to progress within academia; however, disparity has been found between men and women and their publications. Fox (2001) attributed this disparity to the individual academic departments and to how both men and women approach their research. First, she delineated how males and females feel about the concept of inclusion, exclusion and opportunities afforded to both genders with men being more likely than women to report unhappiness with their department and to speak at group meetings. Second, Fox (2001) and Sonnert and Holton (1995) proposed that the difference in the quantity of publications is due to women's tendency to confirm their research findings and report them in more detail than men prior to submitting them for publication.

Aside from the recognition and prestige that publication affords to scientists, it also influences promotional status. In her study conducted in the 1980's involving full professors in the sciences at all Israeli universities, Toren (2000) found that 13 of the 33 participants expressed dissatisfaction with and a desire to leave the field. The respondents felt that they were 'pushed' to make this decision by personal and organizational reasons due to slow promotional rates, stress and 'burn out'. In regards to promotions, the professors acknowledged that there is a significant difference in the timespan required to obtain a higher promotional status between men and women. Basically, women have to work harder and publish more in order to achieve the same success rates in the same time frame as their male colleagues. What is interesting to note though is that none of the women attributed the promotional discrepancy within the organizations to gender but rather they blamed themselves due to their choices during the different stages of their careers. To shed further light on the promotional status of women in the sciences, Fox (2001) found that the academic rankings of women at the university level do not follow suit with the overwhelming increase of women receiving doctoral degrees in the sciences and nor do the promotional status of women adhere to the expected rank as compared to their male colleagues. In other words, sometimes, successful women in science do not achieve the same appropriate progress as successful men in science or engineering. However, in other cases, such as the five women we describe in this chapter, they were and are more successful than men.

Policies

In an effort to address the gender disparity at the organizational level, several anti-gender discrimination policies have been enacted. For example, it has been documented that more women are employed in the 'soft' sciences (i.e., biology, medicine) compared to more technical fields encompassing the 'hard' sciences (i.e., chemistry, engineering) (Bebbington, 2003; Toren, 2000; Wyer, 2003). Due to this difference in employment between men and women scientists, organizations are using non-technical jargon by focusing on the social and environmental benefits of the organization and/or position in the hope of drawing the interest of female students and scientists because these two aspects enhance women's progress in academic life (Barnard, Powell, Bagilhole, & Dainty, 2010). Several organizations have taken a different approach to gender equity by creating structured outlines referring to promotional and fellowship status. Fox (2001) outlined that such approaches include creating and enacting specific benchmarks to mark achievement status and that research funding should be organized and awarded according to a detailed structure rather than by administrators deciding funds according to their personal preference. In return, this process would allow for gender equity to occur without hesitations or opinions from either men or women that gender discrimination is present; rather, standings will be based solely on a pre-scripted structure. Although some improvements have been seen as a result of anti-discrimination policies, Bebbington (2003) found that the pace of change is slow due to the establishment of procedures to execute the new policies. Thus, organizations not only have to create gender equity policies but also they have to initiate procedures that will effectively implement the new policies in a timely and consistent fashion.

In an investigation into women employed at Israeli universities, Toren (2000) found that most of the women who participated in the study elected sciences as a career for the same reasons as their male colleagues; yet, despite the similar reasons for commencement in the sciences, current research emphasizes that there is a perceptual difference between the two genders in regards to their commitment level to the field. Ellemers et al. (2004) conducted research in both the Netherlands and Italy focusing on both female and male doctoral students and faculty members. They found that both male and female doctoral students equally assessed themselves in their commitment to career and time spent at work. In regards to how professors viewed students' level of commitment, there was a distinct difference in opinion. Male professors did not differ in assessing either their male or female doctoral students for their level of commitment but female professors rated female doctoral students as being less committed than their male doctoral students.

It should be noted though that the determination of female doctoral students being less committed to their career originated from the older generation (born between 1921 and 1949) of female professors, which confers with the analysis of Barnard et al. (2010). Ellemers et al. (2004) explained that this opinion was derived from their [the older female professors] struggle to commence their career in the sciences because, at that time, men dominated the workforce and women were unable to find their place in the field or the few women who did manage to gain a foothold in the sciences were out-casted by their colleagues. The second factor attributing to this result was that this generation of professors regarded themselves as possessing a masculine self-image. In return, this image assisted them with their success in the sciences; thus, it may be concluded that female faculty members are inclined to continue the gender stereotype that is prolonged in science-related disciplines.

The results from Ellemers et al.'s (2004) study supported the *Queen Bee syndrome* (Maume, 2011) that attempts to explain the unfavorable behavior of women in a position of power related to their female subordinates. Maume (2011) suggested that the disinclination of associating with other women is because "after demonstrating the same (or stronger) work ethic as their male counterparts in order to get promoted, successful female managers may not be sympathetic to conflicts between work and family life among their subordinates. In seeking to emulate the drive, ambition, and work habits of male superiors, female bosses distance themselves from ''women's issues" in the workplace" (p. 290). He further expressed the view that in order for women demonstrating these characteristics to succeed in their chosen field, they should form distinctive alliances with their male colleagues.

DISCUSSION

The vast majority of research on the progress of women in science and technology thus far has attempted to explain why women are underrepresented in the sciences; however, limited research has been conducted to investigate the gender disproportion within the specific disciplines (Bebbington, 2003; Wyer, 2003).

One perspective of current research practice is to look at the difference by citing the social and cultural aspects of women's roles in society. However, Barnard et al. (2010) suggest that it is imperative to look at the problems themselves rather than emphasizing women as being the cause of the problem. Finally, the opinion of current research findings implies that women in the sciences share a collective view in regards to why women are underrepresented (i.e., gender bias) in the sciences and thus, future research practices should include a broader scale reflecting the multiple views of women and let their voices be heard (Barnard et al., 2010; Toren, 2000).

Entering into a career in the sciences or engineering requires commitment sustained by long hours in and out of the laboratory. To this effect, women are perceived as being less committed than men because they are assessed as not putting in the same long hours as their male counterparts. Hence, their perceived commitment level to their career, profession and organization is lower than that of men (Barnard et al., 2010). Unlike in the humanities where professors may work part time or may continue their research after a hiatus, scientists must invest long and intensive hours in their laboratories which require full-time involvement (Toren, 2000); therefore, organizations take risks in hiring young women in the sciences and other mathematics-related fields due to maternity leave and family obligations. Additionally, Ceci, Williams, and Barnett (2009) found that during their pre-tenure years, young mothers were penalized for their decision to have children, which created a void in the workplace. Consequently, in order to prevail in the sciences, women have to succumb to the demands imposed on them by their career choice (Barnard et al., 2010).

Aside from the persistent nature required of the sciences, women must also apply the same exhaustive level of commitment and long hours to their home life. According to the essentialist approach, women are not able to effectively balance both the work and home spheres of life and as a result, one of these entities will suffer (Barnard et al., 2010). In other words, women who strive for success are unable to be successful at both work and home because they are viewed as being the primary caretakers of the family. With that being said, success is an ambiguous measurement that is subjective to the perception of the individual and how others view them. Researchers have found that women may have success at both home and work; however, this achievement is one of the most significant challenges with which female scientists are faced (e.g. Rosser & Lane, 2002). On one hand, the popular belief is that the underrepresentation of women in the sciences is owed to gender differences and responsibilities at home. On the other hand, researchers (Bebbington, 2003; Fox, 2006; Toren, 2000; Wyer, 2003) have found that gender is not the core reason for the disproportion of numbers of male and female scientists. However, this argument was not supported by studies that included the voices of the female participants. The underrepresentation also cannot be explained by the unequal proportion of publications written by women.

Overall, the help derived from supportive sources assists women with developing academic and social resiliency from the negativity they face with their career choice or from the obstacles and barriers they have to overcome while trying to gain acceptance and admittance into male-dominated scientific fields. Deeply rooted in the social network within the science field lies the *boys club* concept, which includes activities and conversations, associated with the interests of men.

Barnard et al. (2010) suggest that one way of combating the forces imposed by the gender differences is for women to be able to adapt and devise strategies of survival. By not finding ways to conform to their environment, women are faced with the risk of being isolated and having to accept lower ranked positions. A second way to combat the social implications engraved in the existing male-dominated social arena is for women to a) create social networking groups in order to assist them with becoming accepted into the science community, b) promote themselves and their research in more assertive ways, and c) craft an outlet for collaboration and informal mentorship.

This chapter discussed women in science and technology as part of the development of scientific and technological innovations from the beginning of the 20th century. The presentation of five prominent women scientists contributes to raising the awareness that women can perform and achieve at least as well as men in science and engineering in general and in chemistry in particular.

NOTES

[1]   Sabra is a term used to describe a Jewish person born in Israel; the term is also usually inclusive of Jews born before or during the period of the establishment of the state of Israel

REFERENCES

Adams, M. J., & Glusker, J. P. (1995). Dorothy Crowfoot Hodgkin, 1910–1994, *Physics Today*, May 1995.

Bandura, A. (1986). *Social foundations of thought and action: A social cognitive theory*. Englewood Cliffs, NJ: Prentice-Hall.

Bandura, A. (1997). *Self-efficacy: The exercise of control*. NY, NY: W.H. Freeman and Company.

Barnard, S., Powell, A., Bagilhole, B., & Dainty, A. (2010). Researching UK women professionals in SET: A critical review of current approaches. *International Journal of Gender, Science and Technology, 2*(3), 361–381.

Bebbington, D. (2003). Women in science, engineering and technology: A review of the issues. *Higher Education Quarterly, 56*(4), 360–375.

Brooks, J.D. (1996). Living longer and improving health: An obtainable goal in promoting aging well. *American Behavioral Scientist, 39*, 272–287.

Ceci, S. J., Williams, W. M., & Barnett, S.M. (2009). Women's underrepresentation in science: Sociocultural and biological considerations. *Psychological Bulletin, 135*(2), 218–261.

Curie, M. (1911). Nobel lecture: Radium and the new concepts in chemistry. Retrieved from http://nobelprize.org/nobel_prizes/chemistry/laureates/1911/marie-curie-lecture.html

Davis, K.S. (2001). "Peripheral and subversive": Women making connections and challenging the boundaries of the science community. *Science Education, 85*(4), 368–409.

Ellemers, N., van den Heuvel, H., de Glider, D., Maass, A., & Bonvini, A. (2004). The underrepresentation of women in science: Differential commitment or the queen bee syndrome? *British Journal of Social Psychology, 43*(3), 315–338.

Fox, M. F. (2001). Women, science and academia: Graduate education and careers. *Gender & Society, 15*(5), 654–666.

Fox, M. F. (2006). Women and academic science: Gender, status and careers. In C. H. Marzabadi, V. J. Kuck,, & S. A. Nolan (Eds.), *Are women achieving equity in chemistry?* (pp. 17–28). American Chemical Society.

Goldstein, S. (1995). The flight from reason in science. In P. R. Gross, N. L. Levitt, & M. W. Lewis (Eds.), *Quantum philosophy* (pp. 119–125). New York: Academy of Sciences.

Groliers Electronic Encyclopedia (1995). Version 8.0 CD-ROM by Grolier, Inc.

Gupta, R. (2011). Famous women scientists and inventors. Articles Wave. Retrieved from http://www.articleswave.com/articles/famous-women-scientists.html

Hodgkin, D. C. (1967). Nobel Lecture: The X-ray analysis of complicated molecules. Retrieved from http://nobelprize.org/nobel_prizes/chemistry/laureates/1964/hodgkin-lecture.pdf

Joliot-Curie, I. (1935). Nobel Lecture: Artificial production of radioactive elements. Retrieved from http://nobelprize.org/nobel_prizes/chemistry/laureates/1935/joliot-curie-lecture.html

Lent, R. W., Brown, S. D., & Hackett, G. (1994). Toward a unifying social cognitive theory of career and academic interest, choice and performance. *Journal of Vocational Behavior, 45*, 79–122.

Mamlok, R. (1996). *Science: An ever-developing entity*. Rehovot, Israel: The Weizmann Institute of Science.

Mamlok-Naaman, R., Ben-Zvi, R., Hofstein, A., Menis, J., & Erduran, S. (2005). Influencing students' attitudes towards science by exposing them to a historical approach. *International Journal of Science and Mathematics Education, 3*(3), 485–507.

Maume, D. J. (2011). Meet the new boss. . . same as the old boss? Female supervisors and subordinate career prospects. *Social Science Research, 40*, 287–298.

McKeown, T. (1976). *The modern rise of population*. London: Edward Arnold.

National Science Foundation, National Center for Science and Engineering Statistics. (2011). Women, minorities, and persons with disabilities in science and engineering. Retrieved from http://www.nsf.gov/statistics/wmpd/digest/theme2_1.cfm

Nobel Lectures (1966). Chemistry 1922–1941, Amsterdam: Elsevier Publishing Company. Retrieved from: http://nobelprize.org/nobel_prizes/chemistry/laureates/1935/joliot-curie-bio.html

Nolan, S. A., Buckner, J. P., Marzabadi, C. H., & Kuck, V. J. (2008). Training and mentoring of chemists: A study of gender disparity. *Sex Roles, 58*, 235–250.

Porter, R. (1994). *The biographical dictionary of scientists* (2nd ed.). Oxford, UK: Oxford University Press.

Rayner-Canham, M. F., & Rayner-Canham, G. W. (1997). The end of an era and a new generation. In: M. F. Rayner-Canham & G. W. Rayner-Canham (Eds.), *A devotion to their science: Pioneer women of radioactivity* (pp. 230–232). Montreal, Canada: McGill-Queen's University Press.

Read, J. (1995). *From alchemy to chemistry*. New York: Dover Publications, Inc.

Rosser, S. V. & Lane, E. O. (2002). Key barriers for academic institutions seeking to retain female scientists and engineers: Family-unfriendly policies, low numbers, stereotypes, and harassment. *Journal of Women and Minorities in Science and Engineering, 8*, 161–189.

Schiebinger, L. (1989). *The mind has no sex? Women in the origins of modern science*. Cambridge, MA: Harvard University Press.

Shalvi, A. (2009). Ruth Arnon. In: Jewish Women: A Comprehensive Historical Encyclopedia. Jewish Women's Archive. Retrieved from: http://jwa.org/encyclopedia/article/arnon-ruth

Sonnert, G., & Holton, G. (1995). *Gender differences in science careers*. New Brunswick, NJ: Rutgers University Press.

Summers, L. H. (2005, January). Remarks at NBER conference on diversifying the science & engineering workforce. Cambridge, MA. Retrieved from http://shaffner.wikispaces.com/ file/view/ Lawrence+Summers.pdf

Toren, N. (2000). *Hurdles in the halls of science: The Israeli case*. Lanham, MD: Lexington Books.

Vijayan, M. (1995). An obituary of Dorothy Crowfoot Hodgkin, 2 May 1995. Crystallography World Wide Editor, International Union of Crystallography.

Wolff, P. (1967). *Breakthroughs in chemistry, the New York American library*. New York and Toronto. World Book Encyclopedia (1993). World Book, Inc. Volume H.

Wyer, M. (2003). Intending to stay: Images of scientists, attitudes toward women and gender as influences on persistence among science and engineering majors. *Journal of Women and Minorities in Science and Engineering, 9*, 1–16.

Yonath, A. (2009). Nobel Lecture: Hibernating bears, antibiotics and the evolving ribosome. Retrieved from http://nobelprize.org/nobel_prizes/chemistry/laureates/2009/yonath_lecture.pdf

Zeldin, A. L., Britner, S. L., & Pajares, F. (2008). A comparative study of the self-efficacy beliefs of successful men and women in mathematics, science and technology careers. *Journal of Research in Science Teaching, 45*(9), 1036–1058.

Zeldin, A. L., & Pajares, F. (2000). Against the odds: Self-efficacy beliefs of women in mathematical, scientific, and technological careers. *American Educational Research Journal, 37*, 215–246.

Rachel Mamlok-Naaman and Ron Blonder
Weizmann Institute of Science
Rehovot, Israel
Rachel.Mamlok@weizmann.ac.il
Ron.Blonder@weizmann.ac.il

Yehudit Judy Dori
Technion, Israel Institute of Technology
Haifa, Israel and
Massachusetts Institute of Technology
Cambridge, MA
USA
yjdori@technion.ac.il

JOHN K. GILBERT

7. WOMEN CHEMISTS INFORMING PUBLIC EDUCATION ABOUT CHEMISTRY DURING THE 20TH CENTURY

INTRODUCTION

The concerns and ideas of chemistry have a major impact, whether recognized or not, on the personal, social, economic and cultural lives of all individuals. This chapter is an attempt to sketch the role of women chemists in the evolution of public education about chemistry over the course of the twentieth century. Composing such an account is difficult for a number of reasons.

First, chemical education is a subset of science education and cannot be easily distinguished from general trends. So we have to look at the slow change in public science education in general and tease out – often with a high level of inference – what this meant for chemical education.

Second, it is unclear for whom such an education is intended at any one time and what use might be made of it. The field of chemical education has been badly under-researched, in contrast to that of chemistry per se, and the best documentation relates to school- and university-level academic activity. Very little work has been done on the chemical education of the rest of the population – 'the public'. What has been written is spread over many years and published in low-visibility outlets that are now often not easily accessible.

Third, the purposes being addressed in such an education have gradually evolved over the years. At the beginning of the 20th century, the most widely accepted aim was to support a positive appreciation of the social and economic value of chemistry. This remains an implicit aim held strongly by many professional chemists (Lewenstein, 1992), an ambition justified by evidence that the balance between public perceptions of the positive aspects and negative aspects of chemistry tipped steeply towards the latter at the end of the century. By the 1970s there was a concern in scientific circles about the level of the 'public understanding of science', the general knowledge of basic scientific ideas. As surveys showed a persistently low level of such understanding, it was argued that adults might only learn the ideas of science if they had a special purpose for doing so and could actually use that knowledge. Interest then broadened from the basic concepts of science to include the processes by which those ideas were established and their social implications and applications, that is to the idea of 'scientific literacy'. The current emphasis on the 'public engagement of science' – of which

M.-H. Chiu, P. J. Gilmer, and D. F. Treagust (Eds.), Celebrating the 100th Anniversary of Madame Marie Sklodowska Curie's Nobel Prize in Chemistry. 141–166.

'public engagement of chemistry' is a subset - has expanded still further, seeing two-way communication between scientists and the public on what, how, and why scientific research is done and why it is important. To avoid becoming unduly entangled in these epistemological issues, the anodyne phrase 'chemistry and the public', which covers all these concerns, will be used in this chapter.

Fourth and lastly, these changes took place in many, if not most, countries, so no treatment can be comprehensive. What follows is derived from English-language sources and is inevitably brief. In this chapter, I will attempt to address:

– The importance of women chemists in public education about chemistry
– How changes in the factors that affected 'chemistry and the public' during the course of the 20th century impacted on the contribution made by women chemists
– The nature of the contributions made by prominent women chemists, mainly Marie Curie, Irène Joliot-Curie, and Dorothy Crowfoot Hodgkin, to 'chemistry and the public.'

EQUITY OF PROVISION IN PUBLIC EDUCATION ABOUT CHEMISTRY

Equity demands that access to careers in chemistry is gender-neutral. However, although there is today some evidence that this is coming about, girls are still underrepresented in school chemistry classes. Steinke (1997, p. 409) has summarized the research into the factors that lead to this. The barriers are created by evidence of:

– The preferential treatment of boys in classrooms
– The use of curriculum, teaching approaches, and assignments, that favor male intellectual styles
– Unequal experience of practical activities and, most significantly for this essay,
– The lack of role models of women in chemistry.

Increased numbers of female school chemistry teachers and change in pedagogic procedures can address the first three factors. However, this is the theme of a separate literature and cannot be addressed here. Women chemists can however have an impact on public education about chemistry in one of two ways.

The first impact is by presenting a role model of 'women as chemists'. Whilst it is unclear whether being taught by a women science teacher at school has any significant impact on whether girls decide to study science to a higher level (Carrington, Tymmes, & Merrell, 2008), is does seem that positive career choices in favor of science are made by college-age women under the influence of female role models (Lockwood, 2006). Where women chemists do interact with girls and women, both directly, e.g., in public lectures, or indirectly, e.g., through television programs and Internet websites, the content and process of their actions have great significance if an honest and clear role model is to be presented to an audience. Thus Steinke (1997, p. 413) identified the three themes that must be addressed, either directly or indirectly, if such a positive role model is to be presented, namely:

- The establishment of a women chemist's expertise, both by their provision of clear explanations and practical illustrations, backed up by supportive statements from colleagues, especially by males;
- An address to the issues of balancing family life and professional life in terms of time use and commitment.
- Issues surrounding working in a male-dominated field, to which might be added a fourth,
- Representation of a coherent set of humanistic beliefs

The second way that women can have an impact on public education of chemistry is by directly engaging in the dissemination of chemical ideas. The manner and extent on such engagement is influenced by a number of factors.

FACTORS AFFECTING THE CONTRIBUTIONS WOMEN COULD MAKE

A reading of the general literature on 'science and the public' (Gregory, 1998) suggests that the following factors influenced changes in 'chemistry and the public' over the period 1900-2000: the development and impact of feminism; the changing involvement of professional chemistry institutions; changing expectations for what might be included in 'chemistry and the public'; an increase in the number of 'stakeholders' with an interest in 'chemistry and the public'; the presentation of chemistry in the media; increased concern over the environment. Taking each of these in turn in the context of women chemists:

Feminism and Women in Chemistry

Feminism seeks equal political, economic, and cultural rights for women and girls with those of men and boys. The issues that have been and are being addressed are broad in scope: voting in public elections, property ownership, contractual engagement, bodily integrity, employment and workplace rights, and, most importantly for this chapter, educational opportunity. The issue of 'the number of women with an education in chemistry' – indeed 'women educated in science' generally – was probably not widely addressed before 1900. For example, as Baker (1998) writes:

> Educational opportunities for women to study science, until recently, were limited. In most European countries before the 1920s, women were barred from the academic high schools which provided the mathematics, Latin and Greek needed to enter the few universities that accepted women. Poland---- barred women from universities until 1910. The more progressive French allowed women to audit classes at the University of Paris beginning in 1908 and later to attend as full-time students.

This partially explains why distinguished women chemists were so few in number in 1900 and why their number only gradually increased thereafter. But increase it did.

JOHN K. GILBERT

The Place of Women in Professional Chemistry Institutions

The professional associations for chemists in English-speaking countries were established, to varying degrees, by the turn of the century. The American Chemical Society [ACS], founded in 1876, was firmly established by 1900. As its charter makes no mention of the sex of members, it must be assumed that suitably qualified women have always been able to apply for membership. Their progress within the Society seems to have been slow, for example Anna J. Harrison was the first woman president in 1976, i.e., 100 years after its foundation. As one might expect, the Society has always taken a positive view of chemical education for its Mission Statement contains the phrase:

> We... play a leadership role in educating and communicating with public policy makers and the general public about the importance of chemistry in our lives. This includes identifying new solutions, improving public health, protecting the environment and contributing to the economy (ACS, *About ACS*, 2011a, p. 1)

The institutional development of chemistry within the UK was more fragmented. The Chemical Society, founded in 1841, was concerned with chemistry in general per se. The Society of Public Analysts (later The Society for Analytical Chemistry) was formed in 1874 and was concerned with the purity of chemical substances. The Royal Institute of Chemistry founded in 1877 and given a Royal Charter in 1885, was concerned with the establishment and validation of suitable qualifications for professional chemists. In 1980 these four institutions, together with the Faraday Society (founded in 1903), amalgamated to become The Royal Society of Chemistry [RSC]. Its aims are that: '[chemistry] encompasses formal and informal education from the cradle to the grave'. The word 'cradle' here may mean something that you should rock: no woman has ever served as President of any of the five organizations.

It is substantially through these and similar chemical societies that engagement by senior women chemists with pupils and students has historically taken place and will continue to take place. Whilst the pattern of events in history is difficult to perceive, this self-imposed duty of public education was given increased prominence as the 20th century progressed. For example, the International Union of Pure and Applied Chemistry (IUPAC) has established a 'Committee on Chemical Education' which is charged with promoting the 'public understanding of chemistry', in particular with respect to the United Nations-mandated 'International Year of Chemistry 2011'. Both the UK and USA societies now run annual 'National Chemistry Weeks' in which area committees are encouraged a run suitable activities focused on school students (ACS, 2011b.; RSC, 2009). One can only hope that these initiatives continue after their allotted time-span and assume that women play a significant role in them.

Four types of event are provided within these initiatives. First, residential activities for high school students during vacations, e.g., The 'Salters' Chemistry Camps' in the UK (Salters' Institute, 2009). Second, presentations at 'Cafés

Scientifique', informal meetings in a café or restaurant for adults or students at which chemical ideas are discussed (Café Scientifique, 2009). These have been shown to be very successful when carefully related to local cultural social and economic issues (Francis, 2009). Third, and probably the most common and influential form, are 'outreach activities'. Here university staff visits schools in order to run specialist activities e.g., in Australia (Commonwealth Scientific and Industrial Research Organisation [CSIRO], 2009). Fourth is the involvement of school-age students and non-professional adults in chemical research (Center for the Advancement of Informal Science Education [CAISE], 2011). It is reasonable to assume that, as the range and number of these types of activity has progressively expanded, so has the engagement of women chemists in their provision.

Public lectures are still given, albeit mainly in university towns. In the UK, the Royal Institution mounts its 'Christmas Lectures' for (generally older) school children, which are also televised. Although this has taken place since 1825, only four of the lecturers have been by women, the first in 2004 (Royal Institution of Great Britain, 2010). These lectures have not recently been specifically about chemical topics.

Institutional Women Stakeholders in 'Chemistry and the Public'

In about 1900, the main stakeholders in chemical education were the predominately male professional chemists acting through their trade organizations and who were concerned to project a positive image of the subject and its technological applications (Martin, 1911). The rapid expansion of, firstly, organic chemistry and, secondly, pharmaceutical chemistry as the twentieth century progressed seems to have been associated with a steady increase in the number of women chemists.

In common with all the sciences, popular chemistry was prominent in newspapers and magazines in the early 20th century. The period between the two World Wars saw the steady rise of the 'science mediator', somebody who identified things that scientists were doing and presented them to the public through the media in an accessible form. The best of these mediators both understood science thoroughly and commanded the skills of expression, whether in print, in radio, or, later, in television. It does seem that too few of them seem to have been or are women.

Given that scientific research has become very expensive, governments in democracies were anxious to be sure that public money – of increasing importance to science – was spent to best effect. It seems likely that the number of women chemists in such posts has paralleled the steady rise of 'scientific civil servants' in most countries.

The increased influence of women as stakeholders is thus patchy but can be seen.

Changing Perceptions of 'the Public' by Chemists

It seems very likely that, at about 1900, 'the public' was viewed by most academic chemists as being an undifferentiated whole, with only people showing an initial interest and some knowledge, being thought worthy of attention. This perspective has only gradually changed, with the influential USA 'Science Indicators' as late as 1981 assuming that a population could be analyzed in terms of their alertness to scientific ideas generally into 'attentive', 'potential attentive' and 'non-attentive' (Pion & Lipsey, 1981). This tripartite perception is probably still in evidence but weakening as the 'chemical literacy' movement has slowly gained ground.

Changing Expectations for 'Chemistry and the Public'

It is hard to pin down when the broad area of 'science and the public' – including that of chemistry – first became a matter of concern to the professional agencies of science. A landmark was the publication of the Bodmer Report (Bodmer, 1985). The focus was provided by emergent evidence that too high a proportion of the general public were alienated from and ignorant of science in general. The Report thought it very desirable that there was a general 'civic scientific literacy', which was defined with the use of this quotation:

> a vocabulary of basic scientific constructs sufficient to read competing views in a newspaper or magazine... understanding of the process or nature of scientific enquiry... and some level of understanding of the impact of science and technology on individuals and society. (Miller, 1998, p. 205)

This definition and the evidence surrounding its attainment produced by testing in the UK, USA, and elsewhere, led to the adoption of 'the deficit model' of public scientific literacy (Sturgis & Allum, 2004). There has been widespread criticism not only of the 'deficit model' itself but also of the methods used to assess public knowledge and attitudes. For this reason, the nature and degree of this 'deficiency' will not be discussed here. The idea that public should necessarily come to value what the institutions of science thinks are desirable also remains contentious.

In recent years, it has been realized that the public will learn and use scientific ideas if there is a personal reason to do so. The advent of the Internet has made this increasing possible. It has also been realized that a major issue was the quality and level of trust of the public in the work of science and scientists. These factors have led to the emergence of the idea of 'public engagement with science' which seeks to:

- further the public's understanding of, and participation in, the debate of issues of the day;
- facilitate accountability and transparency of researchers, their funders and their employers;
- allow individuals to understand how the results of research affect their lives and, in some cases, assist in making informed decisions in the light of the results; and
- bring to light information affecting public well-being and safety (Bateson, 2006, p. 4).

It remains to been seen how energetically this model will be pursued by the scientific community, carrying as it does implications of loss of complete control over research priorities and possible loss of control of intellectual property rights.

Media in Which Chemistry is Presented

The range of media through which senior women chemists, like other scientists, might present their ideas to diverse audiences has expanded greatly since 1900. In 1900, only lectures, accounts of these in newspapers, and exhibits in museums, were readily available.

The growth of the number of 'science centers' has taken place since the 1970s. Either free-standing or part of a conventional museum, the characteristic of the science centre is that visitors are presented with options of things that they might do in an exhibit and can receive an immediate feedback on the consequences of their action on it. Most 'science centers' have chemistry-related exhibits but very few seem to specialize in them, e.g., Catalyst Science Discovery Centre (2011) in England. The exhibits in Catalyst are of two types, i.e., those that show either the behavior of specific types of chemicals e.g., the nature of plastics (Collard & McKee, 1998), or the behavior of chemical technologies, e.g., the action of sunscreen. As such exhibits have to be robust (student-proof!), easy and cheap to maintain, and capable of giving a response to the visitor in a short time, they are not often developed in respect of advanced or complex chemical ideas.

Newspapers often carry stories about achievements and/or ambitions in chemistry as well as accounts of the personal, social, and economic impacts of chemical technologies. The range and depth of such stories reflects a newspaper's perception of the interests of its readers. There are relatively few magazines of wide circulation, which include a chemistry or chemical technology focus, all of which address a 'science interested' public, e.g., 'New Scientist', 'Scientific American', or 'Forum'. In addition, some more parochial magazines focused exclusively on chemistry do exist (e.g., newsletter from the Chemical Heritage Foundation, 2011). The coverage of science topics by newspapers boomed after World War II but has declined steadily since (Gregory, 1998). Indeed, the heyday of the newspaper seems to be passing, with the number of newspapers declining, and with newsprint being augmented or displaced by web-versions of publications and by entirely web-based news services. A major casualty of these processes is the inclusion of informed news and comment about science and technology under the aegis of a specialist science correspondent (Kennedy, 2010). However, women scientists would nowadays certainly be interviewed or invited to submit articles by all print-media outlets when they have made a 'newsworthy' discovery/invention.

A. Afonso (personal communication, 2010) analysis of publishers' catalogues has shown that there are many books published in English or Portuguese which have a 'chemistry flavor' and which are intended to have a popular appeal. Of the 131 publications so identified as being 'in print,' 25 had at least one author who was female, whilst 105 were entirely male-authored. They fall into the following categories:

- The foundations of chemistry. These are collections of definitions, examples, and explanations;
- Biography of particular chemical compounds. Their discovery or invention, their social reception;

- History of chemistry. These deal with the contribution of a particular individual chemist in history, the evolution of a chemical idea over time, or the chemical technology of a substance;
- Chemistry used in/linked with other sciences. These deal with themes and topics in science in which chemical ideas contribute to a multi-disciplinary explanation;
- Chemistry in everyday life. These deal with the chemistry behind a particular phenomenon or situation that would be familiar to the general public;
- Hands-on chemistry. Chemistry cookbooks and home activities.
- Chemistry in science fiction. These are 'science fiction' books in which a chemistry – real or imagined – plays a major part. Those based on 'forensic science' are particularly popular at the moment;
- Chemistry in comics. Of particular interest to young people and to those with limited reading skills are those comics that have a chemistry component to the story.

As the numbers quoted above show, women authors are under-represented.

Although the field of 'chemistry in fictional film' has not been much studied, the enquiries that have been reported emphasize the negative portrayal of chemists and chemistry (Weingart, 2006). There are some TV programs that have a 'science education' slant, in which chemistry is a frequent sub-theme, for example 'Brainiac: Science Abuse' in the UK at one end of the popularity spectrum and 'Horizon' at the other. In some cases, activities are made available through the Internet that tie-in with TV programs e.g., 'BLAST!' (British Broadcasting Corporation [BBC], 2011). The UK Open University is a source of many science programs, some of which are focused on chemical themes. With the advent of TV, radio has become undervalued as a medium of education, but, in the UK, BC Radio 4 provides a regular output of chemistry-related programs (British Council [BC], 2009). Again, whilst women act as reporters in such programs, relatively few of them seem take a leading or directing ('anchorperson') role.

There seems little doubt that many young people are accessing science sites on the Internet, particularly to support homework and project assignments, although there seems to be no real evidence as to how widespread this is, as to how students evaluate what they find, or what effect it has on their learning (Bell, Lewenstein, Shouse, & Feder, 2009, pp. 260–270). Many science centers are using their experience to make educational materials available on the Internet. Blogs and podcasts with science themes appear in ever-increasing numbers. The nature and extent of the use of the Internet in respect of chemical ideas and chemical technologies by the general adult public seems to be completely unknown as does the engagement of women with them.

The Manifestation of Environmental Concerns

Concerns about the degradation of the macro environment had been expressed in the 1920s; for example, Gregory (1998) cited observations on this theme by Svante Arrhenius. It was only after the publication of the book 'Silent Spring' (Carson, 1964), which drew attention to the effects of the indiscriminate use of pesticides, and of the report 'Limits to Growth' (Meadows, 1974), that public attention began to focus on environmental issues. Even then, the manifestation of that concern was slow to reach the educational system and public lectures. Thus at the end of the century, Hart (1999) reviewed studies that showed low levels of student knowledge of the subject, commented on the need to link cognitive and affective outcomes in student learning, and noted the value of community-based education of the non-formal variety. It was at about that time that the phrase 'sustainability education' began to be used in public discourse. This implied that such education had to be concerned with the future rather than the past, leading to an advocacy of 'futures education' (Lloyd & Wallace, 2004).

Increased concern about the degradation at the micro, or personal level, environment has become increasingly manifest in the promotion of 'health education', 'health' being defined as 'an absence of illness of disease' (Harrison, 2005). To a large extent this concern has been the realization that the costs of 'illness/disease avoidance' are much less than those of 'illness/disease cure'.

Chemicals play a large part in the identification and treatment of both macro and micro level environmental degradations, being the causal (and hence remedial) agents in both. It is therefore to be expected that increased public attention will have been paid to both as the twenty-first century progresses.

ENTER THE DISTINGUISHED WOMEN CHEMISTS

The major conclusion that I draw from the above analysis is that women chemists have gradually increased in number and become increasingly influential in education about 'chemistry and the public' as the 20th century progressed.

Because of their iconic status, women Nobel Laureates in chemistry are particularly important. Four such awards have been made:

– 1911 (Chemistry): Marie Curie
– 'In recognition of her services to the advancement of chemistry by the discovery of the elements radium and polonium, by the isolation of radium and the study of the nature and compounds of this remarkable element'
– 1935 (Chemistry): Frédéric Joliot and Irène Joliot-Curie
– 'In recognition for their synthesis of new radioactive elements'
– 1964 (Chemistry): Dorothy Crowfoot Hodgkin
– 'For her determinations by X-ray techniques of the structures of important biochemical substances'
– 2009 (Chemistry): Venkatraman Ramakrishnan, Thomas A. Steitz, and Ada E. Yonath
– 'For studies of the structure and function of the ribosome'

The influence of the three who are dead (Marie Curie, Irène Joliot-Curie, Dorothy Crowfoot Hodgkin) can best presented in the form of historical case studies (Klopfer, 1969). Some elements that might be included in these are given in the sections that follow. I have omitted discussion of Ada Yonath (personal communication, 2010), who is very much alive, because she feels that too short a time has passed since she received her award for its impact on public education to become apparent.

NOBEL LAUREATE IN CHEMISTRY: MARIE CURIE

Many books have been written about Marie Curie, in which Pierre Curie plays an important role. This chapter draws on two of them. The first of these was a biography by her daughter Eve Curie (1937), which contains much detail of her family life. The second of these is Goldsmith (2005), which seeks to link her emotional and professional lives. Other authors mentioned in this chapter deal with the science per se of her work. This chapter focuses entirely on the impact that she has had and might have had on public knowledge and awareness of chemistry, with especial reference to women.

It is not surprising that she has received so much attention over the years. As has been pointed out:

> She was the first woman to receive a doctorate in France and the first woman anywhere to earn that doctorate in physics. She was the first female professor at that great Parisian university, the Sorbonne. She was the first woman to win a Nobel Prize, for chemistry ---in 1903---. Eight years later, she became the first scientist, male or female, to be awarded a second Nobel Prize-----.'
> (Angier, 2001, p. xiii)

In one respect, Angier was wrong: the 1903 award was for Physics.

She was born in Poland in 1867 at a time when that country was a colony of Russia. Her mother died in 1878, and her father, a schoolteacher, in conditions of considerable poverty, brought her up with her three siblings. At that time, formal education had to be conducted in Russian, in which she was fluent, but she was sent initially to a private school where the Polish language and culture were maintained. After finishing the later course at the academic Gymnasium (with excellent marks and prizes) and being denied, as a woman, access to Warsaw University, she joined a clandestine 'flying (or floating) university' (Goldsmith, 2005, p. 35) of over a thousand women who continued their education illegally. It became clear that, in order to pursue her studies, she would have to move to France, where such things were (somewhat) easier.

One thing that stands out in the biography of Marie Curie (Curie, 1937; Goldsmith, 2005) is the strong support that she received from her family. Her father had encouraged her to learn when young. She gave a large proportion of her first working wage as a governess (at age 16 years) to her sister Bronya who was studying medicine in Paris. This was more than repaid when Marie herself moved to Paris to study in 1891. In 1895 she married Pierre Curie, already a distinguished physicist who also became her closest research collaborator. Indeed, her father-in-law also provided her with great support by managing her home and two children after Pierre was killed in a traffic accident.

The potential portrayal of Marie Curie as a role model could draw on the following analysis:

Establishment of Expertise

Of all the women Nobel Laureates in Chemistry, it is the expertise of Marie Curie that is known in greatest detail, because of the numerous books that have been written about her.

Her professional expertise was manifest in four ways. The first was in her teaching. An initial apprenticeship was in the education of her siblings, as a governess, and of her own children (Curie, 1937). She had significant school teaching experience at Sèvres Higher Normal School for Girls, which she began in 1899 and where she continued to work after her first Nobel Prize (Curie, 1937). The room in which her doctoral examination was conducted was over-crowded, an indication of the standing in which her work was held (Curie, 1937). The second was her publication of books that were widely read at the time, e.g., 'The Work of Pierre Curie' (Curie, 1937) and 'Radiology in War' (Curie, 1937). The third – a really major manifestation – was her organizing, equipping, and operating, mobile X-ray units during World War I. As her daughter Eve records:

> Aside from the 20 motorcars that she equipped, Marie installed two hundred radiological rooms. The total number of wounded men examined in these 220 posts----went above a million (Curie, 1937).

In addition to the men so treated, the attendant nurses and radiography operators, who she also trained, would have readily perceived her example.

The fourth was occasioned by the welcome she received in the USA during a fund-raising tour in 1921. It was ecstatic, not least among women;

> White-robed girls in line along the sunny roads; girls running by the thousand across grassy slopes to meet Mme Curie's carriage; girls waving flags, girls on parade, cheering, singing chorus... (They were) her equals (Curie, 1937, p. 329).

Drawing a Balance Between the Commitments of Home and Work

This became an issue after her marriage. After the birth of her first child, Irène, her health deteriorated but she refused to take an extended rest, for

> She had other things to worry about. She had the laboratory, her husband, her home and her daughter... Marie, panic-stricken, would suddenly fly from the School of Physics towards the Parc Montsouris; had the nurse lost the child? No; she could see afar off... the woman and the little carriage. (Curie, 1937, pp. 150–151)

This tension between home and work was clearly an issue for Marie Curie, for, as Eve Curie (1937) rather histrionically puts it:

> While a young wife [in 1897] kept house, washed her baby daughter and put pans on the fire, in a wretched laboratory at the School of Physics a woman

physicist was making the most important discovery of modern science. (p. 152)

The recruitment of the nurse, a severe blow to the family budget, did help the situation. It seems likely that the major contribution to her peace of mind was made by her father-in-law who, as has already been mentioned, moved into the Curie household on the death of his wife and acted as an 'anchor' in the life of Irène and later Eve.

This dedication to her work –accurately called 'obsessive genius' by Goldsmith (2005) – had a direct impact on relations with her own children. Goldsmith (2005, p. 145) repeats a comment by Eve Curie about her mother:

> I called the book Madame Curie by Eve Curie. I didn't think it was right to call it Marie Curie by Eve Curie: that would have been too intimate.

This comment seems to indicate a degree of coolness, of distance, in relations between Marie and Eve.

Issues Arising from Working in a Male-dominated Environment

There is no doubt that Marie Curie encountered a great deal of male chauvinism in her professional life. This was often present in press coverage, of which a typical example was:

> a charming mother whose exquisite sensibility is accompanied by a spirit curious about the unfathomable. (Curie, 1937, p. 214)

Far worse was the evidence of a conspiracy to deny her a place in scientific history when the letter of nomination to the Nobel Committee failed to mention her and gave prime attribution of the work in question to Becquerel. The fact that she and Pierre did not travel to receive the prize in person gave space for speeches to be biased towards Becquerel (Goldsmith, 2005). This injustice – which seems to have been nearly successful – was compounded by the failure to elect her, even after the award of the Nobel Prize, to the Academie des Sciences (Curie, 1937).

Examples of this chauvinism abound throughout the two books used as sources for this chapter. Marie Curie's approach seems to have been to ignore them and to carry on regardless, despite the real hardship that they often led to. Things may have got somewhat better – or at least not so blatant – during the 20th century, but the contentious cases of Jocelyn Bell Burnell (quasars) and Rosalind Franklin (DNA) do come to mind.

Demonstrating Coherent Personal Beliefs

Marie Curie was a strong Polish nationalist throughout her life and seems to have passively, if not actively, defied the Russian occupying power, not least through her involvement in the clandestine 'floating university.' She was a socialist, for

All her life she had been obsessed by a certain thought: that of the intellectual gifts ignored and wasted in the classes unfavored by fortune. (Curie, 1937, p. 340)

and, later in life, used her fame and fortune to provide scientific scholarships. She saw science as an activity that should not be limited by national boundaries and served on the League of Nations 'International Committee on Intellectual Cooperation' which pursued this ideal (Curie, 1937).

NOBEL LAUREATE IN CHEMISTRY: IRÈNE JOLIOT-CURIE

Irène Joliot-Curie (1897–1956) was initially educated privately at the behest of her mother (Marie Curie) within a group of the children of distinguished academics before entering the Collège Sévigné (1912–14) and then with the Faculty of Science at the Sorbonne. Very little of any substance has been written in English about her, with the valuable eassay by McGrayne (2006) drawing heavily on interviews with her children. Gilmer (2011) in this edited book included various sources on Irène, including McGrayne (1998). It does appear that, in contrast to those of her sister Eve, her relations with her mother were close and cordial. McGrayne (2006) remarks that their letters were

---organized and to the point... Yet they were also tender, affectionate, and respectful of one another. (p. 123)

The picture that can be drawn of her is far less detailed than that for her mother, but the same four elements that contribute to her value as a role model can be detected.

Establishment of Expertise

Irène, in effect, served an apprenticeship as a scientist with her mother, for, after her father's death:

Working with her mother, Irène became more than just a daughter, friend, and collaborator. She functioned as a substitute husband, protecting and caring for a wife. (McGrayne, 2006, p. 126)

Like her mother, she developed a severe professional manner:

In public, she was aloof and brusque... She simply ignored what did not interest or please her. She had eyes only for what was important. (McGrayne, 2006, p. 125)

This professionalism was very quickly necessary, for, with the outbreak of World War I, at 18 years of age, she set up, managed, and employed, mobile X-ray units at the Front (McGrayne, 2006).

Taking an overview of her professional life, it does seem that she was pre-eminently a practical scientist, at pains to get accurate and reproducible results.

However, she was not always able to interpret the significance of her results. McGrayne (2006) notes that she narrowly missed interpretations of data on at least four occasions that led to others being awarded Nobel Prizes.

Drawing a Balance Between the Commitments of Home and Work

Like every professional woman before and since, she had to balance the demands of home and work, for:

> She was a feminist who defined her role as a woman in terms of both work and children. At home, she remained a traditional wife and mother. After Hélène's birth in 1927... she returned to work almost immediately and gave birth to Pierre in 1932. (McGrayne, 2006, p. 131)

Like her mother, she drew great strength from her close professional relation with her husband Frédéric Joliet-Curie:

> They made a good team. Although Fred was considered a physicist, his doctoral thesis was pure chemistry; Irène was considered a chemist, but her thesis was pure physics. Fred thought fast... Irène thought slowly... The combination of approaches made for successes. (McGrayne, 2006, pp. 131–132)

Issues Arising from Working in a Male-dominated Environment

Like Marie, Irène encountered chauvinism, both female and male, throughout her career. For example, immediately after the presentation of her doctoral thesis, a female reporter asked her if a scientific career might not be too taxing for a woman. She replied:

> Not at all. I believe that men's and women's scientific aptitudes are exactly the same... A woman of science should renounce worldly obligations [but] these are possible on condition that they are accepted as additional burdens... For my part, I consider science to be the paramount interest of my life. (McGrayne, 2006, p. 128)

Even the award of the Nobel was popularly attributed mainly to Fred (McGrayne, 2006), whilst, like her mother, Irène was persistently refused admission to the Academy of Sciences (McGrayne, 2006).

Demonstrating Coherent Personal Beliefs

She was Undersecretary of State for Scientific Research in 1936 in the French government, helping to establish the Centre National de la Recherche Scientifique, both of which will have supported chemistry research and, by implication, the role of women in it. After World War II, she was very active in promoting women's education through her membership of the committee of the Comité National de l'Union des Femmes Françoise and the World Peace Council (Irène Joliot-Curie, 2011). She did support left-wing political causes and professionally suffered discrimination because of this towards the end of her life.

NOBEL LAUREATE IN CHEMISTRY: DOROTHY CROWFOOT HODGKIN

Considerably more detail is available about the life of Dorothy Hodgkin, notable, provided by the essay of Dodson (2002) and the very detailed biography by Ferry (1998).

Like the two Curies, Dorothy Crowfoot Hodgkin (1910–1994) also received strong educational support from her parents. Like Joliot-Curie, Hodgkin's mother organized Dorothy's initial education at home, but she later attended a Parents' National Educational Union class. The location of her family oscillated somewhat, for her father worked in Sudan where science educational opportunities were created for her:

> Dr. A. F. Joseph---a close friend of her father---helped Dorothy to perform her first experiments in chemistry, trying to identify the minerals in the garden sand. ---On a later occasion Dr. Joseph gave her a professional surveyor's kit for identifying minerals, which she used for 'many happy hours. (Dodson, 2002, p. 182)

At 11 years she entered Sir John Leman School, where she received strong support from her chemistry teacher. This was reinforced by her mother, who not only bought materials from the local chemist for Dorothy to do analytical experiments at home but also took her to hear the Royal Institution Christmas Lectures by Sir William Bragg, which sparked her interest in crystallography (Dodson, 2002, p. 183). She later went to University of Oxford to study chemistry and stayed there for most of the rest of her working life, evidently receiving sustained support from her husband, Thomas Hodgkin, a Lecturer with the Workers' Educational Association.

Establishment of Expertise

Her professional expertise was manifest in the management of her research group at Oxford. There was a strong atmosphere of what might be termed 'disciplined collegiality'. For example, a visit by an official of a funding agency describes

> a happy, well-managed and effective research group 'under good strong scientific discipline by their gentle lady boss' and 'a lovely small show' (Dodson, 2002, p. 189).

This was achieved because

> Dorothy was generally very easy to work with, unhesitatingly generous and open to discussion---. Successful work was greeted with delight, while failures or mistakes she tried to treat constructively... but when Dorothy

detected some lack of interest or laziness she could be quietly severe (Dodson, 2002, p. 191)

This mentoring of professional behavior would surely have spread as her students went their separate ways.

Drawing a Balance Between the Commitments of Home and Work

Like the Curies, any sense of tension between home and work did not enter Dorothy Hodgkin's life until her marriage. The manner of the marriage itself was a source of great conflict between the socialist ideals of the engaged couple and their conservative, Christian, parents. The fact that she married also caused stress to the relationship with her mentor, J. D. Bernal, but this was quickly resolved (Ferry, 1998). Very unconventionally for the time, she and her husband lived apart for several years (Ferry, 1998). When the Hodgkin family finally coalesced in one place – Oxford - Dorothy, like many other 'blue-stocking' women, found motherhood initially very stressful (Ferry, 1998). However, like the Curies, she was able to carry on with her work through the acquisition of valued domestic servants, albeit paid for – like the Curies - out of a very limited salary (Ferry, 1998).

Issues Arising from Working in a Male-dominated Environment

Reading the Ferry (1998) biography, I am left with the feeling that Hodgkin faced far less gender-based discrimination that did the Curies. Perhaps this was because she worked in England. But a more likely explanation is that she did her work towards the end and after World War II. Social mores had changed over that period. She certainly did face discrimination (Ferry, 1998): she was initially refused membership of the chemistry-research focused Alembic Club at Oxford, but was later admitted; there were allegations of sexism associated with the initial failure of University of Oxford to give her a senior appointment; her election to a Fellowship of the Royal Society was delayed. On the other hand, she was the first member of Somerville College to get paid maternity leave (Ferry, 1998). If she did meet problems, they were fairly readily overcome, for she had considerable support from established male scientists.

Demonstrating Coherent Personal Beliefs

Dorothy Hodgkin was a strong supporter of socialism, a credo which she shared with her husband and which perhaps formed the basis of their evidently successful marriage. Her commitments stem from those beliefs.

She was very concerned about what she saw as the misuse of science in the construction of ever-more powerful weapons. Thus:

After the (1939–45) war she became a prominent figure in the debates on nuclear weapons--- Her own strongly held political beliefs were socialist but these did not interfere with friendships or discussions with others of utterly different views. (Dodson, 2002, p. 214)

In 1975 she became president of the Pugwash Conferences on Science and World Affairs (Ferry, 1998). These commitments show that being a scientist did not excuse her involvement in political affairs, particularly where they involved science and its technological consequences/applications.

She also had a strong interest in science education. Following her appointment at Chancellor of Bristol University, her activities showed that:

Dorothy believed profoundly in the importance of education and that it should be available to all. A reflection of this conviction was her willingness to travel to schools of all kinds, large and small, as well as to distinguished centers of learning and research. There is no doubt that Dorothy got great pleasure from these visits even though they were often onerous, time consuming and distracting. ----. Dorothy put her hosts at ease and communicated her interest, usually very informed, in the teaching and research going on (Dodson, 2002).

WOMEN FELLOWS OF THE ROYAL SOCIETY

Given the very low numbers of women chemists who have received a Nobel Prize, some greater light may be thrown on the potential contribution of distinguished female chemists by looking at that other most prestigious group: Fellows of the Royal Society. Since 1945 –when the first woman was elected to the Royal Society - 110 Fellowships and 14 Foreign Fellowships have been awarded to women out of total of 2080 (P. Collins, personal communication, September 26, 2010). An Internet search suggests that the great majority of the women Fellows are famed for their research in, broadly speaking, the field of genetics. It may be appropriate here to see genetics as the use of chemistry, especially that of DNA, in understanding the causes of specific structures and behaviors in animals and plants. In seems reasonable to assume that, when these Fellows give public lectures etc, they give tacit support to chemistry by having employed those ideas in their work. It is a matter of conjecture whether their audience sees this connection.

THE PUBLIC COMMEMORATION OF PROMINENT WOMEN CHEMISTS

One way that Nobel Prize winners in chemistry – and in other subjects – can achieve public exposure and hence present a positive role model is by the appearance of stamps commemorating their achievement. Figure 1 reproduces these (Yardley, personal communication, 2010):

JOHN K. GILBERT

Fig1. Women Nobel Laureates in Chemistry on postage stamps

Marie Curie has been the most frequently celebrated in this way, most often by her native Poland. Given the time lag in the appearance of stamps, it is to be expected that Israel will do so in the next year or two in respect of Ada Yonath.

The achievements of other notable women scientists is also commemorated on stamps (Figure 2)

Fig 2: More notable women scientists on stamps

As an interesting aside here, even the best-laid plans can go wrong: the USA stamp commemorating Gerti Cori has an error in the structure of the molecule on which her fame rests (Everts, 2009).

A second source of public exposure – well, at least to students - is through the use of eminent women scientists as illustrations in textbooks. Historically, illustrations built around women were not used in school science textbooks and, when they did occur, the presentation emphasized sex-stereotypical roles, e.g., female laboratory assistant to a male research scientist (Sadker, 1991). For chemistry, equity of illustration was increasingly being achieved as the twentieth century progressed (Bazler & Simonis, 1991).

DISCUSSION

As has been argued at the start of this chapter, the factors that influence 'chemistry and the public' have evolved over the last century. The contribution that women chemists make to 'chemistry and the public' has also changed. Whilst the few Nobel Laureates can form the basis of case studies for use in the history of chemistry, both they, and other women chemists, have positively responded to the improved opportunities for public education about chemistry available to them. Thus:

Feminism. The major development over the 20th century was the massive increase in the educational opportunities open in many countries to women, not least for the study of science. This in turn has deepened the pool of women chemists who are available to act as role models of girls and younger women.

The professional institutions. It does seem that, over the course of the 20th century, the professional institutions of chemistry have become gradually more permeable to the involvement of women chemists. At the same time, it has been realized that chemistry is not always recognized a being a 'good thing' and that multiple perspectives on its value are needed: enter more women chemists.

The types of stakeholders. There does still seem to be a shortage of women chemists acting as 'mediators' between chemistry and 'the public'. As the incidence of 'science communication' courses under the umbrella of chemistry degrees increases – as seems to be the case – then the number of women seeking such positions seems likely to rise.

One major form of engagement with the public for chemists is through the provision of lectures for schools. For this type of activity to prosper, it must be recognized as a valuable part of the work of chemists.

The expectations of 'chemistry and the public'. The notion of 'chemistry and the public' has expanded during the 20th century from 'knowing chemical ideas' to 'understanding chemical ideas and how they are produced' to ' being able to use chemical ideas and to engage in discussion about priorities in chemical research'. This has been accompanied by a steady increase in the proportion of the population who were thought able to enter into these issues. The involvement of progressively more women has expanded the envelope of what can be attempted and the audience that can be addressed, but there still is a long way to go.

The media employed. The range of media used in 'chemistry and the public' has expanded massively throughout the last century. Whilst women chemists do make use of many of the newer forms, there are still many avenues of contribution accessible and untenanted. As was pointed out above, women have written relatively few 'popular books' about chemistry.

The rise of environmental concerns. The range and level of concern about environmental issues rose steadily during the 20th century. It does seem that women chemists are rising to this challenge.

WHAT MIGHT THE FUTURE HOLD?

The answer to this question will lie at the intersection to the answers to two other questions: 'what role will women have in society?' and 'what role will chemistry have in science?'

In many countries, the agendas of feminism are being addressed. The pace of change varies greatly from country to country and there are many episodes of revisionism. However, it does seem a reasonable ambition that the current overall trend will be continued until men and women have equal rights in all societies. One manifestation of this equality will be the proportion of senior chemists who are women.

Chemistry, as a subject, does seem to have backed itself into a corner. Rather than garner the praise of societies for the great contributions it has made to the quality (indeed, the length) of life, it is seen as corporately content to accept the blame for the pollution that occasionally results from its activities. However, new avenues are opening up: 'green chemistry' should attract positive engagement.

Whatever the future of chemistry, large-scale and permanent public education about chemistry will be needed. Women chemists have a major role in this, building on the example of Marie Curie and her successors.

ACKNOWLEDGEMENTS

I an most grateful to the following for their invaluable help in drawing together the material with which I have addressed this difficult theme: Jim Al-Khalili, Frank James, Peter Collins, Bruce Lewenstein, Susan Stocklmayer, Léonie Rennie, Chris Yardley, and Ada Yonath. Of course, I take full responsibility for the interpretations laid on the often sparse data.

REFERENCES

American Chemical Society [ACS] (2011a). *About ACS.* Retrieved from http://portal.acs.org/portal/acs/corg/content?_nfpb=true&_pageLabel=PP_TRANSITIONMAIN&node_id=225&use_sec=false&sec_url_var=region1&__uuid=c5426d5f-9b4f-43dc-b693-52627a6de06d

American Chemical Society [ACS] (2011b). *National Chemistry Week 2011.* Retrieved from http://www.acs.org/ncw

Angier, N. (2001). Introduction to the 2001 edition. In E. Curie, *Madame Curie: A biography* (pp. ix–xiii). London: Da Capo Press.

Baker, D. (1998). Equity issues in science education. In B. Fraser & K. Tobin (Eds.), *International handbook of science education* (pp. 869–895). Dordrecht, The Netherlands: Kluwer.

Bateson, P. (2006). *Science and the public interest.* London: The Royal Society.

Bazler, J. A., & Simonis, D. A. (1991). Are high school textbooks gender fair? *Journal of Research in Science Teaching, 28*(4), 353–362.

Bell, P., Lewenstein, B., Shouse, A., & Feder, M. (Eds.) (2009). *Learning science in informal environments.* Washington, DC: National Academies Press.

Bodmer, W. (1985). *Public understanding of science.* London: Royal Society.

British Broadcasting Corporation (BBC) (2011). *BLAST.* Retrieved from http://www.bbc.co.uk/blast/

British Council (BC) (2010). Talking science. Availaable from http://www.britishcouncil.org/talking-science-media.htm

Café Scientifique (2009). *Café Scientifique.* Retrieved from http://www.cafescientifique.org

Carrington, B. T., Tymms, P., & Merrell, C. (2008). Role models, school improvement and the 'gender trap: Do men bring out the best in boys and women the best in girls? *British Educational Research Journal, 37*(3)315–327.

Carson, R. (1964). *Silent spring.* London: Penguin.

Catalyst Science Discovery Centre (2011). Retrieved from http://www.catalyst.org.uk/

Center for the Advancement of Informal Science Education (CAISE) (2011). Retrieved from http://caise.insci.org/

Chemical Heritage Foundation (2011). *Chemical Heritage Newsmagazine.* Retrieved from http://www.chemicalheritage.org/pubs/magazine/index.html

Collard, D. M., & McKee, S. (1998). Polymer chemistry in science museums: A survey of educational resources. *Journal of Chemical Education, 75*(11), 1419–1423.

Commonwealth Scientific and Industrial Research Organisation [CSIRO] (2009). *School Programs (Victoria).* Retrieved from http://www.csiro.au/org/VicSchoolProgram.html

Curie, E. (1937). *Madame Curie: A biography.* New York: Da Capo Press.

Dodson, G. (2002). Dorothy Mary Crowfoot Hodgkin, O.M. 12 May 1910 – 29 July 1994. *Biographical Memoirs of Fellows of the Royal Society, 48,* 179–219.

Everts, S. (2009). Going postal over structural errors. *Chemical and Engineering News, 86*(4), 104.

Feminism (2010). Retrieved from http://en.wikipedia.org/wiki/Emancipation_of_women

Ferry, G. (1998). *Dorothy Hodgkin: A life.* London: Granta.

Francis, J. (2009). Creating culturally relevant cafes - Lessons from abroad. At the Annual Science Communication Conference for the British Science Association, London.

Gilmer, P. J. (2011). Irène Joliot-Curie, a Nobel laureate in artificial radioactivity. In M.-H. Chiu, P. J. Gilmer, D. F. Treagust (Eds.), *Celebrating the 100th anniversary of Madame Marie Sklodowska Curie's Nobel Prize in Chemistry* (pp. 41–57) Rotterdam: Sense Publishers.

Goldsmith, B. (2005). *Obsessive genius: The inner world of Marie Curie.* New York: W. W. Norton.

Gregory, J. (1998). *Science in public: Communication, culture, and credibility.* Cambridge, MA: Perseus Publishing.

Harrison, J. (2005). Science education and health education: Locating the connections. *Studies in Science Education , 41,* 51–90.

Hart, P. N. (1999). A critical analysis of research in environmental education. *Studies in Science Education , 34,* 1–69.

Irène Joliot-Curie (2011). Retrieved from http://en.wikipedia.org/wiki/Ir%C3%A8ne_Joliot-Curie

Kennedy, D. (2010). The future of science news. *Daedalus, 139*(2) 57–65.

Klopfer, L. (1969). The teaching of science and the history of science. *Journal of Research in Science Teaching , 6*(1), 87–95.

Lewenstein, B. V. (1992). The meaning of 'public understanding of science' in the United States of America after World War II. *Public Understanding of Science, 1*(1), 45–68.

Lloyd, D., & Wallace, J. (2004). Imaging the future of science education: The case for making futures studies explicit in student learning. *Studies in Science Education, 40*(1),139–177.

Lockwood, P. (2006). "Someone like me can be successful": Do college students need same-gender role models? *Psychology of Women Quarterly* , *30*(1)36–46.

Martin, G. (1911). *Truimphs and wonders of modern chemistry: A popular treatise on modern chemistry and its marvels, written in non-technical language for general readers and students.* London: Sampson Low, Marston.

McGrayne, S. (2006). *Nobel Prize women in science* (pp. 117–143). Washington, DC: Joseph Henry Press.

Meadows, D. (1974). *Limits to growth: A report for the Club of Rome's project on the predicament of mankind.* London: Pan.

Miller, J. (1998). The measurement of civic scientific literacy. *Public Understanding of Science, 7*(3), 203–223.

Pion, G. M., & Lipsey, M. W. (1981). Public attitudes towards science and technology: What have the surveys told us? *Public Opinion Quarterly, 45*(3), 303–316.

Royal Institution of Great Britain (2010). *The Royal Institution of Great Britain.* Retrieved from *RI Christmas Lectures*: http://www.rigb.org

Royal Society of Chemistry [RSC]. (2009). *Chemistry Week 2009.* Retrieved from http://www.rsc.org/ ChemSoc/Activities/ChemistryWeek/2009/Index.asp

RSC (2009). *Royal Society of Chemistry.* Retrieved from http://www.rsc.org

Sadker, M. (1991). The issue of gender in elementary and secondary schools. In G. Grant (Ed.), *Review of Educational Research #17* (pp. 263–334). Washington, DC: American Educational Research Association.

Salters' Institute (2009). *Salters' chemistry camps.* Retrieved from http://www.salters.co.uk/ camps/programme2.htm

Steinke, J. (1997). A portrait of a woman as a scientist: Breaking down barriers created by gender-role stereotypes. *Public Understanding of Science, 6*(4), 409–428.

Sturgis, P., & Allum, N. (2004). Science in society: Re-evaluating the deficit model of public attitudes. *Public Understanding of Science, 13*(1), 55–74.

Weingart, P. (2006). Chemists and their craft in fictional film. *Hyle--International Journal for Philosophy of Chemistry, 12*(1), 31–44.

John K. Gilbert
Professor Emeritus, The University of Reading
Visiting Professor, King's College, London
john.k.gilbert@btopenworld.com

WILLIAM. P. PALMER

8. FORGOTTEN WOMEN IN SCIENCE EDUCATION

The Case of Mary Amelia Swift

INTRODUCTION

The author has studied the lives of a number of early women scientists and found that little was known about the early textbook author Mary Amelia Swift. The author has written about her several times with the power of the Internet revealing more of her life on each occasion. She is noted for two slim volumes that introduced American children to the study of science in the nineteenth century. Her dates of birth and death are uncertain and different sources contradict each other concerning a number of details of her life. Nonetheless using the power of the Internet and some rare texts, many details of her life are gradually being revealed.

The two textbooks are distinctly religious in tone and apart from their common American usage they were also used in translations in the Burmese Christian missions. Even more surprisingly, evidence can be found that these books were used in Japan during Japan's nineteenth century efforts to westernize its science teaching.

THE EXISTING KNOWLEDGE BASE

In general, the topic of 'women in science' is very thoroughly researched. Some idea of the variety of areas for research may be found by looking at the Wikipedia site (Ref: women in science[1]). This easily accessible article surveys many areas indicating through online links some of these research areas. Alternatively research may begin with hard copy materials.

Biographic works that relate to women scientists where a start to research might be made could include Bailey (1994), Baym (2002), Cooney (1996), Creese (1998), Gornick (1990), Kass-Simon and Farnes (1993), Merchant (1989), Ogilvie (1991), Ogilvie and Harvey (2000), Rayner-Canham (1998), Reed (1992), Rossiter (1992), Shearer and Shearer (1997), Tolley (2003) and Yount (1997). Historically there have been many fewer female scientists than male scientists, but there is still much active research into the achievements of women scientists.

In very early times, about 200–400 AD, probably only Mary Hebrea (Rayner-Canham, 1998, p. 3), Hypatia (Yount, 1997, p. 99) and Hildegard von Bingen (Ramos-e-Silva, 1999) are remembered for their scientific discoveries. In England, the first women scientist of note would have been Margaret Cavendish, Duchess of

M.-H. Chiu, P. J. Gilmer, and D. F. Treagust (Eds.), Celebrating the 100th Anniversary of Madame Marie Sklodowska Curie's Nobel Prize in Chemistry. 167–187.

Newcastle (1623–1673) (Ogilvie, 1991) who was able to spend time on science due to her position in the social hierarchy. Margaret was the first woman to attend a meeting of the Royal Society, founded in 1662 (Schiebinger, 1989). Similarly Alethea Howard, Countess of Arundel (1585–1654) and Elizabeth Grey, Countess of Kent (1582–1651) collected and published medical recipes together (Ref: Countesses). In Germany, Elizabeth of Bohemia was interested in natural philosophy (Ogilvie, 1991, p. 82). In France, Marie Meurdrac (mid 1600s) wrote *La Chymie Charitable et Facile en Faveur des Dames* but little is known about her life (Rayner-Canham, 1998, pp. 9–10); later Gabrielle-Emilie Le Tonnelier de Breteuil, Marquise du Chatelet–Lomont (1706–1749), translated and popularized Isaac Newton's works, in Europe (Ref: Sunshine for Women). Marie Anne Paulze Lavoisier, (1758–1836), Antoine Lavoisier's wife, was an active contributor to the science of chemistry (Ogilvie, 1991, pp. 119–120). Elizabeth Fulhame wrote up her chemical experiments on covering thread with various metals (Palmer, 2008). Over time the number of women involved in science increased, with the biological sciences being the most popular. For example, Wakefield (1807) wrote *An Introduction to Botany*. She was not a wealthy woman but used her skill as a writer to gain an income for her family (Shteir, 1987, p. 40). In the nineteenth century, the first well-known female writer in Britain to write science textbooks for children was Jane Marcet (1769–1858). Her books on chemistry and natural philosophy were very popular (Lindee, 1991, pp. 8–23) and by 1853 Marcet's *Conversations on Chemistry* had sold 160,000 copies in the United States alone (Smith, 1997), though her work was extensively plagiarized. Marcet's books used a conversational approach where a teacher, Mrs. B, and two female students discuss the content.

WOMEN SCIENCE TEXTBOOK WRITERS IN AMERICA

While some women scientists such as Rosalind Franklin, Lise Meitner and Nobelist Marie Curie have a well-documented place on the history of science and its development, women scientists (like Nobelist Irène Joliot-Curie, see Gilmer 2011, in this book) and other science authors have been generally overlooked. There are several reasons for this - the role of women in science in former times was not given sufficient credence and there were no obvious breakthroughs of scientific thought as evidenced by the work of Franklin, Meitner, and Curie. Nevertheless, in the USA, two of the earliest women science textbook writers were Almira Lincoln Hart Phelps and Mary Amelia Swift. This article will initially focus on these two early nineteenth century women science textbook writers. The similarity between them is that they were both teachers and had first-hand experience of what young students needed. This is in contrast to the majority of male science text book writers who were either practicing scientists or academics without classroom experience. Also in America much of the science learning was carried out in homes or isolated schools by parents or inexperienced teachers who looked for a book which made science easy and which also contained support for their religious faith. The textbooks by Phelps and Swift fulfilled these needs. The lives of the two women are apparently very different, especially in terms of the records that exist of them. There is a full-length biography of Almira Hart Lincoln Phelps written by Bolzau (1936); this was originally a dissertation but was later self-published. Arnold (1984) provides a 24–page biography and there are two papers describing Phelps' life and work (Smith, 1926, p. 9–11; Palmer, 2010a). Phelps wrote textbooks for schools covering the various scientific disciplines at both elementary and advanced levels. She also wrote a number of educational books, remained as a principal of well-known schools for most of her life and was frequently in the public eye as a member of the American Association for the Advancement of Science. Among American textbook writers Phelps is certainly one of the best. For example, Gianquitto (2007, p. 21) states:

> Almira Hart Lincoln Phelps (1793–1884) however eclipsed all other authors, male and female, to emerge as the premier textbook writer of the nineteenth century. (Gianquitto, 2007, p. 21)

In her textbooks, Almira Phelps uses straightforward description, whereas Mary Swift uses the question and answer method (catechetical form) that leads to memoriter learning (Nietz, 1966, p. 118). There is a paucity of information about Mary Amelia Swift, so direct comparison with Almira Hart Lincoln Phelps is limited. Most standard biographies of American women scientists omit Mary Swift entirely as in for example, Bailey (1994), Cooney (1996), Gornick (1990), Kass-Simon and Farnes (1993), Ogilvie (1991), Rossiter (1992), and Yount (1997). The fact that there is so little information about her may suggest that she was modest and shied away from publicity. The study will now concentrate on the life and works of Mary Amelia Swift.

The biographical dictionary of women scientists by Ogilvie and Harvey (2000) is a good one that has about 2500 entries. In many entries, there is considerable detail but in the case of Mary Swift there is a very brief entry. Ogilvie and Harvey state that Mary was a 'US naturalist and children's writer' and that 'little is known about Mary Swift except that she wrote books for children' (Ogilvie & Harvey, 2000, p. 1255). There is no evidence that Mary Swift was a naturalist, so that portion of her brief biography is in need of correction.

The current study uses the information given in Ogilvie and Harvey's dictionary as the base knowledge of Mary Swift's life and aims to provide more information as the entry does not do justice to her or her writing. The present author has written about Swift on at least two previous occasions (Palmer, 2004, 2007) and is fascinated by the fact that, with the expansion of the Worldwide Web and the continued improvement of the searching systems, more and more information can be discovered about Mary Swift's life. On each search over the past decade more information about Swift has become available, though there is the minor problem that a few relevant Worldwide Web sites have disappeared. The Internet is thus a hugely powerful tool in exploring of the history of science and it becomes more powerful as each year passes.

The remainder of the paper will examine the evidence, sometimes contradictory, about Mary Swift's life, and the surprising history of the books that she wrote (Swift, 1833, 1836a, 1836b). In terms of general methodology for uncovering information about Mary Swift's life, the methodology indicated in a recent paper (Palmer, 2010b) has been followed. The information has been subjected to triangulation. Triangulation of data can be effective in cases where a number of sources agree or complement each other. However where there is divergence between sources, it is necessary to attempt to evaluate sources. On some occasions there is insufficient evidence to place one source as being trustworthier than another. In relation to the early life of Mary Amelia Swift the different sources provide contradictory information.

One problem lies in the fact that the surname 'Swift' is a common one and that there are many 'Mary Swifts'. Mary Swift's father is known to be Zephaniah Swift and this raises another problem, which is that the name 'Zephaniah', though unusual in modern times, is common within this family. Online genealogies can be confusing and are not necessarily subject to critical review; different authors may present data differently.

MARY AMELIA SWIFT: HER LIFE

Mary Amelia Swift's parentage, date of birth, marriage and death are all, in the last analysis, uncertain; the evidence is reviewed.

Three print based sources, such as dictionaries and encyclopedias, state that Mary is the daughter of Zephaniah Swift (1759–1823) who was a superior court judge (Ref: Law Libraries) in Connecticut from 1801 to 1819. He lived in Windham, Windham County, CT. He is a well-documented (Ref: Congress) and influential historical personage (Ref: Law Libraries). The most thorough biographer of Mary Amelia Swift is Elizabeth Wagner Reed (1992, pp. 161–165). She accepts the statement in *Allibone's Dictionary* (Allibone, 1871) that Mary was the daughter of Zephaniah, the judge. All dictionaries and encyclopedias seen, credit Judge Zephaniah Swift (1759–1823), with being the father of Mary Amelia Swift. The entry 'Zephaniah Swift' in *Appleton's Encyclopedia* (Ref: Famous Americans) agrees with the dates of birth and death of Zephaniah and acknowledges his important legal works and then states:

> His [Zephaniah's] daughter, MARY A., published about 1833 "First Lessons on Natural Philosophy," which was a popular text-book for many years, and was translated into Karen (1846) and into Burmese (1848). (Famous Americans)

There is a practically identical statement in the *Encyclopedia of Connecticut Biography* (Hart, 1917).

> Judge Swift was married to Lucretia Webb, by whom he had seven children; their daughter, Mary A., was the author of "First Lessons on Natural Philosophy," which was translated in Karen (1846) and Burmese (1848) and continued in popular use for many years as a textbook. (p. 93)

Gamely and Carnes (1999, pp. 212–213) confirm that Zephaniah Swift (1759–1823) was a lawyer/ politician/ judge. His first wife was Jerusha Watrous who died in 1792;

he remarried and his second wife, Lucretia Webb bore him seven children (Swift, 1923). The reference to Mary A. Swift (Swift, 1923) in this printed genealogy by Eben Swift is just 'Mary A., authoress (?)', with the question mark being particularly noticeable. The other seven children of Judge Swift have information such as dates of birth, marriage and death detailed, making it appear that Eben Swift was uncertain about Mary A. Swift being the daughter of Judge Zephaniah Swift.

The other genealogical references viewed are online references (Refs: William Swyft of Sandwitch; The Swift Genealogy; The Swift Ancestry; Steve Condarcure's Genealogy; The Swift Archive). Generally these indicate that Mary was the daughter of Zephaniah Swift (1786–1834). The genealogical site (Ref: The Swift Genealogy) lists Mary Amelia Swift as the daughter of Zephaniah Swift of Lebanon, CT, who was born on 15 January 1786 and who died on 21 July 1834. He married Nellie Everett 17 September 1811 and they had three daughters of whom Mary Amelia Swift was the eldest, born on 17 September 1812. It is also stated that Mary married her cousin, Henry Augustus Swift on 6 November 1845. George H. Swift bases *The Swift Genealogy* on a genealogy published 80 years ago (Ref: William Swyft of Sandwitch) with corrections and additions by Kathryn Newkirk Graham. This genealogy can be observed to be very thorough. The searchable online genealogical document, *William Swyft of Sandwitch,* also provides the names, date of birth and decease of Mary Swift's six children, does not list Mary Amelia amongst the Judge Zephaniah Swift's children and appears to be the major source of other online biographies. Eben Swift's genealogy is the only printed document available, but this used the genealogy *William Swyft* as its basis, as acknowledged in the foreword, so all the genealogies are actually versions of *William Swyft.* In terms of Mary Swift's life, few of her children survived to adulthood so her life was certainly replete with distress.

The third genealogy has disappeared over the past ten years but can still be traced using Google archives (Ref: The Swift Archive). The site owner warns that some information may be incorrect where sources are not provided. This is unfortunate as the site gives additional information and it confirms Mary's marriage to Henry Augustus Swift on 6 November 1845 and states:

Mary Amelia Swift was a highly cultivated woman, and a successful teacher in New York. She was a fine Greek scholar, knowing more of the language than was ever attempted to be taught in college, writing modern Greek in Greek script with facility. She never occupied herself with authorship any further than to write *First Lessons in Natural Philosophy*, which was a popular text-book for many years and was translated in 1846 into the Karen language, and in 1848 into Burmese. Mr. and Mrs. Swift had six children. (Ref: The Swift Archive).

One part of the statement above is incorrect in that Mary Swift wrote three books (Swift, 1833; 1836a; 1836b). The information that she also taught in New York is not found elsewhere, but the other data are supported by the existing genealogies.

The only recorded detail (and that unconfirmed) of Mary Swift's early life is that she had been a successful teacher in New York (Ref: The Swift Archive) until her employment at Litchfield Female Seminary as Principal as stated on the front cover of *First Lessons in Natural Philosophy* (first ed., 1833). There is quite detailed information about Litchfield Female Seminary (Barney Buel, & Vanderpoel, 1903), which also refers to Mary A Swift. This is a complete history of the school and its founder Miss Pierce. Matters of curriculum, administration and the students' social life would have been very much the concern of Mary Swift as Principal and some information on these matters will be provided in the next section.

The biographical references clearly record that Mary Swift was the daughter of Zephaniah Swift (1759–1823) whereas the genealogies equally clearly indicate that she was the daughter of Zephaniah Swift (1786–1834). This appears to be a situation that the methodology of triangulation does not solve. The widespread agreement of Swift family genealogists that Mary Swift was the daughter of Zephaniah Swift (1786–1834) makes the possibility that Allibone (1871, p. 2319) made a mistake and that later historians copied this error. One can hope that further records will be found that clarify the situation one way or the other.

LITCHFIELD FEMALE SEMINARY

There were two major educational institutions in the small town of Litchfield, CT. Tapping Reeve and Sally Burr Reeve founded Litchfield Law School in 1773, firstly in a small way with Sally Burr Reeve's brother as the first pupil (Ref: Litchfield Law School).

Miss Pierce founded Litchfield Female Seminary in 1792, at a time when her family was in financial difficulties (Ledes, 1993, p. 27). The Litchfield Female Seminary became the Litchfield Female Academy in 1827 (Stankiewicz, 2002, p. 330). Barney Buel and Vanderpoel (1903) give a detailed picture of the school and show that there were many social occasions arranged allowing the young law students and older girls from the female seminary to mix and many seminary students eventually married these young lawyers in later life. As many as 3000 students, mainly girls, but also 150 boys may have enrolled in the school before it closed in 1833. From the accounts the school was well run by Miss Sarah Pierce with about four or five assistant teachers, but in 1828 Miss Pierce became too elderly to continue as principal and her nephew, Mr. Brace, took over as Principal. Mr. Brace was widely admired as a teacher (Logan, 1934, p. 490) and was 'a gentleman of distinguished literary and scientific attainments, whose time and talents are assiduously devoted to the improvement of the pupils under his charge' (Barney Buel & Vanderpoel, 1903, p. 264). A student also wrote that 'Mr. Brace was one of the most stimulating and inspired instructors of the Academy. He was widely informed, an enthusiast in botany, mineralogy and the natural sciences generally, besides being well read in English classical literature' (Barney Buel & Vanderpoel, 1903, p. 181). However Mr. Brace resigned in 1832 (Barney Buel & Vanderpoel, 1903, p. 266) to take up a principal's position elsewhere and Miss Henrietta Jones became Principal. In 1833 the 'Misses Swift' suddenly appear as joint Principal.

She [Miss Pierce] remained with it [the Academy] until 1832– though for a few years, previous, her nephew, John P. Brace, Esq., was the Principal. More than 2500 young ladies and misses were members of the Academy. It was in 1827.

The successors of Miss Pierce have been Misses Swift, Jones, Heyden and other. (Barney Buel & Vanderpoel, 1903, p. 320).

Possibly instead of a single Miss Swift, there are now two 'Miss Swifts' in the principal's role. This is confirmed (Barney Buel & Vanderpoel, 1903, pp. 264– 265): 'In 1833 Miss Jones, afterward associated with Miss Landod, took charge of the school. Following them were the Misses Swift who lived where Mrs. Kilbourn now lives'. With regard to either of the possible family genealogies, Mary Swift had sisters who could have been the other joint principal. There is a small clue indicating Mary Swift was the daughter of Judge Zephaniah of Windham where Barney Buel and Vanderpoel (1903, p. 201) write 'Taylor has been refused by Miss Swift of Windham', though this is inconclusive.

The school was ahead of its times in ensuring that the pupils were presented with a strong academic curriculum which may be best defined by listing the books actually used:

The text-books used at this institution are Walker's Dictionary, Murray's Grammar, Woodbridge's Geography and Atlas, Miss Pierce's Ancient History, Russell's Modern Europe, Goodrich's American History, Daboll's Arithmetic, Blair's Rhetoric abridged, Allison on Taste, Conversations on Natural Philosophy and Chemistry, Paley's Philosophy... (Barney Buel & Vanderpoel, 1903, pp. 264–265).

Moral and natural philosophy were introduced at the Litchfield Female Seminary as early as 1814 (Beadie, 1993) and prior to Miss Swift's arrival natural philosophy was taught by Mr. Brace and he used Marcet's *Conversations on Natural Philosophy*. There would have been no practical element in teaching natural philosophy. Even blackboards were not in common usage in the 1820s (Ref: Notes). Miss Swift would not have been happy with the textbook *Conversations on Natural Philosophy*, by Jane Marcet, which was the book that the students used. Marcet's book would not have fitted the philosophy of Miss Pierce. In 1811 as Miss Pierce had written her own *Universal History* textbook and had used the question-and-answer method and Mary Swift would have wanted to teach in a way that satisfied the Principal. Mary wrote in the brief preface to the *First Lessons in Natural Philosophy-part first*:

At the time this little work was commenced, the author was teaching a few children; no book on Natural Philosophy suited to their capacity was to be found. It was written for their benefit, and taught to them as it progressed. The form of question and answer was used in the manuscript, and is retained as the simplest method of teaching children. It has been used in this form in several schools, and the satisfaction expressed by the children has induced the author to allow its publication (Swift, 1833, preface, unnumbered).

Jane Haldimand Marcet originally published *Conversations on Natural Philosophy* in England in her name in 1819 (Nietz, 1966, p. 115). Reverend J. L. (1824) and later by Dr. Thomas P. Jones (1826) quickly plagiarized her books in America (Nietz, 1966, p. 115). It is uncertain which of these editions was used at Litchfield Female Academy. At this time, women's writing was very often plagiarized and even half a century earlier Elizabeth Fulhame feared that her ideas would be copied due to 'the furacious attempts of the prowling plagiary' (Fulhame, 1794, p. vii) and Mary Swift's work itself was eventually plagiarized.

First Lessons in Natural Philosophy was published in 1833; Litchfield Female Seminary closed in 1833 (Ledes, 1993, p. 28) with Mary Swift (or Misses Swift) presumably being the Principal/joint Principal on the closure of the academy. Other evidence indicates that Litchfield Female Seminary did not close (Ref: Sarah Pierce) and that Mary Amelia Swift remained associated with it as she signed a receipt of fees for a student 'Receipt to Miss Catherine Tallmadge for Litchfield Female Seminary tuition. Signed by M. A. Swift, October 12th, 1835' (Ref: Tallmadge, Catharine). The evidence regarding the closure of the school is contradictory, but perhaps the school continued on a reduced scale after 1833 with Miss Pierce back as Principal (Ref: Sarah Pierce). The hypothesis that the school did not close is confirmed by the Curator of Library and Archives, Litchfield Historical Society, Linda Hocking, (private communication on 3/01/2011): 'It [The Litchfield Female Academy] continued, but Sarah Pierce was no longer involved in its operation, it was controlled by a board of directors and while the name did not change, it was a much different institution.'

It may be asked whether any correspondence to or from Mary Swift still survives. One of the most noted students of Litchfield Female Seminary was Harriet Beecher Stowe, who wrote *Uncle Tom's Cabin*. Amongst Harriet's correspondence there is a letter to her 'school friend Mary Swift' (Hedrick, 1992, p. 286). The correspondence is also referred to elsewhere 'She was soon able to inform her friend, Mary Swift that she was a *"real school ma'am"*' (Boydston, Kelley, & Margolis, 1988, p. 55). This raises the possibility that Mary Swift and Harriet Beecher Stowe were at school together either at Litchfield or Hartford Female Academy that Harriet attended in 1824; Harriet was born in 1811 (Hedrick, 1992, p. 280) and entered the Litchfield Academy in 1821. However the lists of students in *Chronicles of a Pioneer School* do not include a Mary Swift nor can any information be found about Mary Swift attending Hartford Female Academy.

If Harriet and Mary were school friends they would probably be of similar ages. The Beecher family home, a parsonage, in Litchfield, comprised of up to 25 people, many of whom were boarders at Litchfield Female Seminary (Hedrick, 1992, p. 280), so there is a possibility that Mary was a boarder in the Beecher home. It was Miss Pierce's habit to employ former students as teachers to keep her costs down, which could explain why Mary Swift became a teacher at Litchfield Female Seminary.

FIRST LESSONS IN NATURAL PHILOSOPHY BY MARY SWIFT

Swift wrote three books *First Lessons on Natural Philosophy for Children–part first* (Swift, 1833), *First Lessons on Natural Philosophy for Children–part second* (Swift, 1836a) and *Poor but Happy, or, the Villagers of Ban de la Roche and the Children of Icolumbkill* (Swift, 1836b). The first two books were successful and have interesting histories of publication, whereas the book, *Poor but Happy*, was a very pious work, aimed at encouraging children to live good and useful lives. However it appeared only to have had a single printing. One interesting point is that Mary Swift is not referred to as the Principal of Litchfield Female Seminary in this work but as the author of *First Lessons About Natural Philosophy* showing that even her publisher provided an incorrect title for her natural philosophy book. All three books can be found online at 'Google books' or as OCR reprints.

The greatest variety of different editions of Swift's *First Lessons on Natural Philosophy* can be found on the Internet archive (Ref: Archive) and there are other Internet sites such as the digital library (Ref: Hathi Trust Digital Library), also providing free online access to Mary Swift's books. In the 1862 edition, the second book was extensively revised and contained new chapters on topics including magnetism, the ship's compass, electricity, photography, the daguerreotype and the telegraph. In the preface of her enlarged 1862 edition, she added the following sentence to her 1833 preface 'Its introduction as a text-book throughout the United States, indicated a measure of approval that far exceeded the expectations of the writer, and she presents to the public a new and improved edition' (Swift, 1862, preface, p. 5).

Mary Swift's publishers, Belknap and Hamersley of Hartford, gave her books publicity in a number of different journals and on the back of her books for half a century or more. For example Appendix 1, item 15, shows an advertisement by Hamersley giving Swift's new and enlarged edition of *First Lessons in Natural Philosophy* (Swift, 1862) excellent publicity and also claiming that the book was used nationwide (in every state in the union). In a brief biographical note on William Hamersley it is said that he 'engaged in the business of publishing many famous school books, among which were such books as Swift's Natural Philosophy... (Ref: Various, 1923), so to some extent the publisher's success in business rested on Swift's books. Appendix 1 also details the widespread favorable comment that Swift's books received from many different parts of America. Other evidence that Mary Swift's books were widely used in the United States can be found in the Board of Commissioners of Common Schools of Connecticut curricula where her first book was to be used in Class 3 (Anon, 1840) and also in a private school in Louisiana (Ref: Lake Charles Male and Female Academy) in 1867 (Scarlett, 1938).

The two volumes of *First Lessons in Natural Philosophy* were written in a catechetical style (question and answer) and generally the pupils would recite the answers aloud in unison in order to memorize the content. Appendix 1 shows the comments on the back covers of the books and these are quite revealing as to how the books were used. For example, Mrs. Sigourney (a teacher) stated that she favored the recitations by her young students. Nietz (1966) reviewed two of the major teaching methods of the time, which were conversation (dialogues) and catechetical (memoriter) methods. He commented that 'such dialogues were a much improved modification of the old catechetical (memoriter) method in which numerous elementary school textbooks were written' (Nietz, 1966, p. 114).

What is noticeable about Mary Swift's books, when compared with other books of the period, is that they have a larger typeface, shorter text, a few poems to break the monotony of question and answer and several pictures with at least one in color; these features make Swift's books more easily digestible by younger children. Perhaps this explains their popularity. Reed (1992, p. 161) states that the two volume work ran to 34 printings between 1833 and 1884, though a still later printing of the first part has been identified published by Brown & Gross also from Hartford in 1890. The books were extensively revised and enlarged by Mary Swift in 1859. For example, the 1839 edition of part second had 176 pages and the 1862 edition had 215 pages.

The books are arranged in short lessons which may have increased the appeal to teachers as they could then fit specific content into a given time-slot; this principle was later used with the object lesson 'methodology' where the teacher brings in an object which is going to be the focus of the teaching of that lesson. This gave a practical element to lessons and helps inexperienced teachers with timing.

FIRST LESSONS IN NATURAL PHILOSOPHY

The first book also contains a number of religious poems written by Mrs. Swift that were, at the time, thought suitable for younger students and this may be why the book was used in Christian missions overseas. In the second book there is much less material of a specifically religious nature. Geography, physics and astronomy are all well integrated. The methodology of starting from the known, and proceeding to the unknown is frequently used, for example, beginning with the situation of the town in the United States in which the student lived and eventually coming to the place of the earth in the solar system, was followed over several lessons.

The second book is much closer to a standard physics text with the majority of lessons being on mechanics, but also including air pressure, heat (hot springs), light (including photographs and daguerreotypes), and electricity (including Morse-code telegraphy). Swift does try to include the latest practical applications in each case as well as stories about inventors, so the text is not dull.

Swift defines terms well but on occasions appears to introduce words merely to explain what they mean, usually by giving the Latin derivation. The quality of explanation is generally good but there is some use of simplified language that could give rise to future misconceptions for the students (Swift, 1836a, pp. 102–103):

If you could fill a thin bag with very light air, and throw it into the air, as you do soap bubbles, what would it do?

The bag would rise.

How high would it rise?

Till it came to air of its own weight

The physics, though simplified, is generally accurate; there are instances where our knowledge has changed over time, for example in the number and naming of the planets in *part first*, pp. 66–67 (1839 ed.).

How many planets are there moving round the sun?

Seven.

What are their names?

Mercury, Venus, Earth, Mars, Jupiter, Saturn and Herschel

In the 1859 edition of *part first* Swift had changed this and then added information that was correct prior to 1854, but even in 1859 was out of date:

What are the names of those that we can see most distinctly?

Mercury, Venus, Earth, Mars, Jupiter, Saturn, Uranus, and Neptune.

What are the names of some of those that have been discovered within a few years?

Neptune, Iris, Flora, Victoria, and Irene.

In modern terminology, Neptune is a planet, whereas Iris, Flora, Victoria, and Irene are asteroids. The web site (Ref: Killer asteroids) claims that this fact was generally recognized by 1854. This illustrates the problem of scientific textbooks that stay in print for lengthy periods; the problem is that there are some areas of scientific knowledge, which can change quite rapidly. Although Mary Swift was not always up to date with the latest science, she did seem to write in a way that interested children in her era. Kohlstedt (1978, p. 86, footnote 17) includes Mary Swift among a group of authors who organize their books in a format suited to classroom teaching. Swift's religious sincerity and experience would have made her books popular with parents, who often taught children at home. Sills (Anon, 2004) considers that such books as *First Lessons in Natural Philosophy* were widely used for home instruction in rural areas. Merchant (1989, p. 252) describes the enlarged *First Lessons in Natural Philosophy- part second* of 1859 accurately in terms of its contents. She uses a section on machinery, where Swift described the cotton factories and emphasized the skill of those who make the machines to reducing labor. This in Merchant's view illustrated the idea that women educators/ textbook writers reproduce the social values of their times.

Who teaches man how to save his labor by contriving these machines?

Our creator.

Several historians describing science education in the early and middle nineteenth century mention Swift's little books, for example: Anon (1966, exhibit 46), Ierley (2002, p. 74), Nietz (1966, p. 118), Underhill (1941). All these sources cite and comment briefly on Swift's natural philosophy books.

THE INTERNATIONALIZATION OF FIRST LESSONS IN NATURAL PHILOSOPHY

The most remarkable feature of Mary Swift's two small books entitled *First Lessons in Natural Philosophy* was their popularity and the way in which they spread internationally. The books were really intended for small classes of girls in a Connecticut private school and they eventually appear to have been used throughout America. The two books were also used in the Maritime Provinces of Canada (Norris, 1965), as late as 1885. Norris (1965, p. 610) says little positive about the books and claims that they consist of 'questions and pat responses' giving a couple of exemplars.

In Britain, *First Lessons on Natural Philosophy for Children* (Wilson, 1855) by Rev. T. Wilson (1810–1875) was published in three volumes, but with fewer pages than Swift's books. Rev T. Wilson was a 'nom de plume' for Rev Samuel Clarke who was the Rector of Eaton-Bishop in Herefordshire, England. The name Rev. T. Wilson was principally used by Clarke as author or editor of a series of catechisms on varied subjects for the young learner. These were widely advertised at nine pence each. In this author's opinion Clarke's books are a plagiarized version of Mary Swift's work as he examined a copy at the British Library some years ago.

A very interesting feature of the *First Lessons in Natural Philosophy* was that it was translated in 1846 into the Karen language and in 1848 into Burmese, as listed in the Boston Public Library catalogue (Jewett, Jillson, Vinton, & Bugbee, 1866). The fact that there is a Burmese connection can also be found in Allibone (1871, p. 2319). Allibone also indicates that Mr. Vinton of Maulmain, Burma, translated *First Lessons in Natural Philosophy* into Karen and that Mrs. Stilson of Maulmain, Burma, translated *First Lessons in Natural Philosophy* into Burmese.

Further research indicates that both Mr. Vinton and Mrs. Stilson were missionaries with the American Baptist mission to Burma and had connections with Connecticut through the first Baptist missionary to Burma (Ref: Adoniram, Judson). Internally the books that Swift wrote gave a specifically Christian context to natural philosophy. Why would Mary Swift have allowed her two little books to be translated to further Christian mission? No evidence has been found that permission was given but Litchfield alumni were encouraged to take an interest in Christian overseas mission.

The Litchfield Female Academy students organized to support local missionary, bible and tract societies and raised money for the training of ministers. Many of the academy alumnae carried on these activities in later life... (Ref: Litchfield Female Academy)

There are other connections; for example, very generous praise was given to Mary Swift's book in an article from a Methodist conference published just before her book was translated into Karen and Burmese. It is also of interest that the translation into Karen was only 74 pages whereas the original runs to 107 pages, so the translator may have shortened the work. On the other hand the Burmese edition boasts illustrative woodcuts, which might be the difference between the two translations.

It was more remarkable that Mary Swift's little books were used as a part of the educational effort towards the westernization of Japan (Ref: History of Technology) that started in the 1850s.

Fukuzawa Yukichif (1834–1901) was influential in the process of westernization following the Kanagawa Treaty of 1854 (Yajima, 1964, p. 340) and he emphasized the importance of English in place of Dutch. He managed to travel to the USA with the shogunate ambassador and brought back some American books that helped the modernization process. He wrote the *Kummo Kyuri Zukai* (*Illustration of Natural Science*) in 1872 even though he himself did not have scientific training.

Fukuzawa's book was the first of its kind and served as a model for a numerous variety of similar works. This was the situation in the 1870s in Japan, the period of popularization of scientific knowledge. *Kyuri* was the new fashion. Fukuzawa used as reference mainly Chamber's *Introduction to Science*. Other books then used as the source of popularization were: Quackenbos' *Natural Philosophy,* Swift's *First Lessons on the Natural Philosophy for Children,* an English translation of Ganot's *Cours de la physique,* and Chinese translations such as William Martin's *Natural Philosophy* or William Herschel's *Astronomy.* (Yajima, 1964, p. 350)

As a result of Japanese interest, Mary Swift's books were translated into Japanese, whilst it appears that others were imported untranslated. Evidence of translated versions is available in a number of libraries such as the World catalogue (Swift, 1866) or Kagawa University (Swift, n.d.). Just one example with an interesting story was available commercially; the whole advertisement appears below:

SWIFT, MARY A. *First Lessons on Natural Philosophy, for Children – in two parts. New edition, enlarged and improved.* Yedo [i.e. Tokyo], 1867–66. $1,000

2 parts in 3 volumes, 16mo, pp. [104]; [88]; [107]; illustrated with woodcuts throughout (that of the rainbow hand-colored); original tan wrappers sewn in the Japanese manner, printed paper labels on upper covers; last 40 pp. of the first volume heavily annotated over the text and obscuring the same, so this is accompanied by another copy of the first volume in a different wrapper; occasional spots and stains, ink stamps; good copy. The interesting part of the overwriting is that it was written by an officer by the name of Hiroshi Yuchi in the Sino-Japanese War (ca. 1894–95), and as such constitutes a sort of diary, making notes on military strategy, the raining down of bombs and hand-grenades, deaths of comrades, longing for his girl friend, etc. The imprint in vol. II is Hartford: William J. Hamersley, publisher; Philadelphia: J. B. Lippincott & Co., 1866. Columbia University only in OCLC. (Rulon-Miller Books)

The chance events that took Mary Swift's books to Burma are amongst the earliest records of a textbook being translated for what would now be called 'the third world'. This probably means that natural philosophy/ physics was being taught at a primary level in Burma earlier than it would be taught in many other countries. In the case of Japan, Swift's little books played a part in helping Japan (then a developing country technologically) to modernize. In Japan there is still an interest in her books as a recent exhibition of children's textbooks at Kobe University demonstrates (Ref: Kobe University Library).

By the end of the nineteenth century, Mary Swift's little books were no longer used and were forgotten. In 1966, the educational journal, *School Science and Mathematics,* republished *First Lessons in Natural Philosophy* in three successive issues, which may illustrate an educational turning point, as a time when educators started to pay attention to the textbook writers of past eras.

CONCLUSION

A more convincing and accurate story of Mary Swift's life has been created than is available elsewhere using the power of the Internet. As better Internet systems develop it is probable that more will become known of Mary Swift's life.

Accurate knowledge of even Swift's genealogy and circumstances is limited. The only sure knowledge of her life is that she was once Principal of Litchfield Female Seminary and wrote three books. However, this brief article indicates a probable date of birth and marriage and that she may have been Principal of Litchfield Female Seminary both before and after the Seminary's temporary closure. It indicates that she married and had six children and that few of these children lived to adulthood. Perhaps the paucity of information on her life implies that she was a quiet, good and self-effacing woman. It also provides some remarkable stories of the books that she wrote.

Swift's work is of interest for its usefulness and popularity for younger children and for the fact that it was translated into three Asian languages. She should be remembered better than she is remembered in the current biographies. Her books, which are still easily and cheaply available, are her main memorials.

NOTES

[1] References to URLs are given within the References at the end of this chapter.

REFERENCES

Adoniram, J. (2011). Retrieved from http://www.wholesomewords.org/missions/bjudson3.html

Allibone, S. A. (1871). *Allibone's critical dictionary of English literature. British and American authors living and deceased from the earliest accounts to the latter half of the nineteenth century* (Three vol.) (p. 2318). Philadelphia: J. B. Lippincott.

Anon (1840). Report of school visitors, *Connecticut common school journal,* Vol. 1–4 (p. 226). Connecticut Board of Commissioners of Common Schools.

Anon (1966). *Science in nineteenth-century children's books: An exhibition based on the Encyclopedia Britannica historical collection of books for children in the University of Chicago Library held during the celebration of the University's seventy-fifth anniversary year, August through October.* Chicago, IL: University of Chicago Library.

Anon (2004). Why collect old physics textbooks? *American Institute of Physics History Newsletter, 36*(1). Retrieved from http://www.aip.org/history/newsletter/spring2004/physics-texts.htm

Archive. Retrieved from http://www.archive.org/

Arnold, L. B. (1984). *Four lives in science: Women's education in the nineteenth century*. New York: Schocken Books.

Bailey M. J. (1994). *American women in science: A biographical dictionary*. Denver, CO: ABC-CLIO Inc.

Barney Buel, E. C. (Ed.), & Vanderpoel E. N. (Compiler) (1903). *Chronicles of a pioneer school, from 1792 to 1833 being the history of Miss Sarah Pierce and her Litchfield school*. Cambridge, MA: University Press. Retrieved from http://nrs.harvard.edu/urn-3:FHCL:664615

Baym, N. (2002). *American women of letters and the nineteenth-century sciences: Styles of affiliation*. New Brunswick, NJ and London: Rutgers University Press.

Beadie, N. (1993). Emma Willard's idea put to the test: The consequences of state support of female education in New York, 1819–67 [Special issue]. *History of Education Quarterly, 33*(4), 543–562.

Blake, J. L. (1824). *Conversations on natural philosophy, in which the elements of that science are familiarly explained, and adapted to the comprehension of young pupils*. Boston, MA: Lincoln and Edmands.

Bolzau, E. L. (1936). *Almira Hart Lincoln Phelps: Her life and work, Vol. 1*. Philadelphia, PA: Self-published.

Boydston, J., Kelley, M., & Margolis, A. T. (1988). *The limits of sisterhood: The Beecher sisters on women's rights and woman's sphere* (p. 55). Chapel Hill, NC: University of North Carolina Press.

Congress. Retrieved from http://bioguide.congress.gov/scripts/biodisplay.pl?index=S001119

Cooney, M. P. (Ed.) (1996). *Celebrating women in mathematics and science*. Reston, VA: National Council of Teachers of Mathematics.

Countesses. Retrieved from http://en.wikipedia.org/wiki/Elizabeth_Grey,_Countess_of_Kent

Creese, M. R. S. (with contributions by Thomas M. Creese) (1998). *Ladies in the laboratory? American and British women in science, 1800–1900: A survey of their contributions to research*. Lanham, MD and London: The Scarecrow Press, Inc.

Famous Americans. Retrieved from http://www.famousamericans.net/zephaniahswift/

Fulhame, Mrs. E. (1794). *An essay on combustion, with a view to a new art of dying and painting, wherein the phlogistic and antiphlogistic hypotheses are proved erroneous*. London: printed for the author by J. Cooper.

Gamely, J., & Carnes, M. (Eds.) (1999). *American national biography, 21*, 212–213. Oxford and New York: Oxford University Swift.

Gilmer, P. J. (2011). Irène Joliot-Curie, a Nobel laureate in artificial radioactivity, In M.-H. Chiu, P. J. Gilmer, D. F. Treagust (Eds.), *Celebrating the 100th anniversary of Madame Marie Sklodowska Curie's Nobel Prize in Chemistry* (pp. 41–57). Rotterdam: Sense Publishers.

Gianquitto, T. (2007). *Good observers of nature: American women and the scientific study of the natural world, 1820–1885*. Athens, GA: University of Georgia Press.

Gornick, V. (1990). *Women in science: 100 journeys into the territory*. New York: Touchstone.

Hathi Trust Digital Library. Retrieved from http://catalog.hathitrust.org

Hart, S. (1917). *Encyclopedia of Connecticut biography: Genealogical-memorial: Representative citizens*, Vol. 1. Boston and New York: The American Historical Society, Inc.

Hedrick, J. D. (1992). Parlor literature: Harriet Beecher Stowe and the question of 'Great Women Artists'. *Signs, 17*(2), 275–303.

History of Technology. Retrieved from http://d-arch.ide.go.jp/je_archive/english/society/biblio_17.html

Ierley, M. (2002). Wondrous contrivances: technology at the threshold. New York, NY: Clarkson Potter.

Jewett, C. C., Jillson, W. E., Vinton, F. & Bugbee, J. M. (1866). *Index to the Catalogue of Books in the Bates Hall of the Public Library of the City of Boston* (p. 612). Boston, MA: Boston Public Library.

Jones T. P. (1826). *Conversations on natural philosophy, in which the elements of that science are familiarly explained*. Philadelphia, PA: Grigg & Elliot.

Kass-Simon, G., & Farnes, P. (Eds.) (1993). *Women of science: Righting the record*. Bloomington and Indianapolis: Indianapolis University Press.

Killer asteroids, Slide 7. Retrieved from http://kska.org/wp-content/uploads/2010/04/Jedi-Talk-web.pdf

Kobe University Library, Exhibition of Mari Suuifuto (Mary Swift). October 22, 2010 - December 21, 2010). Retrieved from http://www.lib.kobe-u.ac.jp/www/html/tenjikai/2010tenjikai/mokuroku2010. pdf

Kohlstedt, S. G. (1978). In from the periphery: American women in science, 1830–1880. *Signs*, *4*(1), 81–96.

Law Libraries. Retrieved from http://www.jud.ct.gov/lawlib/history/swift.htm

Ledes, A. E. (July, 1993). Female education in the early republic, *The Magazine Antiques*, *144*(1), 27-28.

Lindee, M. S. (1991). The American career of Jane Marcet's conversations on chemistry, 1806–1853. *Isis*, *82*, 8–23.

Litchfield Female Academy. Retrieved from http://www.litchfieldhistoricalsociety.org/history/ academy.php

Litchfield Law School. Retrieved from http://www.litchfieldhistoricalsociety.org/history/histlawschool. html

Logan, C. T. (1934). Composition teaching in America before 1850. *The English Journal*, *23*(6), 486–496.

Merchant, C. (1989). *Ecological revolutions: Nature, gender, and science in New England* (p. 252). Chapel Hill and London: University of North Carolina Press

Nietz, J. A. (1966). *The evolution of American secondary school textbooks* (1st ed.). Rutland, VT: Charles E. Tuttle Company.

Norris, S. (1965). Biology teaching: An historical perspective. *The American Biology Teacher*, *27*(8), 607–614.

Notes (2011). Retrieved from http://www.pballew.net/mathbooks.html

Ogilvie, M. B. (1991). *Women in science: Antiquity through the nineteenth century*. Cambridge, MA: Massachusetts Institute of Technology Press.

Ogilvie, M., & Harvey, J (Eds.) (2000). *The biographical dictionary of women in science: Pioneering lives from ancient times to the mid 20th century*, Vol. 2, (p. 1255). New York and London: Routledge.

Palmer, W. P. (2004). How significant has women's contribution to the progress of science been? IPSI-2004 Montenegro conference from 2/10/04 to 9/10/04.

Palmer, W. P. (2007, July) Mary Amelia Swift: A little known children's science textbook author. Symposium conducted at conference of the Australasian Science Education Research Association, Fremantle, WA, AUS.

Palmer, W. P. (2008). Elizabeth Fulhame, woman chemist of the chemical revolution. *Science Teaching*, *54*(4) 12–16. Retrieved from http://findarticles.com/p/articles/mi_6957/is_4_54/ai_ n31161065/

Palmer, W. P. (2010a, January). Almira Hart Lincoln Phelps (1793–1884): Her life, her textbooks and her educational influence. In symposium, *Envisioning the future: The role of curriculum materials and learning environments in educational reform* conducted at The Sixth International Conference on Science, Mathematics and Technology Education. (In W-H Chang, D. Fisher, C-Y Lin, & R. Koul (Eds.), *Proceedings of the Sixth International Conference on Science, Mathematics and Technology Education* (pp. 387–396) [as CD], Hualien, Taiwan).

Palmer, W. P. (2010b, November). Seeking the elusive: The stories of science writers at contemporary approaches to research in mathematics, science, health and environmental education. In presentation at Deakin University, Melbourne Campus at Burwood. Retrieved from http://www. deakin.edu.au/arts-ed/efi/conferences/car-2010/papers/palmer.pdf

Ramos-e-Silva, M. (1999). Saint Hildegard von Bingen (1098–1179): The light of her people and of her time. *International Journal of Dermatology*, *38*(4), 315–320. doi:10.1046/j.1365–4362.1999.00617.

Rayner-Canham, M. & G. (1998). *Women in chemistry: Their changing roles from alchemical times to the mid twentieth century*. New York: American Chemical Society.

Reed, E. W. (1992). *American women in science before the Civil War*. Minneapolis: University of Minnesota.

Rossiter, M. W. (1992). *Women scientists in America: Struggles and strategies to 1940.* Baltimore, MA: John Hopkins University Press.

Rulon-Miller Books. Retrieved from http://www.biblio.com/books/261123676.html

Sarah Pierce (1767–1852). Retrieved from http://www.eaww.uconn.edu/author_pages/pierce_sarah.html

Scarlett, L. A. (1938) (Trans. by L. White, January 2007). *The history of education in Lake Charles prior to 1907.* The Department of Education, Louisiana State University and Agricultural and Mechanical College, in partial fulfillment of the requirements for the degree of Master of Arts.

Schiebinger, L. (1989). *Mind has no sex: Women in the origins of modern science.* Cambridge, MA: Harvard University Press.

Shearer, B. F., & Shearer, B. S. (Eds.) (1997). *Notable women in the physical sciences: A biographical dictionary.* Westport, CT and London: Greenwood Press.

Shteir, A. B. (1987). Botany in the breakfast room: Women and early nineteenth British plant study. In P. G. Abir-Am & D. Outram (Eds.), *Uneasy careers and intimate lives: Women in science, 1789–1979.* New Brunswick, NJ: Rutgers University Press.

Smith, M. V. (1926). A pioneer in education. *The Vermonter: The state magazine, 31*(1), 9–11.

Smith, P. D. (1997). German literature and the scientific world-view in the nineteenth and twentieth centuries. *Journal of European Studies, 27*(4), 389–416.

Stankiewicz, M. A. (Summer 2002) Middle class desire: Ornament, industry, and emulation in 19th-century art education. *Studies in Art Education, 43*(4) 324–338.

Steve Condarcure's Genealogy, p. 2154. Retrieved from http://www.genealogyofnewengland.com/f_869.htm

Sunshine for Women. Retrieved from http://www.pinn.net/~sunshine/whm2001/chatelet.html

Swift, E. (1923). *William Swift and descendants to the sixth generation.* Yarmouthport, MA, privately printed by Charles W. Swift.

Swift, M. A. (1833). *First lessons on natural philosophy for children–part first.* Hartford CN: Belknap and Hamersley.

Swift, M. A. (1836a). *First lessons on natural philosophy for children–part second.* Hartford CN: Belknap and Hamersley.

Swift, M. A. (1836b). *Poor but happy, or, villagers Ban Roche children Icolumbkil.* Hartford CN: Belknap and Hamersley.

Swift, M. A. (1862). *First lessons on natural philosophy for children–part first (new edition-enlarged and improved).* Hartford CN: W. J. Hamersley.

Swift, M. A. (1866). *First lessons on natural philosophy for children.* Yedo [Tokyo]: s.n. (from World Catalogue) in Japanese.

Swift, M. A. (1966, reprint). *First lessons on natural philosophy for children: in two parts, School Science and Mathematics,* (part1) *66*(3), 290–306; (part 2) *66*(4), 345–359; (part 3) *66*(5), 447–454.

Swift, M. A. (n.d.). *First lessons on natural philosophy for children,* 2 vols. Reprinted in Japan (William J. Hamersley) (from Kagawa University Library). Retrieved from http://www.lib.kagawa-u.ac.jp/www1/kanbara/moku/ymoku.html

The Swift Ancestry. Retrieved from http://wc.rootsweb.ancestry.com/cgi-bin/igm.cgi?op=GET&db=ssimonw&id=I46071

The Swift Archive. Retrieved from http://web.archive.org/web/20041128210434/http://www.sawyer-family.org/sawyer1/i9655.htm

The Swift Genealogy (based on *William Swyft of Sandwitch* compiled by George H. Swift, published by Round Table Press, Millbrook, N.Y. 1900, with corrections and additions by Kathryn Newkirk Graham). Retrieved from http://www.nashfamilyhistory.com/winglibrary.org/swiftgenealogy.html

Tallmadge, C. (1835 October 12) in Folder 82: Receipt, signed by M. A. Swift. Retrieved from http://www.litchfieldhistoricalsociety.org/archon/?p=collections/findingaid&id=2&rootcontentid=238.

Tolley, K. (2003). *The science education of American girls. A historical perspective.* New York and London: Routledge Falmer.

Underhill, O. E. (1941). *The origins and development of elementary-school science*, etc. [A thesis. with a bibliography] (pp. xii–347). Chicago, IL: Scott, Foreman & Co.

Various (1923). *Encyclopedia of Connecticut biography, genealogical memorial, representative citizens* (p. 163). New York and Chicago: The American Historical Society Inc.

Wakefield, P. (1807). *An introduction to botany, in a series of familiar letters, with illustrative engravings.* (5th ed.). London: printed by and for Darton and Harvey, also for Vernon and Hood, J. Walker, & J. Harris.

Women in Science: Retrieved from http://en.wikipedia.org/wiki/Women_in_science

William Swyft of Sandwitch and some of his descendants, 1637–1899 by Swift, George H. 1820–1908, published 1900 online (Searchable see p. 56). Retrieved from http://babel.hathitrust.org/cgi/ls?q1=mary+a+swift&a=srchls

Wilson, T. (1855). *First lessons on natural philosophy for children*. London: Darton & Co. (British Library, seen).

Woolbridge, W. C. (1836). Notices of books. *American Annals of Education and Instruction, 4,* 47.

Yajima, S. (1964). The European influence on physical sciences in Japan. *Monumenta Nipponica, 19*(3/4), 340–351.

Yount, L. (1997). *A biographical dictionary A to Z of women in science and math.* New York: Facts On File Inc.

APPENDIX 1

From back cover of: *First Lessons on Natural Philosophy for Children part first* By Miss Mary A. Swift, Principal of the Litchfield Female Seminary.

1. *From the Hartford Watchman.*

> This author has unusual skill in writing a child's book of natural science. We can testify to the adaptedness of her former work to the minds of children from observation; and this last surpasses it in some respects. Children are better pleased with ideas than words, and it would not be easy to find a spare word in the whole of this little book, it is beautifully concise and simple.

2. *From the New Haven Palladium.*

> Its contents are admirably adapted to their capacities, the science being illustrated by the things most familiar to their sight and understanding. The "First Part" of the same work was extremely well received.

3. *From the New York Weekly Messenger.*

> So simple, plain, easy, instructive and entertaining, that the child, under the care of a suitable teacher, is anxious to go forward until the whole is learned. When the tasks of children are thus rendered pleasing instead of painful there is not only a *hope* but a *certainty* of improvement.

4. *From the Connecticut Observer*

> This little volume is an admirable counterpart to the first that was published, and which exhibited the *tact* of the writer for addressing youthful minds on subjects of this nature. It shows how such a subject can be made interesting to those who, in the earliest developments

of thought, begin to enquire into the sense of things, and are full of curiosity with regard to the objects around them. The modes of explanation are very judicious; the style, as it should be, simple; and the chain of consecutive reasoning clearly and brightly preserved. It is a matter of rejoicing to all parents and teachers all youth that minds like those of the writer are devoting their powers to such works – forming a new era in the juvenile literature of the country.

5. *From the Fall River Messenger*

The lessons are admirably adapted to the capacities of children. Part First is now used in the schools of this town and we hope Part Second may be introduced without delay.

From back cover of: *First Lessons on Natural Philosophy for Children- part second.*

6. The "First Lessons About Natural Philosophy," is well calculated to interest the minds of youth. It brings down the popular parts of Natural Philosophy to the level of the capacities of children, with a degree of simplicity and accuracy which I have seldom seen excelled. I wish Miss Swift all success in the useful literary labors in which she is engaged, and in her endeavors to arrest the attention of the young, and simplify useful knowledge,—Thomas Dick, LL. D, author of the Christian Philosopher, &c. &c.

7. FIRST LESSONS ABOUT NATURAL PHILOSOPHY —part first. By Miss MARY A. Swift, Principal of the Litchfield Female Seminary. The lessons are admirably adapted to the capacities of children. Part First is now used in the Schools in this town, and we hope Part Second may be introduced without delay.—Fall River Monitor

8. The '*First Lessons in Natural Philosophy*', I am now submitting to the best of all modes of criticism – the daily recitations of little children and I am happy to add, that hitherto they stand this severe test admirably.
(Mrs. Sigourney, 1859, back cover).

9. *First Lessons on Natural Philosophy.—Parts 1 and 2.—*By Mary A. Swift. ...These books for clearness of explanation and illustration are unequalled by any other work on the subject for young children. They are used in every State in the Union.

10. It is the peculiar merit of these 'lessons' that they not only teach philosophy well, but what is of paramount importance, they teach it in a truly Philosophical manner – that is, in harmony with the progressive expansion of the juvenile mind. No person, I am persuaded, who has given his days and nights to the science of teaching, can peruse this book without admiring this prominent feature in every lesson in it. It is this which commends it to universal acceptation.
(E. H. Burritt, Esq., Author of *Geography of the Heavens*, 1859, back cover)

Other Reviews

11. Woolbridge, W. C. (1836). Notices of books, *American Annals of Education and Instruction*, No 4, p. 47.

The whole exterior of this book, if we except, perhaps, a few engravings, is superior to most of the books we have seen for children; nor does it seem to be behind many in intrinsic excellence. If we were at all in favour of the catechetical method of instruction, we should not hesitate to commend this neat little volume as one of its most happy specimens.
(Woolbridge, 1836, p. 47)

12. *The Plaindealer* (Saturday, January 7th, 1837, Vol. 1, no. 6, p. 86)

> *First Lessons About Natural Philosophy for Children.* by Mary A. Swift, Principal of the Litchfield Female Seminary. Hartford, Belknap & Hamersley. This book is obviously the production of one who understands the wants and capacities of very young students, and, what is more rare, understands how to accommodate herself to their immature intellects.

13. *The Knickerbocker; or, New-York monthly magazine,* (February, 1837, Vol. 9, No.2, p. 208)

> *First Lessons About Natural Philosophy*, a small volume for children, from the pen of Miss Mary A. Swift, Principal of the Litchfield Female Seminary, and from the press of Messrs. Belknap and Hammersley, Hartford (CT), is an admirable little book, remarkable alike for the large amount of useful information which it contains, and the clear and simple manner in which it is conveyed to the juvenile mind.

14. *New York Mirror: a weekly journal devoted to literature and fine arts.* (Saturday, April 22nd, 1837, vol. 14, p. 343).

> *First Lessons About Natural Philosophy for Children part second* -Belknap and Hamersley does more than her share in providing the excellent little works for the rising generation. The present volume by Miss Mary A. Swift of Litchfield is a good specimen of the class to which it belongs and we have pleasure in recommending it to our juvenile readers.

15. Methodist Episcopal Church. (1845). Natural philosophy (Excerpt) *The Ladies' repository*, No. 5, p. 256. Cincinnati: J.F. Wright and L. Swormstedt.

> I have been put upon this train of reflections, having lighted upon a little book entitled, '*First Lessons on Natural Philosophy*', by Miss Mary A. Swift. It is the *second* part that I saw. I have never seen a book on any subject so well adapted to the very young as this—*so simple*. There is hardly anything in it that is not well explained; and the incidental admissions (though they render the book not quite so "artistical") are well calculated to interest and please the youthful student, without interfering with or confusing the proper idea. It is indeed an excellent book, and no doubt a delightful one to those to whom it is dedicated.

> I would recapitulate by observing, that the present acquisition must not be accounted at a simple value as stopping *here,* but as regards its availableness in the series of science, and, above all, in reference to the *discipline of mind.* C. M.

Publisher's advertisement in a Greek Grammar of 1867.
Published by WM. JAS. HAMERSLEY, HARTFORD, CON., and to be obtained through the principal booksellers of the country.

16. *Swift's First Lessons on Natural Philosophy. Part First and Second.* Revised and enlarged editions, with numerous illustrations, containing new chapters on electricity, the daguerreotype, &c.

> The remarkable success of the first editions of these books has abundantly proved that natural science can be made clear to the minds of young children, and that these books are eminently adapted to that purpose, having gained for themselves a circulation in every State in the Union. Their great success has induced the publisher to bring out an enlarged edition.

For simplicity of style and aptness of illustration, Miss Swift has obtained a reputation as wide as our country.

William P. Palmer
Science and Mathematics Education Centre
Curtin University
bill_palmer15@hotmail.com

SECTION 3: POLICY IMPLICATIONS

ANITA HUSSENIUS AND KATHRYN SCANTLEBURY

9. WITCHES, ALCHEMISTS, POISONERS AND SCIENTISTS

Changing Image of Chemistry

Chemistry is a science well suited to the talents and situation of women; it is not a science of parade; it affords occupation and infinite variety; it demands no bodily strength; it can be pursued in retirement; it applies immediately to useful and domestic purposes; and whilst the ingenuity of the most inventive mind may in the science be exercised, there is no danger of it flaming the imagination, because the mind is intent upon realities, the knowledge that is acquired is exact and the pleasure of the pursuit is sufficient reward for the labour. (Edgeworth, 1795, p. 21)

INTRODUCTION

On north side of Stortorget in the old part of Stockholm sits the Nobel Museum, opened in 2001. The museum honors the awardees and summarizes their accomplishments on posters that move above the patrons on a ceiling track. Alfred Nobel (1833–1896) a chemical engineer famous for his invention of dynamite founded the Nobel Prizes. By the time of his death in 1896, he had 355 patents and when his will was read it came as a surprise that his fortune was to be used for Prizes in Physics, Chemistry, Physiology or Medicine, Literature, and Peace. Marie Curie (Nobelprize.org, 1903) is the only person to win two Nobel Prizes in separate fields of science and one of the few women to win any. Since the inception of the Nobel Prize in chemistry in 1901, 160 scientists have received the award, only four were women: Marie Curie in 1911 (Nobelprize.org, 1911), Irène Joliot-Curie in 1935, Dorothy Crowfoot Hodgkin in 1964) and Ada E. Yonath in 2009. The Nobel Prize in Physics has been awarded 104 times to 189 laureates, and of these, the only two women laureates are Marie Curie in 1903 (Nobelprize.org, 1903) and Maria Goeppert Mayer in 1963 (Nobelprize.org, 1963). The corresponding number of laureates who have been awarded prizes in physiology or medicine is 196 (for 101 times) with eight women. Only 2.5% of Nobel Prize recipients in the natural sciences or medicine are women, which is a low number that at the same time announces who might be predestined for a career and accolades in science and who might not.

The laureates' autobiographies are posted on the official Nobel Prize (Nobelprize.org, 2011) web site. Starting in the late 1970s to an increasingly larger

M.-H. Chiu, P. J. Gilmer, and D. F. Treagust (Eds.), Celebrating the 100th Anniversary of Madame Marie Sklodowska Curie's Nobel Prize in Chemistry. 191–204.

extent these biographies have been written by the laureates themselves, giving a broader and more personal picture of the scientist and her/his achievements, than the descriptions given of earlier awardees. It is somewhat striking when reading the autobiographies of the female scientists who received the Nobel Prize before the 1970s, how these biographical essays differ from those of male awardees. For example, Marie Curie (Nobelprize.org, 1903) is described as being in possession of personal characteristics such as "quiet, dignified and unassuming," characteristics that are not value neutral and are absent in the biographies of men. Another example is Maria Goeppert Mayer, Nobel laureate in Physics in 1963. Her biography states:

> She is deeply indebted to Max Born, for his kind guidance of her scientific education. ...

> She was also employed by the Argonne National Laboratory with very little knowledge of Nuclear Physics! It took her some time to find her way in this, for her, new field. But in the atmosphere of Chicago, it was rather easy to learn nuclear physics. She owes a great deal to very many discussions with Edward Teller, and in particular with Enrico Fermi, who was always patient and helpful. (Nobel Lectures, *Physics 1963–1970*, 1972)

Such quotes convey a picture that women succeed in research because of patient and helpful men, and diminish women's work and achievements with expressions such as "it was rather easy to learn nuclear physics."

Some of the autobiographies written by the female laureates present a personal insight into the struggles of being a woman in academia with a desire and commitment to science. Rosalyn Yalow shared the 1977 Nobel Prize in Physiology or Medicine for the development of the radioimmunoassay (RIA) technique, powerful for detection of peptide hormones. In her autobiography she described how a part time position as a secretary to a leading biochemist, provided her an entrée into graduate courses, although she had to enroll in stenography. She studied physics and received A's in two of her physics courses: an A in Optics and an A⁻ in the associated laboratory. When the Chairman of the Physics Department reviewed her record, he commented, "That A⁻ confirms that women do not do well at laboratory work."

What about academia? Is the picture that appears above balanced by a more equal distribution of women and men in academic positions today, *e.g.,* professors in science generally, and in chemistry specifically? We provide two snapshots, one from Europe, using Sweden as an example, and one from the USA. Sweden has a reputation as one of the most gender equitable countries in the world. Equality is a social aim influencing the society, through formal structures such as the Equal Opportunity Act (Swedish Code of Statutes, 1991, p. 433). Public as well as private work places are obliged to comply with the laws stated in the act. These laws influence policies impacting preschool to higher education, in both the Education Act (Swedish Code of Statutes, 1985, p. 1100) and in the national curriculum. In spite of these laws and policies, this same Swedish labor market is highly divided between the sexes, and academia reflects this pattern. In 2009, female professors in natural sciences at the five biggest universities ranged between 8.6 and 22%, and the prediction is that during the coming years the proportion of women professors will decrease (Swedish National Agency for Higher Education, 2011). The participation of women in academic chemistry follows a similar trend. In Swedish chemistry doctoral programs, there is an equal distribution among female and male students, while in undergraduate education female students comprise about 60%. For the last 15 years, these percentages have remained consistent. But the proportion of women in positions as senior lecturers and professors decreases. The more prestigious the position, the fewer the number of women.

In 1972, the US government established Title IX Act states,

> No person in the United States shall, on the basis of sex, be excluded from participation in, be denied the benefits of, or be subjected to discrimination under any education program or activity receiving Federal financial assistance (U.S. Department of Labor, 1972, p. 1).

While the act has primarily been used to ensure women and girls equal access to education opportunities in the US, Government Accounting Office (2004) noted that the four key STEM (Science, Technology, Engineering, and Mathematics) funding agencies (Department of Education (Education), the Department of Energy (Energy), the National Aeronautics and Space Administration (NASA), and the National Science Foundation (NSF)) did not complete any monitoring activities as per Title IX requirements. Moreover, the agencies investigated complaints and provided assistance for grantees to comply with the Title IX act, only Education conducted reviews to ascertain if universities and grantees adhered to the act. Further investigation found that many scientists and engineers had the perception that Title IX dealt with providing persons equal access to sports, and did not understand that the act covered all education programs.

The NSF produces a yearly report on the status of women, minorities and persons with disabilities in science and engineering, but the specific data regarding chemistry is not accessible as it is reported as physical sciences. However, Corbett, Hill, & St. Rose (2008) conducted further analysis and in 2006, women attained 52% of undergraduate chemistry degrees and 34% of the doctoral degrees in chemistry. Nelson and Bremmer (2010) conducted a study that examined the participation of women in the top 50 departments chemistry departments. In 2007, in the same year, 21% of assistant, 20% of associate and 10% of full professors were women. Chemistry departments had a low utilization of women in assistant professor positions compared with the 'pipeline' of women with doctoral degrees in chemistry. A major concern with the image of chemistry is that its image is becoming increasingly diversified at the undergraduate and graduate levels but the upper echelons remain mainly male and white (Nelson & Bremmer, 2010). Further, 33% of the professionals in chemistry and materials science[1] and 13% of chemical engineers were female.

In recent years Swedish policymakers have promoted research within science, technology and medicine through targeted funding to "centers of excellence." The Council for Gender Equality in Higher Education has recently evaluated these targeted efforts. The report, *"His Excellency: About billion investments in strong research environments"* concluded that the targeted research investments have systematically disadvantaged women scientists, *e.g.* top qualified women are screened out in the application process and over time an estimated one billion Swedish crowns (about 160 million USD) of research funds have transferred from women to men (Sandström, Wold, Jordansson, Ohlsson, & Smedberg, 2010). Thus, fiscal resources are transferred from many researchers to a small, predominantly male, group. Often these researchers cannot spend the grants received which accumulates fiscal resources within their research groups and universities, rather than being disbursed to other researchers.

Moreover, the report questioned whether the excellence efforts are worth the price as the scientific quality and productivity declined in the vast majority of research groups that received the grants. The conclusion was that "In fact, there is no scientific support for the large and costly experiment that not only the Swedish government, but much of the western world, embarked on" (Sandström, et. al., 2010, p. 103, translated from Swedish by Hussenius).

In the United States, funding agencies have also moved towards funding collaborative grants involving multiple researchers at different career stages. No systemic review has been conducted; but men submit the majority of these large grants. Further disparity between women and men may occur in the US STEM research funding stream because larger grants are more likely awarded to research and higher ranked institutions where women are less likely to work (Hosek, Cox, Ghosh-Dastidar, Kofner, Ramphal, Scott, & Berry, 2005).

Printed Source of Chemistry's Image

Looking at advertisements for higher education in chemistry and other natural sciences provides an idea of what image is held by and what kind of message is conveyed and disseminated by academia and society today. In a recent study, Salminen-Karlsson (2009) investigated higher education's promotional materials, to see if the way different educational programs described themselves produced differences in recruiting students. She compared programs within two areas, caring professions and technical education as a number of projects have started recently in attempts to recruit more students of the underrepresented sex. Salminen-Karlsson (2009) found that in the university education brochures different words are used for similar phenomena. These different ways to depict programs, or abilities associated with the future profession, follow society's perceptions of feminine and masculine traits and stereotypes. For example, girls are responsible and boys seek excitement and, women are content to do a good job that is easier while men make a career because of their expert skills and ability to express their ideas. The descriptions of caring profession educations include words and expressions with a feminine connotation and *vice versa*. In this way gender stereotypes and expectations are cemented and reconstructed.

In the spring 2011 the image of a full-page advertisement for chemistry education at a Swedish university was as follows: A picture dominates the page. In the middle of the picture, is a young man wearing a white lab coat and with untidy hair in an *Einstein-like* manner. He is the subject of the picture, looking straight into the camera, straight into the eyes of the observers. He holds an Erlenmeyer flask containing a blue liquid. In front of him is a lab trolley with chemistry equipment; pipettes, round bottomed, volumetric and Erlenmeyer flasks, tripods and racks. All flasks containing colorful liquids of which some are bubbling and fuming. What is mediated is something that has a taste of a juggler's tricks, e.g., what Edgeworth already in 1811 stated as something that should be avoided. This deep-rooted image of a chemist is an image that is found again and again in a variety of situations and contexts. But that is not all. In the advertisement, the young man, dressed in a lab coat is surrounded by five attractive, women dressed as flight attendants in suits and wearing high-heeled shoes. In the background is also a man dressed as a flight attendant. All are looking at the "chemist" with admiration in their eyes. The text beneath the picture says that you will get a flying start to your career by studying chemistry at the university.

Where does the image of the chemists come? The image of a mad, male scientist surrounded by flasks with colored liquids, boiling, bubbling and fuming. One should note that the 21st century scientist is no longer pictured by himself (sic) but has a cadre of admirers. The image itself is not new, but in an historical retrospective very similar to two apparitions specifically: the witches and alchemists. The view of witches is closely connected to herbalism, which is a traditional folk medicine practice that uses plants and plant extracts to treat and cure diseases and ailments. Such medical practices have occurred since Egyptian time ~3000 BC. The oldest written source is papyrus rolls such as the Ebers Papyrus from about 1550 BC, which is the most important one from a medical perspective. It contains about 800 prescriptions and mentions more than 700 domestic and foreign drugs (Göthberg 1982). At that time, physicians prepared concoctions and pastes of different textures as well as pills, ointments and plasters. The equipment they used was very similar to modern day tools: mortars with pistils, mills to crush the drugs, sieves, crucibles and scales, glass bottles or pots of earthenware stored the drugs.

In the Middle Ages, the power of the evil mastered people's imagination, and the devil and his witches were the origin of disease and death. In several old churches from the 15th century are paintings of witches stirring in their pots. The ceiling paintings in churches were the bible for the illiterates, showing how people could be protected from the evil powers. There was also the evil itself illustrated and you could see what happened to the poor sinner. Those who were found guilty of witchcraft were severely punished and witch trials and burnings at the stake occurred until the late 18th century. The climax was reached in the middle of the 17th century when a wave of witchcraft trials went through Europe and New England. Although a witch in principle may also be a man, in 78% of trials the accused was a woman (Reis, 2003).

During the early Middle Ages, the cultivation of medicinal plants occurred mainly in monasteries. Monks and nuns engaged in health care and used knowledge from traditional folk medicine. The clergy had the literacy skills to preserve and disseminate this knowledge. But, this same knowledge among country people became a severe risk factor during the witch trials, and people with knowledge of herbal medicine were often suspected of witchcraft and sentenced to burn at the stake. Most often women, so-called wise old female quacks who cured the peasants in the countryside with a mixture of superstition and knowledge of herbs and their medicinal properties, died because of their knowledge and skills.

Alchemy's roots lie in Hellenistic Egypt built from a mixture of practical knowledge about metallurgy, pharmacy and glass making combined with the philosophical practice of analyzing and theorizing about the world. The alchemists searched for nature's secret quinta essentia, which would give people the ability to transform base metals into gold. During the Middle Ages, unlike witches who were female, alchemy as a profession had high status and its practitioners were men.

Even today, the stereotypical image of a chemist continues to be an elderly man with an unkempt appearance and surrounded by flasks, bearing great similarities to ancient times' images of witches and alchemists. Is this a surprising and totally wrong image? A very important and fundamental aspect of chemical activities is the engagement with experiments. And it is not just media and society around us that conveys the stereotyped image of the chemist; it is conveyed again and again by chemists themselves. It is also the image often presented by chemistry students when they participate in different types of recruiting activities to attract young people to choose the same education, career and future as themselves. The image shows what many of us perceive as the essence of our work: the work in a laboratory. The problem is perhaps that chemistry activities are much more diverse than this image. The picture is simplified and in a way an unfair image is not attracting young people today. A question that rises then is how do we want the chemist of today to be presented, in a credible manner without being nerdy/geeky and stereotyping?

The Chemist as a Poisoner

Although not chemistry's most favorable image, historically (and still to this day) using poison to kill a person was regarded as one of the more sophisticated murder methods. In antiquity and middle ages, princes and lords did not feel safe from one meal to another, as placing poison in food was common. At that time professional poisoners existed and acted, and they also constituted a historic link to the image of the chemist.

Socrates was forced to drink the poisoned cup containing probably the juice of hemlock, mixed with opium and wine in 399 BC. According to Pliny this mixture was the Greeks' means to execute convicted criminals. The active component of hemlock, conine, has a sedative, analgesic and antispasmodic effect. Six to eight fresh leaves of hemlock can kill an adult. After drinking hemlock a person would suffer a paralysis starting in the feet. The body temperature drops, skin discoloration occurs, and death is caused by respiratory paralysis. The poisoned person is conscious until death. The execution of Socrates is a real event, but you also find the use of poison in the literature such as in Shakespeare's plays: Hamlet, Romeo and Juliet, or for example Macbeth in which the witches cook a strange brew of toxic herbs and other satanic ingredients. The portrayal of the three witches and their brew reflects the ingredients that people assumed were used.

Arsenic toxicity was known before Christ, and used during 1400's and 1500's by the families interested in attaining and keeping power and privilege such as the Borgias. Catherine de' Medici tried to murder Henry of Navarre by wetting book pages with arsenic acid, so that the unsuspecting Henry, when he licked his finger to turn the book pages, was gradually poisoned. This technique of administering poison was used in Eco's (1983) novel *The Name of the Rose*. Dorothy Sayers, Agatha Christie and Maria Lang are women writers who made great use of poison as a murder weapon in their crime fictions. In particular, Agatha Christie published some 80 detective novels and in more than half, poison was the method to murder people. Twenty-five of Christie's books have a female killer and 22 of them used poison. She showed a great knowledge in the variety and diversity of toxins used. Christie was a trained nurse and in the beginning of World War I she worked as such, but from 1916 on, she was responsible for pharmacy and medicine distribution. And again she worked in a pharmacy during the World War II, which is where she most likely acquired her knowledge of poisons.

Utilizing chemistry to identify a murderer is often the theme of the plethora of television crime shows that foreground the use of forensic science, and in particular, chemistry. The popularity of these shows can attract and renew students' interest in the subject. Universities with forensic science programs in their chemistry degrees recruit more students than other programs. Knowledge of chemistry may produce a poisoner, or the person who provides the evidence to identify a criminal.

Female Chemistry Role Models

In school chemistry textbooks, males dominate the images and text. Marie Curie is often the only female scientist mentioned (see below). Today, feminist historians and philosophers have increased our knowledge of the history of female scientists. Yet many of these women are still unknown to a broader population. Moreover, in recent decades most Western countries have invested human and fiscal resources into science, engineering and technology. A key assumption from policymakers and stakeholders is that women would choose science if they only understood how exciting and interesting the subject is. One strategy to achieve this goal is to include female scientists as role models in textbooks. Although the number of female Nobel laureates is low, Marie Curie is not the only example. Several of the physiology or medicine prizewinners are chemists and could be used to illustrate the close connection between biochemistry and medical improvements. For example, Gerty Theresa Cori (Nobelprize.org, 1947) a biochemist received the Nobel Prize in Physiology or Medicine in 1947 for the discovery of the steps in the catalytic conversion of glycogen. Gertrude B. Elion's research produced important principles for drug treatment and development of medicines for treatment of diseases such as leukemia, anemia, hepatitis, rheumatoid arthritis and herpes, and to prevent rejection of transplanted organs. When Elion received the Nobel Prize in Physiology or Medicine in 1988 a colleague commented to her that she had done more for the humanity than Mother Teresa (McGrayne, 1993).

Other women's contribution to chemistry could modify the discipline's masculine image. Historically Mary Somerville (1780–1872; cited in Neely, 2001) is one of the few female scientists recognized in her lifetime by science societies. Although she could not participate in the institutions' events, Somerville received one of Britain's first state pensions for scientific activity. That a similar sum was awarded Michael Faraday was an indication of her reputation. Somerville wrote several science books that became widely used by the universities, yet neither she nor her daughters were permitted to study there. In Somerville's 1834 book, *On the connexion of the physical sciences* she dedicated her book to women of her country, and no doubt she had a strong opinion of women's intelligence, an opinion that may have been strengthened by the researchers, such as Faraday with whom she socialized. His interest in chemistry was originally inspired by the book of Somerville's friend Jane Marcet called *Conversations on Chemistry* which became a bestseller when published anonymously in 1806 (Neely, 2001). Another reason for scientific women's invisibility is that they, like Jane Marcet, had to anonymously publish their scientific work. It was undignified for a woman to publish under her own name. And several male scientists who received recognition for their discoveries worked closely with their wives, sisters or other female relatives or friends. Men have had access to the academic arena, where women have been banned. Mary Somerville never became a member of the Royal Society, and was an exception as she signed her books with her own name. Somerville's husband was not a scientist but could enter the science society's institutions. He borrowed books from the science library and he introduced her to researchers that he, but not she, could meet at the institutions (Neely, 2001). If Somerville had been married to an eminent scientist, her work would have probably merged with her husband's and presented as his work. That was the usual story, with examples of a famous male scientist with a publicly unknown wife include Albert Einstein and his first wife Mileva Maric, Antoine Lavoisier and Mari-Anne Paultze, and Louis Pasteur and Marie Laurent.

Historical examples of female chemists can often broaden the stereotypic image of a chemist and the work that characterizes chemistry. The historical canon includes the story of the brilliant, lonely man who has contributed to major scientific discoveries, and paradigms shifts (Harding, 1986). This image of a natural scientist as a genius may have an exclusive function in the sense that there is a hidden message stating that not everyone can or should engage in such activities. An extraordinary talent is needed and teachers conveyed implicitly or perhaps even explicitly this message (Lemke, 1990). In the biography of Barbara McClintock and her genetic research, Keller (1983) showed that objectivity and rationality could be complemented with sympathetic understanding and emotional commitment to provide a fuller description of natural science. Researchers like McClintock and Einstein pointed to the importance of *letting the material speak to you*. They argued that it was easier to make discoveries if you became part of the system rather than being an observer from outside, that is, you need to *feel for the organism* (Keller, 1996).

The role of vision in her (Barbara McClintock's) experimental work provides the key to her understanding. What for others is interpretation, or speculation, for her is a matter of trained and direct perception. McClintock has pushed her special blend of observational and cognitive skills so far that few can follow her. She herself cannot quite say how she knows what she knows. She talks about the limits of verbally explicit reasoning; she stresses the importance of her feeling for the organism in terms that sound like those of mysticism. But like all good mystics, she insists on the utmost critical rigor, and, like all good scientists, her understanding emerges from a thorough absorption in, even identification with, her material. (Keller, 1983, xxi–xxii)

Like McClintock pointed out the necessity of "feeling for the organism," in order to change the image of chemistry, chemists could acknowledge the emotional aspect of their research and laboratory work and the connection that occurs between the researcher and her (sic) tools - the instruments, equipment, and chemicals, that provide the pathway to discovering new knowledge. There are chemists who are very skilled using certain instruments. The equipment becomes an extension of their bodies and is perceived almost as embodied, but the chemists have developed their skills such that the practical aspect of the subject is as important as the outcome of the handicraft. This image of the chemist may be perceived as equally nerdy as the common stereotypical view. However, compare the image of a chemist using her tools to produce knowledge with an artist, a painter. For a painter, the painting in itself is certainly a driving force and not just the idea of the finished painting. S/he would also have a strong emotional connection with the process and the material medium to produce the painting. Chemists can experience a similar emotional feeling with laboratory work, a feeling where the material speaks to, with and through the chemist.

Representation of Chemistry in Textbooks

Another aspect of the image of chemistry is the way the subject is presented in textbooks. For over 50 years, researchers have studied the pictorial and written representation of scientists/chemists in all forms of textual materials and also asked students their perceptions of scientists through verbal and pictorial representations (Chambers, 1983; Mead & Metreaux, 1957). In a study of 10 Turkish middle school and 10 chemistry books, Kahveci (2010) found that in the high school chemistry textbooks, males dominated the images and text and Marie Curie was the only female scientist mentioned. Turkey supports textbook adoption, thus teachers would have to introduce other materials to counteract the masculine image of chemistry. Similarly a study of lower secondary science textbooks used in Brunei noted that males were overrepresented compared to females in the images and diagrams (Elgar, 2004). More recent studies suggested that the stereotypic images of a chemist as white and male have a negative impact on girls' attitudes and achievement. But when girls are presented with a counter image of a chemist during science lessons their science anxiety decreased and achievement increased. So teachers may consider counteracting the stereotypic image of a chemist by introducing photographs and other textual materials that highlight women in the discipline (Good, Woodzicka, & Wingfield, 2010). Researchers have also suggested that making explicit connections of chemical concepts to the 'real world' and 'authentic events' is another approach to changing students' image of chemistry from a subject that is done by eccentric white men wearing white laboratory coats, to a discipline that is important to humans, their environment and the worlds they live in (Glaser & Carson, 2005). The modification of textbooks has included information about 'chemistry in action' that is presented in a framed box with the text, or 'boxed essays.' However, if used as an authentic learning task, on-line resources such as *Chemistry is in the News* can provide students the opportunity to expand their image of chemistry and chemists. Younger students may develop their perceptions of scientists through trade books that are often used to teach science in elementary school. These text sources also reinforce the stereotype of the scientist as male, white and dedicated to his work (Ford, 2006). Texts often portray the scientist in a heroic stereotype--a white male that is incredibly smart, and *if* a female then an additional characteristic is she is hardworking (Milne, 1998).

Students' Attitudes Towards Chemistry/Science

There are few studies directly examining students' attitudes towards chemistry. In 2006, PISA (OCED, 2009) noted that while 93% of students viewed science as important to their lives, only 57% saw it as relevant. Students' interest in science declines throughout schooling but when this is examined at the discipline level students' interest in chemistry declines more than for biology, and this is particularly true for girls (Krapp & Prenzel, 2011). A recent study in England and Wales found that when asked if chemistry was a favorite lesson, 85% of 11-year olds said yes, 75% of 14-year olds and 65% of 16-year olds also agreed with the statement. The authors concluded that the students enjoyed the practical work associated with chemistry. While, chemistry started with a higher popularity than biology or physics with 11-years olds, there is a significant decline in students' interest in the subject between ages 11–14 and more than boys are interested in the subject. Girls were more likely than boys to report that they saw little relevance of chemistry to their lives (Bennet & Hogarth, 2009). A similar pattern held for 79 American high school students, while there were no significant differences between girls and boys liking of biology, there was a significant difference in 'liking chemistry'. Boys reported higher preference to study chemistry than girls (Miller, Slawinski Blessing, & Schwartz, 2006).

In her study of German ninth graders, Nieswandt (2006) examined their attitudes towards chemistry as a discipline, not how the students experienced the subject in a class. The students were surveyed, and reliabilities for the scales ranged from .70 and .83. Students who had a positive perception of their success in chemistry along with a strong interest in chemistry had a deeper conceptual understanding of the subject. Another attitude survey instrument was developed to examine Greek students' difficulty (6 items), interest (9 items), usefulness of chemistry course (3 items), and importance of chemistry (5 items) (Salta & Tzougraki, 2004). Given to eleventh graders, students answered questions on a five-point Likert scale. The subscales had the following reliabilities: difficulty (0.87), interest (0.89), usefulness (0.71), importance (0.61). The sample had 576 students who were enrolled in one of three categorizations: 1) science-medicine, 2) humanities and 3) engineering. At the college/university level, Dalgety, Coll & Jones (2003) developed *Chemistry Attitudes and Experiences Questionnaire* (CAEQ) to measure first-year university chemistry students' attitude toward chemistry, chemistry self-efficacy, and learning experiences. The authors modified questions from previous attitudinal scales such as TOSRA (Fraser, 1978) and College Biology Self-efficacy Instrument (CBSEI) (Baldwin, Ebert-May, & Burns, 1999). The resultant instrument had three scales (attitude toward chemistry, chemistry self-efficacy, and learning experiences), with five subscales contributing to attitude toward chemistry. Those five subscales are attitude toward chemists, skills of chemists, attitude toward the role of chemistry in society, leisure interest in chemistry and career interest in chemistry. The attitude towards chemistry subscales' reliability ranged from 0.72-0.93. The self-efficacy scale has a reliability of 0.96. The learning experiences scale was comprised of four subscales: lecture learning experiences, tutorial and tutor learning experiences, practical learning experiences, and demonstrator learning experiences whose reliability ranged from 0.84 to 0.90. Overall the CAEQ had an average reliability of 0.74. One study, by Dalgety and Coll (2006) utilized the CAEQ and found that students intending to enroll in a second year of chemistry have a significantly more positive attitude towards chemists and leisure interest in chemistry compared with students who did not plan to continue with chemistry. The students planning a second year also had higher mean scores on the self-efficacy scale. Students dropped out of chemistry during their first year, but there were no students who picked up the subject. Although programs of study required some first year students to study chemistry, these students were as likely as their peers who chose to study chemistry to indicate that they would enroll in a second year of the subject.

There is a gap in the research on students' attitudes towards chemistry and science. Increasingly, Western countries are becoming ethnically and racially diverse. While there are equal numbers of girls and boys engaged in chemistry at the high school level, the field has not examined participation patterns from a racial perspective. White students remain the dominant group in chemistry. Moreover, with the recommendations that teachers provide students the 'real-world' applications for chemistry these examples should be provided in a socio-cultural context. Recent studies have examined students' perceptions of scientists and scientific practices but that work focused on biology, a discipline that has for several decades has attracted and retained students' interest.

FEMINIST/GENDER STUDIES AND CHEMISTRY

The image of chemistry remains male, and those who practice the discipline, especially at its highest ranks remain largely male and white. In contrast to mathematics, physics and biology, there are very few feminist critiques of chemistry either from feminists from within the discipline or from those who offer critiques from a standpoint perspective. In a recent autobiographical book, several women chemists described their experiences as chemists and chemistry educators in the USA. Gilmer (2010) and Lewis (2010) both used the wind as a metaphor to describe their experiences as chemists. For Gilmer, the wind in her face was stimulating but also represented the men who acted as obstacles and obstructions to her academic career in chemistry. While Lewis viewed the wind metaphor as wind in her back, something that helped propel her forward and change her direction away from that of a scientist who was a role model for younger students interested in science because she now is a science educator and collects data from people and not molecules.

Over a decade ago in the USA, a group of senior women chemists and chemical engineers formed COACh (Committee on the Advancement of Women Chemists, n. d.) because of their "common concern about the gender-based obstacles women scientists face in trying to attain their career goals." The group has developed workshops to provide female chemists with professional skills, established networks and mentoring programs and conducted research on the barriers to female chemists' careers. This comprehensive and extensive effort to change and challenge the image of chemistry in the United States from male and white could also benefit from feminists outside of the discipline to engage in the theoretical work to understand why the image of scientist remains stereotypically a chemist… a chemist who is male, white, with unruly hair and very heroic.

NOTES

[1] Data are reported as combined, that is chemistry and materials science.

REFERENCES

Baldwin, J., Ebert-May, D., & Burns, D. (1999). The development of a college biology self-efficacy instrument for nonmajors. *Science Education, 83*, 397–408.

Bennett, J., & Hogarth, S. (2009). Would you want to talk to a scientist at a party? High school students' attitudes to school science and to science. *International Journal of Science Education, 31*, 1975–1998.

Chambers, D. W. (1983). Stereotypic images of the scientist: The Draw-A-Scientist Test. *Science Education, 67*, 255–265.

Committee on the Advancement of Women Chemists (n.d.). Retrieved from http://coach.uoregon.edu/

Corbett, C., Hill, C., & St. Rose, A. (2008). *Where the girls are: The facts about gender equity in education*. Washington, DC: AAUW.

Dalgety, J., & Coll, R. (2006). The influence of first-year chemistry students' learning experiences on their educational choices, *Assessment & Evaluation in Higher Education, 31*(3), 303–328.

Dalgety, J., Coll, R., & Jones, A. (2003). Development of chemistry attitudes and experiences questionnaire (CAEQ), *Journal of Research in Science Teaching, 40*(7), 649–668.

Eco, U. (1983). *The name of the rose*. London: Everyman.

Edgeworth, M. (1795). *Letters for literary ladies*. London: Everyman.

Education Act (1985). Swedish code of statutes, Svensk författningssamling, 1100. Skollagen.

Elgar, A. G. (2004). Science textbooks for lower secondary schools in Brunei: Issues of gender equity. *International Journal of Science Education, 26*(7), 875–894.

Equal Opportunity Act. (1991). Swedish code of statutes, Svensk författningssamling, 433. Jämställdhetslagen.

Ford, D. (2006). Representations of science within children's trade books. *Journal of Research in Science Teaching, 43*(2), 214–235.

Fraser, B. J. (1978). Development of a test of science-related attitudes. *Science Education, 62,* 509–515.

Gilmer, P. (2010). Going upwind in chemistry. In K. Scantlebury, J. B., Kahle, & S. Martin (Eds.), *Re-visioning science education from feminist perspectives: Challenges, choices and careers* (pp. 69–78). New York: Sense Publishers.

Glaser, R., & Carson, K. (2005). Chemistry is in the news: Taxonomy of authentic news media-based learning activities. *International Journal of Science Education, 27*(9), 1083–1098.

Good, J., Woodzicka, J., & Wingfield, L. (2010). The effects of gender stereotypic and counter-stereotypic textbook images on science performance. *The Journal of Social Psychology, 150*(2), 132–147.

Göthberg, G. (1982). Växterna i läkekonstens historia. In Lindeberg, I., Gustafsson, O., Hellströ, S., Johansson, U., Järnebrand, M., Larsson, L.-G., Löfveberg, S., Pagoldh, S., von Sivers, C., Säthersten, S. & Wahlsten, N. (Eds.), *Örtmedicin och växtmagi* (pp. 12–42). Spain: Anfang Förlag.

Harding, S. (1986). *The science question in feminism.* Ithaca, NY: Cornell University Press.

Hosek, S. D., Cox, A. G., Ghosh-Dastidar, B., Kofner, A., Ramphal, N. R., Scott, J., & Berry, S. (2005). *Gender differences in major federal external grant programs.* Arlington, VA: RAND Corporation.

Kahveci, A. (2010). Quantitative analysis of science and chemistry textbooks for indicators of reform: A complementary perspective. *International Journal of Science Education, 32,* 1495–1519.

Keller, E. F. (1983). *A feeling for the organism.* New York: W. H. Freeman.

Krapp, A., & Prenzel. M. (2011). Research on interest in science: Theories, methods, and findings. *International Journal of Science Education, 33*(1), 27–50.

Lemke, J. L. (1990). *Talking science.* Westport, CT: Greenwood Publishing Group.

Lewis, J. (2010). Whistling for a wind. In K. Scantlebury, J. B., Kahle, & S. Martin (Eds.), *Re-visioning science education from feminist perspectives: Challenges, choices and careers* (pp. 79–88). New York: Sense Publishers.

McGrayne, S. B. (1993). *Nobel Prize women in science. Their lives, struggles, and momentous discoveries.* New York: Birch Lane Press.

Mead, M., & Metraux, R. (1957). Image of the scientist among high-school students: A pilot study. *Science, 126,* 384–390.

Miller, P., Slawinski Blessing, J., & Schwartz, S. (2006). Gender differences in high-school students' views about science. *International Journal of Science Education, 28*(4), 363–381.

Milne, C. (1998). Philosophically correct science stories? Examining the implications of heroic science stories for school science. *Journal of Research in Science Teaching, 35,* 175–187.

Neely, K. A. (2001). *Mary Somerville: Science, illumination and the female mind.* Cambridge: Cambridge University Press.

Nelson, D. J., & Bremmer, C. (2010). *A national analysis of diversity in science and engineering faculties at research universities.* Retrieved from http://chem.ou.edu/~djn/diversity/Faculty_Tables_FY07/07Report.pdf.

Nieswandt, M. (2006). Student affect and conceptual understanding in learning chemistry. *Journal of Research in Science Teaching. 44,* 908–937.

Nobel Lectures (1972), *Physics 1963–1970,* Elsevier Publishing Company, Amsterdam, 1972. Retrieved from Maria Goeppert Mayer - Biography. http://nobelprize.org/nobel_prizes/physics/laureates/1963/mayer.html

Nobelprize.org (1903). *Marie Curie, nèe Sklodowska.* Retrieved from http://nobelprize.org/nobel_prizes/physics/laureates/1903/marie-curie.html

Nobelprize.org (1911). *Marie Curie.* Retrieved from http://nobelprize.org/nobel_prizes/chemistry/laureates/1911/b

Nobelprize.org (1947). *Theresa Cori Gerty, nèe Radnitz.* Retrieved from http://nobelprize.org/nobel_prizes/medicine/laureates/1947/cori-gt.html

Nobelprize.org (1963) *Maria Goeppert Mayer.* Retrieved from http://www.nobelprize.org/nobel_prizes/physics/laureates/1963/mayer.html

Nobelprize.org (2011). Nobelprize.org – All about the Nobel Prize awarded achievements. Retrieved from http://nobelprize.org

Organization for Economic Cooperation and Development (OECD) (2009). *Equally prepared for life? How 15-year-old boys and girls perform in school.* Retrieved from http://www.pisa.oecd.org/dataoecd/59/50/42843625.pdf

Reis, E. (2003). Confess or deny? What's a "witch" to do? *OAH Magazine of History, 17*(4), 11–15.

Salminen-Karlsson, M. (2009). *Att välja utbildning utan innehåll – gymnasisters värderingar av utbildningskatalogernas reklamfraser* [Choosing education without a content – upper secondary school students' values of advertising phrases in university education information catalogs]. Resultatdiaologen 2009, Swedish Research Council.

Salta, K., & Tzougraki, C. (2004). Attitudes toward chemistry among 11th grade students in high schools in Greece. *Science Education, 88*(4), 535–547.

Sandström, U., Wold, A., Jordansson, B., Ohlsson, B. & Smedberg, Å. (2010). *Hans Excellens: om miljardsatsningarna på starka forskningsmiljöer* [His Excellence: About billion investments in strong research environments]. Council for Gender Equality in Higher Education. Stockholm, Sweden.

Sommerville, M. (1834). *On the connexion of the physical sciences.* John Murray: England.

Swedish National Agency for Higher Education (2011). *Forskarkarriär för både kvinnor och män? – statistisk uppföljning och kunskapsöversikt,* [Research career for both women and men? – statistical follow-up and knowledge review] Report 2011:6 R

U.S. Department of Labor (1972). *Title IX of the Education Amendments of 1972.* Washington, DC: Author.

U.S. Government Accountability Office. (2004). W*omen's participation in the sciences has increased, but agencies need to do more to ensure compliance with Title IX* (GAO-04–639). Washington, DC: Author.

Anita Hussenius
Center for Gender Research
Uppsala University
anita.hussenius@gender.uu.se

Kathryn Scantlebury
Department of Chemistry and Biochemistry
University of Delaware
kscantle@udel.edu

PNINA G. ABIR-AM

10. MME CURIE'S 2011 CENTENNIAL AND THE PUBLIC DEBATE ON THE UNDERREPRESENTATION OF WOMEN IN SCIENCE

Lessons from the History of Science

INTRODUCTION

During the calendar year 2011 the scientific community, science literati, women scientists, historians, and various others in the world-at-large celebrate the centennial (100th anniversary) of Mme Marie Curie's (1867–1934) Nobel Prize in Chemistry (Nobelprize.org, 1911), awarded to her in 1911 in recognition for her discovery of the new elements—radium and polonium—and study of the properties of radium in compounds. The 1911 Nobel Prize was as a sole award, reaffirming her share in the 1903 Nobel Prize in Physics (divided between M. Henri Becquerel (1/2), M. Pierre Curie (1/4) and Mme Marie Sklodowska Curie (1/4)) (Nobelprize.org, 1903) and also accepting the greater challenge posed by her interdisciplinary discoveries for the field of chemistry.

The 2011 Centennial is a major event for several converging reasons: first, it marks the recognition of Mme Curie's interpretation of radioactivity as an atomic property—a step that revolutionized our understanding of atoms, the ultimate constituents of matter, as no longer immutable. The phenomenon of radioactivity had been initially observed by Becquerel in 1896 and referred by him as *uranium rays*. Mme Curie's conception of radioactivity as an atomic property left an indelible mark on science, as well as on the history of the 20th century. That conception became the basis for the discovery of artificial radioactivity in 1935 (by Mme Curie's daughter and son-in-law, Irène and Frédéric Joliot-Curie – see chapter by Gilmer, 2011) and of the new field of nuclear chemistry. A decade later, in 1945, the construction and use of the atomic bombs, a technoscientific feat that built upon the concepts of both natural and artificial radioactivity, led to an earlier conclusion of World War II in the Pacific Theater, thus saving the lives of many combatants, both American and Japanese, albeit at the price of so many Japanese civilian casualties (Goldberg, 2000).

Second, the 2011 Centennial of Mme Curie, recognizing the best known woman scientist in the world and the only one widely known in the public realm, outside of science, comes only six years since a yearlong public debate on the underrepresentation of women in science, which unfolded in 2005 and has continued to occasionally erupt well into the present (Abir-Am, 2010).

M.-H. Chiu, P. J. Gilmer, and D. F. Treagust (Eds.), Celebrating the 100th Anniversary of Madame Marie Sklodowska Curie's Nobel Prize in Chemistry. 205–223.

Third, the sheer rarity of a scientist winning twice the much-coveted Nobel Prize ensures that even 100 years later, scientists and the public at large would like to know more about how and why Mme Curie twice received such a rare honor in separate fields of science.[1]

The current Centennial should thus provide a unique opportunity for taking stock of 100 years of changes in the status of science in society, as well as in the status of women in science. In this chapter, I focus on the above mentioned second topic, i.e., how and why the 2011 Centennial of Mme Curie's Nobel Prize in Chemistry can be viewed as a barometer for the public response, within and outside the scientific community, to the ever present issue of the underrepresentation of women in science.

My assessment is based on the *early birds*, i.e., commemorative events held in the first half of 2011. Indeed, the purpose of this chapter, written by an historian of science with expertise in scientific commemorations as a historical and cultural phenomenon, as well as in the history of women in science, is to stimulate a more serious engagement—both inside and outside the scientific community—with a wide range of science policy issues raised by Mme Curie's life in science, issues that still challenge us a century later.

CURIE COMMEMORATIVE EVENT AT AAAS 2011

I start by examining a commemorative event that rose to the challenge of learning lessons from Mme Curie's life in science, namely a symposium at the recent Annual Meeting of American Association for the Advancement of Science (AAAS, 2011a), held in Washington DC between February 17–21, 2011.

The AAAS Program Committee scheduled the symposium, "Celebrating the 100th anniversary of Mme Curie's Nobel Prize in Chemistry" (AAAS, 2011b), in an ideal time slot, on the first full-day of the meeting. This fortunate timing and spacing, in addition to the topic that combines the best known woman scientist with the science and history of the Nobel Prize, ensured that the session was well patronized, almost to capacity (~160), including both women and men attendees. The latter deserve to be mentioned because men rarely attend topics focused on women scientists; no doubt the Nobel Prize has such a great appeal to men that they overcame their reticence from *women's topics*.

Co-sponsored by AAAS Sections C (Chemistry; AAAS, 2011c), and L (History & Philosophy of Science (AAAS, 2011d), this session was co-organized by Professors Penny J. Gilmer of Florida State University (FSU), a biochemist, and leader at FSU of the Alliance for the Advancement of Academic Women in Chemistry and Engineering (AAFAWCE, 2011)—a National Science Foundation (NSF)-ADVANCE-PAID grant, part of a consortium of five Florida universities that engages in advancing the professional status of academic women chemists, physicists, and engineers—and Alan J. Rocke of Case Western Reserve University, a historian of European chemistry, and outgoing Chair of Section L who also chaired the session and introduced the speakers. Lemonick (2011) provided e-coverage of this symposium.

The first speaker, Patricia Ann Baisden (2011)—a nuclear chemist at the Lawrence Livermore National Laboratory (LLNL), a government-owned, national facility but managed by the University of California and four industrial contractors—discussed Mme Curie's experimental procedures in discovering two new radioactive elements, radium and polonium, with amazingly detailed graphics. Baisden displayed many original photographs given to her by a former director of the Radium Institute in Paris, while asking intriguing questions, such as whether Mme Curie had sufficient experimental basis to claim the discovery of polonium when she did (yes, indeed, even by current standards). Baisden's presence further enlightened us on subtle distinctions between nuclear chemists such as herself and radiochemists, both *descendants* of Mme Curie's discoveries, but one branch being more physical and the other more chemical, as befits the progeny of the interdisciplinary field of radioactivity.

The second speaker, historian Julie Des Jardins (2011) of Baruch College/City University of New York spoke on the long-lasting American fascination with Mme Curie, ever since her visits to the US to raise money to purchase radium in 1921 and 1929. She emphasized how Mme Curie's public image as a woman scientist was adjusted to fit gender stereotypes, such as the claim that her science was *maternal* or that she practiced science primarily for the sake of curing cancer. The impact of such a distorted public image on generations of women scientists is further elaborated in Des Jardins' recent book, *The Madame Curie Complex: The Hidden History of Women in Science* (2010), which builds upon the scholarship on women in science in America by historians of science, most notably, Rossiter (1982, 1995), and scientists, most notably Howes and Herzenberg (1999), among others.

My talk, the third and final one (Abir-Am, 2011a), entitled, "Historical perspectives on the public memory of Marie S. Curie—2011, 1911," discussed the concept of commemorative practices in science, the nexus of reinterpretation that they provide while interrogating the present's relationship to the past; the stimulus they provide for conducting new research in history of science; and their potential ramifications for science policy. I began with analyzing new data on the changing international profile of Mme Curie's commemorations throughout the 20th century. Earlier anniversaries were marked only in France and Poland (her adopted and native countries, respectively), culminating with Marie and Pierre Curies' reburials in the Pantheon, the graveyard of great French minds (or as Mona Ozouf (1984) put it jokingly, *L'Ecole Normale des Morts*). This symbolic act made Mme Curie the first woman to be so honored for her own scientific accomplishments, albeit belatedly, coming six decades after her death.

I reflected on the AAAS 2011 symposium in the Newsletter of the History of Science Society (Abir-Am, 2011b).

THE DEBATE THAT WILL NOT GO AWAY

On January 18, 2005, *New York Times* discussed then Harvard President Lawrence Summers' defense of his ideas he had presented four days earlier on innate differences between women and men in science (Dillon, 2005). The text of his speech during a conference on diversity in the labor force, held at the National

Bureau of Economic Research, a think tank in Cambridge, MA is available (Summers, 2005). Summers triggered a large response, with people surprised by the provocation in tone and manner, as former Association of Women in Science Executive Director, Catherine Didion, now with the National Academy of Engineering, noted in the *New York Times* a few days after Summers' delivery (Dillon, 2005). Summers' comments generated international coverage as well, for example, in the *UK Guardian*:

> The president of Harvard University has provoked a furor by arguing that men outperform women in maths and sciences because of biological difference, and discrimination is no longer a career barrier for female academics. (Goldenberg, 2005, p. 1)

A follow-up article in *New York Times* three months later which interviewed M.I.T. faculty member and notable gender scholar Evelyn Fox Keller, called it the debate 'that will not go away' (Dean, 2005). Around that time, I became the principal investigator on a National Science Foundation-Small Grants for Innovative Research (hereafter NSF-SGER), which has examined the public unfolding of this debate from the viewpoints of history and science policy (Abir-Am, 2005–2006).

As its name suggests, the 2005 public debate triggered persistent coverage in the media during and after 2005. The Committee on Maximizing the Potential of Women in Academic Science and Engineering, National Academy of Sciences, National Academy of Engineering and Institute of Medicine (2007) published a comprehensive book that brought to the debate some measure of closure. But it also gave rise to an ongoing literature on this topic, both policy-oriented and academic, well into the present. For example, recent items, including a paper published by Ceci and Williams (2011) on understanding current causes of women's underrepresentation in science was published in time to be mentioned during our symposium at the AAAS 2011 Annual Meeting.

After drawing attention to the recent and recurrent context of the underrepresentation of women in science as a key policy issue pertinent to my AAAS presentation (Abir-Am, 2005–2006), I proceeded to showcase the work of several historians of science whose research helped dispel the gender stereotypes long shrouding Mme Curie's public memory. Such stereotypes included attributing her research in radioactivity to the goal of curing cancer, presumably a more suitable goal for a woman scientist than Mme Curie's other key preoccupations with industry, metrology, and institution building. Hence, I highlighted the recent work of historians of science, which clarified the centrality of Mme Curie's industrial connections (Roque, 1997), her key role in international standardization of units of measurement for radioactivity (aptly named the curie) (Boudia, 2001), and her role as leader of a research school of great social diversity including men and women, and international and French scientists (Davis 1995; Rayner-Canham & Rayner-Canham, 1997; Boudia, 2011).

All these aspects of Mme Curie's actual past have in common one dimension that has long been overlooked, namely her astute exercise of power. Historical research on Mme Curie rarely engaged the role of power in Curie's career, a role that contrasted so much with the patriarchy that existed within and outside of science, which meant that most women were deprived of power, especially formal power.

Only recently historians of science have finally drawn attention to her uses of power as an integral part of her historical persona. The reference here is mainly to the work on Mme Curie as head of a research school (Davis, 1995), her success in having her laboratory accepted as the source of the international standard of a unit of radioactivity, aptly termed the "curie" (Boudia, 2001), and her substantial involvement with the radium industry in both Europe and the US (Roque, 1997).

Some of the many biographical studies of Mme Curie, works that are already well known because they cater to a wider public (Brian, 2005; Dry, 2003; Giroud, 1981; Goldsmith, 2005; Pasachoff, 1996; Pflaum, 1989; Quinn, 1995; Reid, 1974) attempted to go beyond the above-mentioned patriarchal mythology created around Mme Curie since the 1920s, often by expanding upon lesser-known episodes from her life. For example, Giroud's account (1981, 1986) focused on the press coverage of the public scandal that erupted in 1911 around Mme Curie's love relationship with physicist Paul Langevin, thus shedding new light on the private life of a woman scientist best known for her around-the-clock laboratory life. Along these lines, Quinn (1995) drew attention to the collaboration and parallel careers of Curie, mother and daughter (Bensaude-Vincent, 1996).

In my 2011 AAAS presentation, I included a scene from the French film, *Les Palmes de M. Schutz*, directed by Pinoteau (1997), in which Isabelle Huppert played Mme Curie. This was at the same time as the recent death of Greer Garson, who played Mme Curie in the 1943 American film, *Madame Curie*, directed by LeRoy and Lewin (1943) and adapted from Mme Curie's first biography (published by her younger daughter, E. Curie, 1938). Some attendees in our AAAS audience still remembered the unforgettable Greer Garson! A comparison between these two films should be instructive for suggesting how the imagery of a woman scientist has changed over the last half of a century in both French and American cinematographic cultures.

I also drew attention to the pertinence of Mme Curie's work, life, and career for public debates in our own time on the underrepresentation of women in science. Half a dozen or so lessons from her historical case study were offered, including emigration as a condition for pursuing science by women from peripheral countries; diversified collaborative strategies with other scientists, including one's own spouse, so as to preserve the scientific credit—especially for members of disadvantaged groups; and cooperation with industry as a source of financial independence.

I also emphasized how Mme Curie's life also constitutes a resourceful case study in balancing an intense and demanding career with family life, including spouse, children, and relatives in two countries. With the help of a photo portraying Mme Curie and her two young daughters (Figure 1), I drew attention to the exhibition on Curie at the AAAS annual meeting by standing next to the magnified exhibit of the trio's joint photograph. Irène was born in 1897, before Marie's discovery of radium in 1898, and Eve was born in 1904. As I stressed in a humoristic manner to an appreciative audience, this fact remains noteworthy a century later, when the balancing of career and family life by women in science is still considered one of the most challenging parts of women's careers.

The AAAS symposium, which went remarkably well, i.e., without glitches, (except for failing to get the Skype to connect to co-organizer Penny J. Gilmer, then still recovering from an automobile accident, to watch us from afar), seemed to set a precedent for how model sessions should be. With collaboration between symposium co-organizers—a scientist and a historian, a woman and a man (co-organizers Penny Gilmer and Alan Rocke)—it further produced a spectrum of speakers—a scientist, a general historian, and a historian of science.

But the most unexpected and telling experience with our AAAS Symposium was the opportunity to share a petition (Appendix A) with my audience calling upon scientific organizations to practice gender inclusiveness in seeking contributors for the ongoing Curie Centennial (e.g., special issues of scientific magazines and special symposia and lectures). Shortly before our AAAS session took place, I became aware that our symposium might be exceptional in having had an adequate, perhaps even more than adequate, representation of women speakers and organizers. In retrospect, our symposium may have inadvertently existed so as to compensate for a surprisingly low or no presence of women scientists in commemorations of Mme Curie's Centennial by scientific organizations other than AAAS. This remains a telling phenomenon, which deserves some elaboration, especially since it occurred just a few years after the long debate on the underrepresentation of women in science.

OTHER CURIE COMMEMORATIVE EFFORTS IN BOTH THE US AND EUROPE

I examine other commemorative efforts in both the US and Europe that, at least so far, have attempted to engage with the meaning and opportunities afforded by Mme Curie's Centennial in areas such as the public understanding of science, and of science education. However, these efforts failed to engage with the Centennial's pertinence to stimulating new work in the history of science, and especially to addressing the science policy aimed at the persisting issue of the underrepresentation of women in science.

Chemistry International's Centennial Issue for Marie Curie

For example, *Chemistry International* (*CI*), the news magazine of the International Union for Pure and Applied Chemistry - IUPAC) featured no single woman among its four guest-editors for its special issue on the Mme Curie Centennial in January-February 2011. As I put it to the audience at our AAAS Symposium, "By comparison, no anniversary issue honoring Martin Luther King would be published without an African-American guest-editor!" The special issue had eight men and four women authors, numbers that can be viewed as encouraging and not that far from parity. When one examines the contents of the *CI* issue, a clear gender demarcation appears with all the male authors writing on a wide variety of scientific topics, some related to Mme Curie, or to her history. However, none of the four female authors wrote about the science because, intentionally or otherwise, the editors assigned them to *female topics* such as family, traditional female occupations, or women in science.

This relegation of women's topics for the women *CI* authors is particularly disturbing because it further obscures the fact that two of the four women authors have high technical expertise. Instead of signaling that fact, the all-male four guest editors, even though they worked with a woman managing editor, evidently considered that all the women authors should be associated with *female topics*. This is a stance that is not only historically inauthentic by obscuring the progress made by women scientists in fields pioneered by Mme Curie (e.g., radiochemistry, nuclear chemistry; see above the presence of a woman nuclear chemist in the AAAS Symposium) but also obtuse to major science policy efforts currently underway to combat the underrepresentation of women in science. Any woman student reading this news magazine will conclude that even for the centennial celebration of the best known woman scientist, Mme Curie, women's presence as authors is still defined by gender stereotypes (i.e., association with family, women's issues, and traditional female occupations, rather than science proper).

For example, *CI* recruited Mme Curie's granddaughter, Hélène Langevin-Joliot (2011) born in 1927, current age of 84. Langevin-Joliot, Professor of Nuclear Physics at the Institute of Nuclear Physics at the University of Paris and Director of Research at the CNRS, remained the only woman scientist the organizers could think of as suitable! This reminds us of the 17th century when the new founders of science such as Galileo and Descartes conversed with aristocratic women (e.g., Grand Duchess of Tuscany and Queen Christina of Sweden, respectively) but had no use for ordinary women practitioners of science who were formally excluded at that time from science's first institutions, the academies. Indeed, Mme Curie's granddaughter was asked to share her memory of her family of four generations of scientists, so as to provide an understandable measure of authenticity for the commemorative effort. This means that such an authenticity still came at the expense of embodying recognition of women scientists as contributors on science per se, because no other woman scientist contributed on science proper.

Along these lines, two other women authors in the *CI* centennial issue on Marie Curie provided curatorial compilations of Curie memorabilia and eponymic practices, thus exemplifying a traditional female occupation. Though this information, coming as it did from Polish authors dedicated to the public memory of Mme Curie as a great scientist of Polish descent, is in principle a good idea, still, in the context of the special issue it functions as an instance in which nationalist considerations trumpet considerations of gender equity. Such considerations were also evident in the inclusion of two out of four guest editors from Poland, at a time when no single woman—French, Polish, American, Japanese, etc.—was a guest editor! These four countries are most active in commemorations of Mme Curie and/or her discoveries, details of which I provided during my AAAS talk. Once again, the desire to balance Western and Eastern European guest editors—a progressive political move in the context of the European Union—came at the expense of gender balance. Must we remind these editors that Mme Curie's symbolic heritage is not limited to her being a French scientist, or a scientist of Polish descent and a Polish patriot, but also a woman scientist—indeed the best-known woman scientist. As such, her Centennial is not something that can be partitioned between France and Poland but must include respect for her gender and inclusion rather than exclusion of women in science in her Centennial events.

The last, or the only woman author ostensibly invited for her professional expertise to the special issue of *CI*, commemorating Marie Curie, i.e., unrelated to her status as family member or practitioner of traditional female occupations, was Soraya Boudia, a historian of the Curie Laboratory (Boudia, 1997, 2001). However, much as with Hélène Langevin-Joliot, Boudia was not asked to write in her own technical area of expertise, i.e., Curie's metrology, but rather to cover a *women's topic*, namely the history of Mme Curie as Head of a laboratory with many women researchers (Boudia, 2011). The implication being that a woman historian's presumed gender relevance in covering a *women's topic* outweighed the value of her technical expertise in determining the rationale for her status as an invited author.

Furthermore, though Boudia is an excellent choice for an author on Mme Curie's laboratory, asking her to write on the women in Mme Curie's laboratory further reveals the editors' lack of understanding that the history of women in science had been a designated area of historical expertise, at least since 1987 when the History of Science Society (2011) had begun to distribute awards for *outstanding research* in that field. Contrary to *CI*'s editors' superficial understanding, women scientists or women historians are not necessarily experts on the history of women in science. There is by now a sufficient body of specialized work, in both award winning books and article formats for a quarter of a century, to the effect that serious editors should first try to secure such expertise rather than using women with expertise in other fields, as if the mere fact that one is a woman makes one an expert on a specific aspect of women's history in science. To sum up, on the issue of gender and science the *CI* editors made it clear that all the women scientists from Mme Curie onward are still to be found below the radar of both *CI*, and its sponsor, IUPAC. This is a serious and disturbing conclusion to be reached during 2011, the Centennial Year of Mme Curie's Nobel Prize in Chemistry, and a mere six year since a year long public debate on women in science. It is also possible that the root cause of producing a *tribute* for Mme Curie's Centennial that ironically both embodies and promotes gender stereotypes stems from a low level of historical consciousness, or of history of science more widely, on the part of *CI* scientist editors.

The organizers of the AAAS Symposium demonstrated the supreme value of collaboration between scientists and historians in producing a spectrum of commemorative topics and speakers that included scientists, historians, and historians of science. However, CI's scientist editors did not aim for a partnership with historians of science, even though a centennial is a topic that requires a specialized understanding of bridging between the present and the past, a topic that has emerged in the last decade as a sophisticated area of inquiry within the history of science. For example, collective volumes on how scientific commemorations, ranging from the quinquicentennial of Copernicus to the bicentennials of Lavoisier and the centennials of Darwin, Pasteur, Planck, Royer, among other scientists, refashioned the nexus between the past and the present, invariably under the aegis of what had become known as the *politics of public memory* have been available for over a decade in both English and French (Abir-Am & Elliott, 1999).

To conclude this disappointing encounter with *CI*'s foray into Mme Curie's centennial, scientists who seek to organize anniversaries and commemorations of discoveries, discoverers, or laboratories would find it most useful to inform themselves of the pertinence of historians of science in such endeavors. Though historicity may challenge the presentist, even futurist ethos of science, ignoring it altogether has transformed an intended tribute into its very opposite, by using Mme Curie's fame as an occasion to reinforce the status quo, a status quo which means ongoing underrepresentation of women in science. Displaying ignorance of the public upheaval surrounding the underrepresentation of women in science only six years ago, as well as ignorance of scholarship in the history of science is not a professional way to celebrate the Centennial of one of the world's most accomplished and courageous women scientists.

Chemical Heritage Foundation

Several other scientific organizations that planned events for Mme Curie's Centennial also seem to suffer from a similar malaise of memory, having *forgotten* to even mention in otherwise highly publicized events that IYC–2011 was so named in honor of Mme Curie's Centennial. For example, the Chemical Heritage Foundation, (hereafter CHF) describing itself in a brochure distributed at the 2011 AAAS Annual Meeting as a "Library, Museum, and Center for Scholars" in Philadelphia, conducted several kick-off events in the first half of February 2011 to promote the International Year of Chemistry-2011 (IYC–2011, 2011). Those included a lecture, an artistic exhibition, an inaugural book club meeting and a panel with speakers from industry, business, and academia—the launch event. But nowhere was it mentioned that ICY-2011 was so declared in honor of the Centennial of Mme Curie's Nobel Prize in Chemistry as if this fact is an embarrassment rather than being a source of pride. Nor were any activities advertised so far related to addressing Mme Curie's role in combating gender bias against women in science. Apparently, CHF, whose most notable accomplishments may well be in the area of fundraising as evident from a varied list of sponsors it boasts, including corporations, individual donors, and foundations, had no time to contemplate the pertinence of Mme Curie's Centennial for its activities, or even to inform its audience that ICY–2011 was so declared because of the Mme Curie Centennial and not the other way around.

However, the CHF does highlight five women out of 11 scientists, with its theme of atomic and nuclear structure on their web site (CHF, 2011) and includes Joseph J. Thompson, Ernest Rutherford, Marie Sklodowska Curie, Iréne Joliot-Curie, Frèdéric Joliot, Otto Hahn, Lise Meitner, Fritz Strassman, Glenn Seaborg, Darleane Hoffman, and Helen Vaughn Michel. The CHF does not explicitly mention the Centennial of Mme Curie's Nobel Prize in Chemistry in 2011, or her visits to the radium industry in Pennsylvania in the 1920s, even though CHF in Philadelphia is mainly sponsored by the local industry with a mission to foster "an understanding of chemistry's impact on society" (CHF, 2010, p. 1).

International Commission on the History of Modern Chemistry

Yet another international organization, the Commission on the History of Modern Chemistry (CHMC, 2011a, 2011b) just announced its 2011 biennial symposium (Renewing the Heritage of Chemistry in the 21st Century, 2011) but has declined to include the Centennial of Mme Curie as a topic in its program. This organization is one of the Commissions associated with the International Union for History of Science and Technology (IUHST, 2011), the worldwide professional organization in that field. The only relevance between the Commission's symposium and Mme Curie's Centennial was described by CHMC's colorful program as geographical, namely, holding the meeting in Paris where Mme Curie lived her life as a scientist.

This is a disingenuous excuse, because holding a meeting in Paris does not require any special justification; moreover, the decision to do so had been taken two years earlier when the Commission met during the 23rd IUHST in Budapest for reasons related to a commission member willing to host the biennial meeting. The CHMC discovered that its upcoming meeting coincides with Mme Curie's Centennial only after Professor Margaret Rossiter of Cornell University, a leading historian of women in science, drew its attention to this fact. Still, it chose not to rectify this incredible oversight. Both the preliminary and final programs thus have no session that refers to Mme Curie's Centennial, even though her Centennial is a most suitable topic for any historical or scientific meeting held in 2011 (Symposium of the Commission on the History of Modern Chemistry, 2011).

Ostensibly the focus of the CHMC meeting in June 2011 is "Preservation, Presentation and Utilization of Sources Sites and Artifacts." In that context, the decontamination of the Curies' notebooks in the 1990s, which enabled the historians cited above to conduct original research on Mme Curie's laboratory for the first time, could have made a perfect topic. Again, Mme Curie, her Centennial, and women chemists, whether her students or otherwise, all remained below the radar of CHMC, an international commission in the history of chemistry. Much as the IUPAC's *CI,* the CHMC is yet another international body which missed the opportunity and the challenge of Mme Curie's Centennial, even at the price of making its own program less timely. Hopefully, CHMC, among other organizations whose initiatives are still in planning stages, will manage to enrich its program with topics pertinent to Mme Curie's Centennial, as well as the very idea of preserving the often neglected and little known heritage of women nuclear chemists and radiochemists.

Ironically, organizations on the history of chemistry such as the above mentioned CHF and CHMC proved more resistant to marking the Centennial of Mme Curie's Nobel Prize in Chemistry than organizations in the history of science as a whole. Thus, both the International Commission on Women in the History of Science, Technology, and Medicine (affiliated with the above mentioned International Union for History and Philosophy of Science) and the History of Science Society (2011) in the US currently plan symposia on Mme Curie's centennial. While the former circulated a call for paper in April 2011 with Mme Curie's Centennial being one of its five themes at its biennial meeting in Paris in September 2011, the latter had already approved a proposed session with five participants for its November annual meeting. In both cases the initiative came from women historians who specialize in the history of women in science; this outcome raises the issue of whether men scientists and scholars, who form the majority of practitioners in both science and history of science, are willing and able to commemorate the contributions of women scientists, or are they more interested in maintaining the status quo, relegating both women scientists and their *female topics* to the margins of both science and its commemorative practices?

PROTESTING THIS STATE OF AFFAIRS

Given all these examples, one wonders why some of the above organizations, and probably others (IUPAC's upcoming meeting in Puerto Rico late in July 2011 boasts the presence of seven Nobel Laureates but does not have, as yet, anything on its preliminary program that pertains to Mme Curie's Centennial), tend to hide or play down the fact that the International Year of Chemistry-2011 (IYC–2011) was declared in honor of the Centennial of Mme Curie's Nobel Prize in Chemistry. Readers may remember the numerous events scheduled during 2005 to mark the centennial of Mme Curie's friend, Albert Einstein (Fox & Keck, 2005), especially his multiple-discovery *annus mirabilis* of 1905 (much as 1898, had been for Mme Curie, the year she discovered radium and polonium in collaboration with Pierre Curie (see Nobelprize.org, 2011)

The identity of the discoverer, Einstein, was not hidden at all, quite the contrary, it bordered on a cult of scientistic personality! So why does this double standard continue to exist a quarter of a century after the History of Science Society began formally recognizing excellence on the topic of the history of women in science (in 1987), and four decades after the passage of affirmative action executive orders and legislation in the mid-1960s and early 1970s, respectively, in the US (Affirmative action, 2011)?

Could it be that those organizations ignore the name of Mme Curie in the year of her Centennial (IYC–2011) in order to avoid addressing the issue of underrepresentation of women in science—an issue that inevitably highlights those organizations' ongoing practices of gender inequality? Is this widespread denial of institutional responsibility for the underrepresentation of women in science a generational issue, stemming from the slow to die attitudes of an earlier generation of Cold War scientists who always knew that the best place for a woman scientist was someone else's laboratory?

The convergence of these three *offenders* (CI, CHF, and CHMC) was thus experienced as a rude awakening, coming as it did on the heels of the AAAS symposium. That symposium, as noted above, was not only a model commemorative event but was also well received by its audience, suggesting in a way that the message on the historical role of women in science was being absorbed. But it suddenly became obvious that there are still large pockets of colleagues, and their organizations, which despite a quarter of a century (and more) of professionally rewarded outstanding research on women in science, they remain uninformed about the historical place of women in science or the social urgency of addressing the underrepresentation of women in science.

What can one do in such a demoralizing situation? As a scholar and community builder in the area of the history of women in science, I felt that all my efforts in the last quarter of a century as well as those of my colleagues in various collective volumes and other venues were in vain. This counting started in 1986 when the 12-author book I co-edited, *Uneasy Career and Intimate Lives: Women in Science, 1789–1979* (Abir-Am & Outram, 1987) went to press—the book won a History of Science Society award for outstanding research in 1988.

The idea of protesting this state of affairs, i.e., of either ignoring or downplaying the status of women in science, was inspired by having already included in my PowerPoint presentation at the AAAS Symposium, a slide on the centennial of Émile Zola's (2011) *J'accuse…! a* letter of protest, written to the President of the French Republic and other organs of state and published in the newspaper *L'Aurore* on January 13, 1898. It remains the most famous public appeal in modern times. The letter was concerned with the miscarriage of justice in the case of Captain Alfred Dreyfus who was falsely accused of treason and imprisoned. I referred to Alain Pages' (1998) book as an example of the wider cultural context of the centennial of the discovery of radium because both centennials took place in 1998. As I put it, on their way to and from the laboratory in which radium was discovered, the Curies would have heard Zola's petition being read on many Parisian street corners.

Zola's petition changed the world, giving rise to the concept of the public intellectual, in addition to stimulating far-reaching political ramifications within and beyond France. Those far-reaching changes included a long-lasting dichotomy in the political map of France between Dreyfusards and their opponents, well into the Fifth Republic. Those far-reaching changes also included the idea that European Jews, as a quintessential minority, may need to seek individual civil rights at a collective rather than at the individual level (as the Third Republic so famously failed to defend the civil rights of Captain Alfred Dreyfus—a member of a minority group). Within half a century, that idea led in 1948 to the establishment of Israel (Sachar, 1976; 3rd ed., 2007)—in itself a transformative event for the geopolitics of the Middle East as well as for the civil rights of Jews and other minorities worldwide.

Moreover, having been affiliated for the last several years with the Women's Studies Research Center (WSRC, 2011) at Brandeis University (whose motto is "Scholarship, activism, and art") I let the readers, much as the AAAS attendees did beforehand, judge whether my jocular efforts at satirizing the distortion of Mme Curie's public memory so as to fit gender stereotypes qualify as a form of art… at the very least it made the audience laugh on several occasions as if it was exposed to a comic performance. This Brandeis interdisciplinary center exposed me to efforts of other colleagues in promoting a wide variety of gender-related public causes ranging from freedom of speech to wage equality, by a wide variety of means, including such petitions.

It remains to be seen whether the proposed petition on mandating and monitoring an adequate representation of women scientists in the programs of scientific commemorations, or any other scientific symposia and events, may also change the world by bringing science, the most influential institution of our time, closer to accepting the ideal of gender equality.

NOSTALGIC MEMORIES STIRRED AT 2011 AAAS ANNUAL MEETING

In this respect, the 2011 AAAS Annual Meeting proved encouraging because its outgoing President, Alice Huang of California Institute of Technology, mentioned the status of women in science as a key issue in her Presidential Address (Huang, 2011). She also told me during the reception afterward that she was happy to see that our symposium was well placed at the beginning of the AAAS Program. She seemed more aware of the reality for women in science both in the past and nowadays, than many scientists, both men and women, who become distinctly uncomfortable when the topic of the underrepresentation of women in science is mentioned. It was also interesting to compare notes with her on well known case studies of gender discrimination in the recent history of women in science—cases I know from my research as a historian of science but she knew from personal encounter with those involved.

Other colleagues involved in the issue of the underrepresentation of women in science that I was able to meet at the AAAS meeting included Sue Rosser, the Provost of San Francisco State University (SF State News, 2009), who was elected to the AAAS Board of Directors in 2010 (SF State News, 2010). She was a principal architect of NSF-POWRE (a program that preceded the current NSF-ADVANCE grants) (Rosser, 2004; Rosser & Taylor 2009), which still stirs in me a great deal of nostalgia. Among other things, I was reminded of an eventful flight to a POWRE awardee meeting at NSF headquarters in the late 1990s, from my then location at University of California, Berkeley, in the company of my by then 10-year old daughter. She informed all in the airport that if she would not get upgraded to first class, then her mother was a bad one. Too bad the *New York Times*, which covered that meeting, missed such telling comments about balancing work and family a century after Mme Curie balanced her discovery of radium with taking care of one year old Irène, who like her mother would also become a Nobel Laureate in Chemistry (Nobelprize.org, 1935).

Nostalgia also applied to opportunities given to the topic on women in science by AAAS on previous occasions. On one such occasion, the 1989 Annual Meeting, we also had a symposium on women in science, entitled "Uneasy careers and intimate lives – Great women in science during the late 1800s and the 1900s," (History of Physics Newsletter, 1988), co-organized by Caroline L Herzenberg of Argonne National Laboratory and me, and chaired by Professor Stephen Brush of the University of Maryland at College Park, a former President of the History of Science Society who has written one of the early essays on women in science (Brush, 1985). A *New York Times* science journalist (Norman, 1989) covered our symposium in *Science*. It not only included quotations from my own talk but also our coverage was published in parallel with that of the AAAS Presidential Address! Then, as now, the topic of women in science has remained timely because change toward gender equity has remained slow (Valian, 1999), though perhaps the sense of urgency which gave us top coverage in 1989 has disappeared in the aftermath of the 2005 year-long debate on women in science, which saturated anyone's appetite for coverage. That unusual coverage, prompted in part by the *celebrity* status of some participants in the debate, and other factors beyond its core issue of gender inequality, contrasted with the paucity of actual or meaningful policy action.

Let's hope that those who wish to speed such change will sign the enclosed petition, while those who organize scientific commemorations, or other symposia, will remember or otherwise be reminded by their organizations' bylaws, to be inclusive of women in science, whether as speakers, organizers, or *mere* topical presences. How Mme Curie's Centennial is marked by science and society in 2011 remains a sensitive barometer of their determination, or lack of it, to solve the problem of the underrepresentation of women in science. Mme Curie's Centennial is a perfect timing for house cleaning of vestiges of sexism, so as to engage now in a concerted action by a combination of science policy and social policy for women in science—an idea advanced almost two decades ago (Abir-Am, 1992).

Figure 1. Author, Pnina G. Abir-Am, shows one frame of the poster display at the 2011 AAAS annual meeting in Washington, DC on Marie Curie's life. The largest photograph on this particular poster is of Marie Curie, taken with her two daughters, with infant Eve on her lap and Irène sitting beside Marie.

NOTES

[1] Fred Sanger (1958, 1980 in chemistry) and John Bardeen (1956, 1972 in physics) are the only other scientists who twice received a Nobel Prize in science. Linus Pauling received a 1954 Nobel Prize for Chemistry and a 1963 Nobel Prize for Peace. See also http://nobelprize.org/nobel_prizes/ nobelprize_facts.html for the number of scientists who received a Nobel Prize since its inception in 1900, per field.

REFERENCES/BIBLIOGRAPHY

Abir-Am, P. G. (1992). Science policy or social policy for women in science: Lessons from historical case studies, *Science and Public Policy, 12*, 11–12.
Abir-Am, P. G. (2005–2006). Women in science: The debate (on under-representation) that won't go away; Historical roots, social dynamics, policy ramifications. Retrieved from http://people.brandeis.edu/~pninaga/women_in_science.html
Abir-Am, P. G. (2010). Gender and technoscience: A historical perspective. *Journal of Technology Management & Innovation, 5(*1), 152–165.
Abir-Am, P. G. (2011a). Historical perspectives on the public memory of Marie S. Curie. Retrieved from http://aaas.confex.com/aaas/2011/webprogram/Paper2977.html
Abir-Am. P. G. (2011b). How science, policy, gender and history meet each other once a year. *Newsletter of the History of Science Society*, 40(2). Retrieved from http://www.hssonline.org/ publications/Newsletter2011/April-cross-discipline-meeting.html
Abir-Am, P.G., & Elliott, C.A. (Eds.) (1999). *Osiris, 14, Commemorative practices in science, Historical perspectives on the politics of collective memory*. Chicago, IL: University of Chicago Press.
Abir-Am, P. G., & Outram, D. (Eds.) (1987). *Uneasy careers and intimate lives: Women in science, 1789–1979*. New Brunswick, NJ: Rutgers University Press.
Affirmative action (2011). Affirmative action in the United States. Retrieved from http://en.wikipedia.org/wiki/Affirmative_action_in_the_United_States
Alliance for the Advancement of Academic Women in Chemistry and Engineering (AAFAWCE, 2011). Retrieved from http://web3.cas.usf.edu/main/depts/ANT/advancepaid/
American Association for the Advancement of Science (AAAS) (2011a). Retrieved from http://news.aaas.org/
American Association for the Advancement of Science (AAAS) (2011b). Celebrating Marie Curie's 100th anniversary of her Nobel Prize in Chemistry. Retrieved from http://aaas.confex.com/ aaas/2011/webprogram/Session2793.html
American Association for the Advancement of Science (AAAS) (2011c). Chemistry section. Retrieved from http://www.aaas.org/aboutaaas/organization/sections/chem.shtml
American Association for the Advancement of Science (AAAS) (2011d). History and philosophy of science section. Retrieved from http://www.aaas.org/aboutaaas/organization/sections/hist.shtml
Baisden, P. A. (2011). Marie Curie, the premier chemist, co-discoverer of radiation an radioactivity. Retrieved from http://aaas.confex.com/aaas/2011/webprogram/Paper2956.html
Bensaude-Vincent, B. (1996). Star scientists in a Nobelist family: Irène and Frèdèric Joliot-Curie. In H. M. Pycior, N. Slack, & P. G. Abir-Am (Eds.), *Creative couples in the sciences*. New Brunswick, NJ: Rutgers University Press.
Brian, D. (2005). *The Curies: A biography of the most controversial family in science*. Hoboken, NJ: John Wiley & Sons, Inc.
Boudia, S. (1997). The Curie laboratory: Radioactivity and metrology. *History and Technology, 13*, 249–265.
Boudia, S. (2001). *Marie Curie et son laboratoire*. Paris: La Decouverte.

Boudia, S. (2011). An inspiring laboratory director: Marie Curie and women in science. *Chemistry International, 33*(1), 12–15. Retrieved from http://www.iupac.org/publications/2011/3301/3_boudia. html

Brush, S.G. (1985). Women in physical science: From drudges to discoverers. *Physics Teacher 23*, 11–19.

Ceci, S. J., & Williams, W. M. (2011). Understanding current causes of women's underrepresentation in science. *Proceedings of the National Academy of Sciences, 108*(8), 3157–3162 (doi: 10.1073/pnas.1014871108).

Chemical Heritage Foundation (CHF, 2010). About us. Retrieved from http://www.chemheritage.org/ about/index.aspx

Chemical Heritage Foundation (CHF, 2011). Atomic and nuclear structure. Retrieved from http://www.chemheritage.org/discover/chemistry-in-history/themes/atomic-and-nuclear-structure/index.aspx

Commission on the History of Modern Chemistry (CHMC, 2011a). Collque, Paris, 21–24. Juin 2011. Retrieved from http://www.chmc2011.fr

Commission on the History of Modern Chemistry (CHMC, 2011b). International Union of History and Philosophy of Science. Division of History of Science. Retrieved from http://www.uni-regensburg.de/Fakultaeten/phil_Fak_I/Philosophie/Wissenschaftsgeschichte/CHMC.htm

Committee on Maximizing the Potential of Women in Academic Science and Engineering, National Academy of Sciences, National Academy of Engineering and Institute of Medicine (2007). *Beyond bias and barriers: Fulfilling the potential of women in academic science and engineering.* Washington, DC: The National Academies Press.

Curie, E. (1938). *Madame Curie: A biography by Eve Curie.* New York: Doubleday, Doran & Co., Inc.

Davis, J. L. (1995). The research school of Marie Curie in the Paris faculty, 1907–1914. *Annals of Science, 52, 310–340.*

Dean, C. (2005). Theorist drawn into debate 'that will not go away.' *New York Times,* April 12. Retrieved from http://www.nytimes.com/2005/04/12/science/12prof.html

Des Jardins, J. (2010). *The Marie Curie complex: The hidden history of women in science.* New York: Feminist Press. Retrieved from http://www.feministpress.org/books/madame-curie-complex

Des Jardins, J. (2011). The Marie Curie complex: The hidden history of women in science. Retrieved from http://aaas.confex.com/aaas/2011/webprogram/Paper2957.html

Dillon, S. (2005). Harvard chief defends his talk on women. *New York Times,* January 18. Retrieved from http://www.nytimes.com/2005/01/18/national/18harvard.html

Dry, S. (with Seifert, S.) (2003) *Curie.* (London: Haus Publishing).

Fox, K. C., & Keck, A. (2005). Einstein A to Z. Retrieved from http://www.einsteinatoz.com 2005_02_01_news.shtml

Gilmer, P. J. (2011). Irène Joliot-Curie, a Nobel laureate in artificial radioactivity. In M.-H. Chiu, P. J. Gilmer, & D. F. Treagust (Eds.), *Celebrating the 100th anniversary of Madame Marie Sklodowska Curie's Nobel Prize in Chemistry* (pp. 41–57). Rotterdam: Sense Publishers.

Giroud, F. (1981) *Marie Curie, une femme honorable.* Paris: Fayard (in English: *Marie Curie, a life.* New York: Holmes & Meyer, 1986).

Goldberg, S. (2000). The Enola Gay affair: What evidence counts when we commemorate historical events? In P. G. Abir-Am & C.A. Elliott (Eds.), *Commemorative practices in science, historical perspectives on the politics of collective memory.* Chicago, IL: University of Chicago Press.

Goldenberg, S. (2005). Why women are poor at science, by Harvard president. *Guardian,* January 18. Retrieved from http://www.guardian.co.uk/science/2005/jan/18/educationsgendergap.genderissues

Goldsmith, B. (2005). *Obsessive genius: The inner world of Marie Curie.* New York: W.W. Norton.

History of Physics Newsletter (1988). Retrieved from http://www.aps.org/units/fhp/newsletters /upload/Vol-III-4-Oct1988.pdf

History of Science Society (2011). The society: About the history of the science society. Retrieved from http://www.hssonline.org/about/society.html

Howes, R., & Herzenberg, C. (1999). *Their day in the sun, women of the Manhattan Project.* Philadelphia: Temple University Press.

Huang, A. (2011). Huang Presidential address: Science diplomacy must "avoid arrogance" to succeed. Retrieved from http://news.aaas.org/2011_annual_meeting/0221alice-huang-plenary.shtml

International Union of History and Philosophy of Science, Division History of Science (IUHPS, 2011). Retrieved from http://www.icsu.org/publicdb/frmDisplayMember?docid=97d44bb2b86ba6e1458 72f68db2d0d62

International Year of Chemistry-2011 (IYC-2011). International year of chemistry 2011. Retrieved from http://www.chemistry2011.org/

Langevin-Joliot, Hélène (2011). Retrieved from http://en.wikipedia.org/wiki/H%C3%A9l%C3% A8ne_Langevin-Joliot

Lemonick, S. (2011). Stories for, by and about women in science. Under the microscope where women and science connect. Crossing borders with Curie and AAAS. Retrieved from http://www.underthemicroscope.com/blog/crossing-borders-with-curie-and-aaas

LeRoy, M., & Lewin, A. (1943). Madame Curie (film). Retrieved from http://www.imdb.com/title/tt0036126/

Nobelprize.org (1903). Nobel Prize in Physics 1903. Henri Becquerel, Pierre Curie, Marie Curie. Retrieved from: http://nobelprize.org/nobel_prizes/physics/laureates/1903/

Nobelprize.org (1911). Nobel Prize in Chemistry 1911. Marie Curie. Retrieved from http://nobelprize.org/nobel_prizes/chemistry/laureates/1911/

Nobelprize.org (1935). Frèdèric Joliot and Irène Joliot-Curie. Nobel Prize in Chemistry. Frédéric Joliot, Irène Joliot-Curie. Retrieved from http://nobelprize.org/nobel_prizes/chemistry/laureates/1935/joliot-curie-bio.html

Nobelprize.org (2011). Marie and Pierre Curie and the discovery of polonium and radium. Retrieved from http://nobelprize.org/nobel_prizes/physics/articles/curie/

Norman, C. (1989). AAAS meeting draws a crowd. Science, 243, 474–475 (doi: 10.1126/science. 243.4890.474).

Ozouf, M. (1984). Le Panthéon: L'école normale des morts. In Pierre Nora (Ed.), Les lieux de mémoire Vol. 1, pp. 139–166. Paris: Gallimard. Retrieved from http://www.wsfh.org/Style%20Sheet% 20for%20Authors%20%20Lafayette%202010.pdf

Pages, A. (1998). Le 13 janvier, 1898, J'accuse... Paris: Albin.

Pasachoff, N. (1996). Marie Curie and the science of radioactivity. New York: Oxford University Press.

Pflaum, R. (1989). Grand obsession, Marie Curie and her world. New York: Doubleday.

Pinoteau, C. (1997). Les palmes de M. Schutz (film). Retrieved from http://www.imdb.com/title/tt0119855/

Quinn, S. (1995). Marie Curie: A life. New York: Simon & Schuster.

Rayner-Canham, M., & Rayner-Canham, G. (1997). A devotion to their science, pioneer women of radioactivity. Philadelphia: Chemical Heritage Foundation.

Reid, R. W. (1974). Marie Curie. New York: Dutton.

Renewing the heritage of chemistry in the 21st century (2011). Retrieved from http://www. chemistry2011.org/participate/activities/show?id=274

Roque, X. (1997). Marie Curie and the radium industry. History and Technology, 13, 267–291

Rosser, S. (2004). The science glass ceiling: Academic women scientists and the struggle to succeed. New York: Routledge.

Rosser, S., & Taylor, M. Z. (2009). Why are we still worried about women in science? Academe Online. Retrieved from http://www.aaup.org/AAUP/pubsres/academe/2009/MJ/Feat/ross.htm

Rossiter, M. W. (1982). Women scientists in America: Struggles and strategies, 1880–1940; Baltimore, MD: The Johns Hopkins University Press.

Rossiter, M. W. (1995). Before affirmative action: Women scientists in America, 1940–1972. Baltimore, MD: The Johns Hopkins University Press.

Sachar, H. M. (1976; 3rd ed., 2007). A history of Israel. New York: Knopf.

SF State News (2009). SF State announces new provost Sue Rosser. Retrieved from http://www. sfsu.edu/~news/prsrelea/fy08/042.html

SF State News (2010). Provost Rosser elected to AAAS Board of Directors. Retrieved from https://www.sfsu.edu/~news/2010/spring/15.html

Summers, L. (2005). Remarks at NBER conference on diversifying the science & engineering workforce. Retrieved from http://president.harvard.edu/speeches/summers_2005/nber.php

Symposium on the Commission on the History of Modern Chemistry (CHMC, 2011). Retrieved from http://chmc2011.fr/spip.php?article14

Valian, V. (1999). *Why so slow? The advancement of women*. Cambridge, MA: The MIT Press.

Women's Studies Research Center (WSRC. 2011). Retrieved from http://www.brandeis.edu/wsrc/

Zola, É. (2011). *Émile Zola*. Retrieved from http://en.wikipedia.org/wiki/%C3%89mile_Zola

APPENDIX A

Petition for mandating inclusiveness of women in the Mme Curie Centennial and related symposia

2-28-2011

Dear Colleague,

As you may know, *various efforts* are currently under way to honor the centennial of Mme Curie's Nobel Prize in Chemistry (1911) this year, declared the International Year of Chemistry-2011 (IYC-2011) by UNESCO. This is a great opportunity to reflect upon the progress that Mme Curie's discovery of two new elements, radium and polonium, made in combating social *bias and barriers* both she and other women scientists and scholars have encountered and still do.

We were very disappointed that some early efforts marking this Centennial seemed to *reinforce gender stereotypes*. For example, the January-February 2011 issue of Chemistry International (*CI*), an IUPAC official magazine, featured *no* woman scientist among its four guest editors of its special issue on the centennial of Mme Curie. By comparison, no anniversary issue honoring Martin Luther King would be published without an African-American guest-editor! The *only* woman scientist contributor in that issue is Curie's granddaughter scientist who reminiscences about her family! *CI* further limited its selection of three other women contributors to traditional female occupations or topics. Eight men authors are the only ones in charge of scientific aspects. Such gender stereotypes suggest that the actual purpose of its tribute may not be to honor Mme Curie *but rather use her Centennial to reinforce the status quo* of underrepresentation of women in science. Not including women scientists among the eight men scientific contributors sends the wrong message worldwide; it falsely implies that there are *no* worthy women scientists to be included in a tribute to the best-known woman scientist.

This occurred rather soon after the yearlong public debate on the underrepresentation of women in science, dubbed the "debate that will not go away" (*New York Times*, May 12, 2005). It just resurfaced in the February 7, 2011 issues of the *Chronicle of Higher Education* and the *Proceedings of the National Academy of Science.* We conclude that if left to their own devices, leaders of public opinion in science would fail to include their women scientist colleagues, most ironically even when they claim that they seek to honor Mme Curie.

In order to ensure that all scientific anniversaries reflect both gender inclusiveness and desegregation of women from a sole association with traditional women's topics (e.g., family, traditional occupations) we call upon pertinent scientific and other organizations to adopt an *official policy of monitoring* that the *representation* of women scientists and scholars among all ranks of invited contributors and all kinds of topics *is adequate*.

The petition will be addressed at organizations for their planning special events or publications on the Centennial of Mme Curie's Nobel Prize in Chemistry in 1911. Please return your signed copy to the first signatory below at pninga@brandeis.edu (sample of signatories follows below).

Your name, position, institution, and comments, if any:

- Dr. Pnina G. Abir-Am, Resident Scholar, WSRC, Brandeis University, "Women's greatness should not be ignored or hidden!"
- Dame Gillian Beer, Professor Emeritus, Cambridge University, "Marie Curie is an icon but not alone among women."
- Joy Harvey, Independent Scholar, Somerville, MA.
- Prof. Rusty Shteir, Chair, Women's Studies, York University, Toronto
- Prof. V. Betty Smocovitis, Zoology & History, University of Florida at Gainesville

Pnina G. Abir-Am
Resident Scholar, Women's Studies Research Center
Brandeis University
pninaga@brandeis.edu

SHERRY A. SOUTHERLAND AND SIBEL UYSAL BAHBAH

11. EDUCATIONAL POLICY OF ACCOUNTABILITY AND WOMEN'S REPRESENTATION IN SCIENCE

The Specter of Unintended Consequences

INTRODUCTION

Our world continually presents us with anomalies: Things we don't expect. Things that don't fit our norms. These anomalies can be rejected out of hand, or they can be examined more closely to challenge our expectations for how the world works. Certainly during her lifetime, Marie Curie was seen as an anomaly. She was one the first women to be awarded a Ph.D. in Science in Europe, the first woman to win the Nobel Prize and as well as the first scientist of either gender to receive the Nobel Prize for science twice in her lifetime. She received the Nobel Prize in Physics jointly with her husband, Pierre Curie, and with Henri Becquerel in the same year she finished her doctorate in 1903. Despite these achievements and serving as a reflection of the view of women held by many in the scientific community of the day, this outstanding scientist became, in Marie Curie's (1923) own words, "chief of the work in the laboratory that was to be created for him [Pierre Curie]" (p. 191). Pierre Curie, who had been named professor after receiving the Nobel Prize in 1903 with his wife, died in 1906 in a horse and carriage accident. It was only at that point in time that the university asked Marie Curie to occupy her husband's professorship. Thus, through much of her working life, Marie Curie was viewed as an anomaly that was to be rejected or accepted only reluctantly.

In contrast, from our vantage point from this second decade of the 21st century, we understand Marie Curie's success not as an anomaly but as a challenge to the expectations the culture of the time held for women. One could ask, what was it about her as an individual that allowed to her succeed—what was her upbringing, her work ethic, her intellect? Or one could examine the educational institutions and norms of the day that simultaneously allowed for the production of this outstanding scientist while at the same time denied safe passage into the scientific community to other such women. We find the latter approach to understanding Curie's success, that of focusing on educational institutional norms, to be particularly compelling. However, as interesting as an analysis of her history is, we are drawn to understanding the current educational context in terms of the promise it provides in supporting the development of the next generation of outstanding woman scientists.

In this chapter we examine the data describing the current trends in the role of women in Science, Technology, Engineering, and Mathematics (STEM) fields. This

M.-H. Chiu, P. J. Gilmer, and D. F. Treagust (Eds.), Celebrating the 100th Anniversary of Madame Marie Sklodowska Curie's Nobel Prize in Chemistry. 225–238.

is followed by a review of educational research into gender and learning, particularly science learning. We begin this review by describing the theoretical frames through which we view women and science, followed by a review of the empirical educational research literature exploring this topic. We then report a synthesis of the research that investigates the influence of the current educational policies of accountability, science teaching, and the learning of girls. This synthesis allows for a prediction about the influence such policies will have in the science education of the next generation of young women. As much of the world moves toward systems of accountability as a lever for change in schools, are we building a system that only allows for the occasional anomaly, or are we challenging the norms so that the science learning of all girls is fostered?

THE CURRENT ROLE OF WOMEN IN STEM FIELDS

While women have made tremendous progress in terms of their participation in science over the past 50 years, their continued underrepresentation in science, technology, engineering, and mathematics (STEM) fields is well documented (American Association for University Women [AAUW], 2010; National Science Foundation [NSF], 2008). Women comprise only 29% of the total full time doctoral workforce in the Biological, Agricultural and Environmental Life sciences, and only 19% of the full time doctoral workforce in computer and information sciences (Hallman, 2009). As described by Ceci, Williams, and Barnett (2009), women earned 31% of chemistry Ph.D. degrees between 1993 and 2003 but in 2002, women only held 21.5% of incoming assistant professorships. A similar situation is found in physics, engineering, and mathematics. In 2006, the percentage of women receiving Ph.D. degrees has increased to 25%, but the percentage of female assistant professors lags far behind this figure. As Ceci et al. (2009) describe, women are not being hired as assistant professors at the rate that they are earning PhD degrees. The number of women represented in academia is of particular importance, as these individuals will be responsible for the education of the next generation of scientists and mathematicians (De Welde, Laursen, & Thiry, 2011).

When one examines the entire STEM workforce, including those holding doctorates, the picture is more equitable, with nearly 45% of all biological scientists being women, and 32% of all chemists being women. Although, according to Census Bureau's 2000 results, the percentage of women in physics (14%) and engineering (11%) continues to bare evidence of gender inequities in these disciplines (AAUW, 2010).

As we continue to look down the pipeline, the more equitable portrayal of STEM continues, with over 62% of all Bachelor's degrees in the Biological Sciences being awarded to women, 41% of all Earth, Atmospheric and Ocean Science BS degrees, 42% of all Physical Science BS degrees, 45 % of all mathematics BS degrees, and 20% of all Engineering BS degrees (NSF, 2009). Each of these figures represents a notable increase in the participation of women in the same fields from 30 years earlier, as the number of women engaged in STEM fields both in and out of college has increased. This increase can also be seen in the participation of girls in mathematics and science in high school. Hallman (2009) reports that on average, girls are taking slightly more credits than boys in science and math and earning higher grades in these classes, although boys are still outnumbering girls in terms of the number taking advanced placement exams.

As described by De Welde et al. (2011), many of the gender patterns in STEM found in the United States are also seen in other countries. DeWandre (2002) describes that in the United Kingdom, women were awarded 50% of all undergraduate biology degrees, but hold only 9% of all full professorships. In Italy's national laboratories, women are promoted at half the rate of their male counterparts. Wennerås and Wold (1997) describe that in Sweden, women had be scored 2.5-times more productive in the merit review process to be rated the same as men.

WAYS TO UNDERSTAND GENDERED ISSUES IN STEM

Thus, it seems that the continuing gender "lag" of women in STEM is very real and can be found in countries throughout the world. Over the past 20 years there have been concentrated efforts within science education to understand the basis behind these gendered patterns in STEM participation and to alter these patterns. We will draw on the work of Scott Sowell (2004) to characterize some of these attempts with his description of three waves of feminist thought. The first wave of feminist thought, liberal feminist thought, focuses on increasing the numbers of women involved in science. Work within this theoretical frame concentrates on the disparities in women's participation in science in comparison to that of men. (This work also began and fostered discussions of disparities in success in science along social class, ethnic, and racial groups.) Sowell describes that much of this first wave of feminism has a deficit approach, so that interventions that this wave fosters attempts to bring women and other groups of students 'up to speed' so that they could be successful in the sciences by focusing on students' attitudes toward science, their achievement and their participation in science activities. Sowell (2004) argues that while such Liberal feminist activities have been successful in creating programs to get girls into science, this wave of work is limited because it focuses on only one half of the equation, girls, leaving science unexamined. Both Barton (1998a) and Sowell understand these equity interventions from first wave feminism as "placing the burden of change on the marginalized group of people as opposed to the marginalizing discipline" (Sowell, 2004, p. 48).

Second wave feminism moves away from a deficit view of women and girls, and begins to critique the project of science. Following in work of Harding (1998) and Keller (1985), a major assumption underlying these second wave feminist activities is the view that science itself includes positivistic, masculine traditions and norms, and it is these traditions and norms that actively work to exclude women. As Barton (1998a) describes:

Science is not a practice completely separated from other ways of knowing or doing. It is connected to, and influenced by, ways of knowing and doing that permeate every other aspect of life, from religion to survival, and that the knowledge produced within the science community is not value-free or independent (p. 4).

Second wave feminist thought illuminates the socially embedded aspects of the nature of science to explain the cause of current gendered inequities. As Sowell (2004) describes, because science is socially and culturally embedded, the knowledge and experiences of those that participate in science become important. Second wave feminist thought calls for the inclusion of those traditionally marginalized by science in an effort to enhance science. In second wave feminist thought, it is not the women that need science, but "science who needs women"—because of their particular subjectivities and unique views (Barton, 1998a).

Sowell (2004) explains that many of the women's program arising from first and second wave feminist thought can be characterized as 'female friendly' or espousing a 'women centered perspective.' But Sowell (2004) and Barton (1998a) suggest that both first and second waves of feminism are separatist in nature in that they emphasize the differences between the genders and work to involve both genders in the doing of science.

In contrast, third wave feminism does not rely on *gender differences* (males versus females) to create equity interventions, and so it avoids avoid essentializing some supposed "natural" characteristics of males and females, assumptions that find a home in first and second waves of feminist thought. Instead "third wave feminism constantly questions how relationship and knowledge are situated within webs of knowledge and power" (Barton, 1998a, p. 27). As Sowell (2004) describes, this emphasis on situatedness of the third wave of feminism focuses our attention on the connection between the production and use of scientific knowledge. Within this framework, understanding science and who is allowed to "do science" is central to understanding our larger society.

Findings of Research into Gender and Science

Baker (2002) provides a brief history of the treatment of gender equity within science education research over the previous 30 years, and this history is useful in that it allows us to see how research has evolved over time. The treatment of gender equity found in the 1970's was propelled by largely first wave feminist thought, which focused on differences between the sexes and cognitive capabilities.

> These studies were either psychological in orientation and used White male performance as the benchmark... They were conducted under what I call the "My Fair Lady" framework, or "Why can't a woman be more like a man?" When there were differences or correlates, the White male model was the right model. (p. 660)

Kahle (2004) characterizes such work as using a "characteristic lens", explaining that it is because of the characteristics that girls do or do not have that causes them to be maladapted to science. The work which continued throughout the late 1980's was propelled by the first wave of feminist thought and "the psychological perspective still held sway, and no one was yet questioning whether the so-called problem of girls and science had less to do with the nature of girls and more to do with the nature of science" (p. 660).

By the late 1980's, the literature that had once revolved around explaining differences based on sex moved toward getting more girls involved in school science and the second wave of feminist thought had begun. In second wave feminist thought differences between men and women are acknowledged, but changes are sought in science teaching to make it more gender-inclusive, that is to provide more access to girls in science. Second wave feminist research often challenges the very nature of school science, and in this tradition 'fixing school science takes precedent over fixing the girl science student" (Southerland, Smith, Sowell, & Kittleson, 2007, p. 57). In Kahle's (2004) terms, this research uses a response lens to understand the low numbers of women in science, as this research is constructed on the assumption that girls' underachievement in the science is due to their response to teaching. Research in this tradition often focuses on how instruction can be adjusted to be more "friendly" to women, emphasizes cooperative or collaborative groups and teacher questions and attitudes.

The late 1990's was a time of gender research that was informed by the a more third wave conception of gender, and much of the work of this period focused on understanding the relationship of gender to the nature of science. Third wave feminist thought problematizes a simplistic biological dichotomy of sexes and rejects overly simplistic essentialized notions of gendered behavior (i.e., girls aren't competitive, boys don't like group work). Most importantly, work in this third wave began to acknowledge the connections of gender to other markers of difference (class, ethnicity). Much of this research focuses on how classroom portrayals of science intersect with the identities of learners. Third wave feminist research often focuses on how science is portrayed in the classroom as well as who students think they need to be in order to successfully participate in that science:

It is from this perspective that questions of representation in science (what science is made to be) and identity in science (who we think we must be to engage in that science) become central (Barton, 1998b, p. 380).

Thus, gendered research now often intersects with discussion of the nature of science ("what science is made to be"). The research community is coming to understand that a robust understanding of the nature of science (NOS) can function as an important political tool to achieve more equitable science teaching (Southerland, Golden, & Enderle, 2011).

Of equal importance in the Barton quote above, much of the third wave of feminist research in science education focuses on the construct of identity and how that influences students in the science classroom. This work describes equitable science teaching as that which provides students with access to scientific understandings and habits of mind without reinforcing the difficulties involved in navigating between home and school science identities. Thus, having multiple ways of looking at issues of identity allows us as teacher educators to validate the importance of identity politics, while at the same time, recognize its limitations. For example, with regard to gender, Brickhouse, Lowery, and Schultz (2000) make an important conclusion by declaring, "When teaching girls science and trying to explain why it is they are or are not doing well in science, we need to know more than that they are girls. We need to know what kinds of girls they are" (p. 457). Clearly the essentialized notions of girls (and boys) that characterized the first wave of feminist work have undergone significant evolution in the third wave of feminism.

Integrating the Findings of Gender Research to the Science Classroom

The discussion above is overly simplistic, and it is important to point out that each of the succeeding waves of feminist thought have not overtaken and replaced those earlier. Instead, many science educators and science teachers interested in gender equity and furthering inclusion of women in science now largely operate from a fused, multidimensional feminist framework. As an example, in a recent meta analysis conducted by Hill, Corbett, and St. Rose (2010), sponsored by the NSF and the AAUW, eight reasons are cited to explain the continued underrepresentation of women. It is important to note that some of the reasons cited do hearken to earlier waves of feminist thought (i.e., girls aren't good at x), but these are often beliefs held by the social actors. Indeed, it seems that it is through the lens of the perceptions of women and girls that some of these factors become important. The eight causal factors identified as influencing women's choice of the sciences for a career include: beliefs about intelligence, stereotypes, self-assessment, spatial skills, the college student experience, university and college faculty, implicit bias, and workplace bias.

Boys and girls often view the significance of science education differently, especially in the STEM fields (Brickhouse, 2001). Girls and boys start school with same the interest and performance rate in science during the elementary grade level. In the middle school years, girls' interest and performance in science begins to gradually decline (NSF, 2007). Following this trajectory, female students' enrollment in advanced science courses drops significantly during the high school years (Simpson & Oliver, 1985, 1990; Weinburgh, 1995).

These different degrees of interest in science, perceptions of ability, and attendant course taking patterns may be due to the larger culture, they may be due to some fundamental difference in abilities held by boys and girls, or they could be due to the differential treatment girls receive in schools. For instance, it has long been known that teachers' expectations from their female students are not equal to those from their male students (Beal, 1994; Rosser, 1995). From grade school to graduate school, research shows that boys enrolled in science classes garner more attention from their teachers than female students. Males are called upon more often to answer questions, are given positive feedback on their work effort, are given more freedom to call out answers, and also receive more comprehensive answers from their teachers (Jones & Wheatley, 1990; Sadker & Sadker, 1994; Tobin, Kahle, & Fraser, 1990). Furthermore, male students are often evaluated on their achievement success in class while female students are evaluated on their behavior (Jones & Wheatley, 1990; Sadker & Sadker, 1994). Teachers generally do not want to give female students direct feedback or criticism presumably because they do not want to discourage them, but lacking such feedback girls are not pushed to excel (AAUW, 1998).

While each of the reasons discussed above seem to be linked to perceptions and bias, the first wave feminist notion that girls lack some skills necessary to succeed in the sciences does carry some empirical weight. One of the largest gender gaps in cognitive skills is seen in the area of spatial skills with boys consistently outscoring girls (Hill et al., 2010). However, even this seemingly immutable difference is susceptible to change. Indeed, work of Sorby and Baartmans (2000) suggests that if women are placed in an environment that enhances their spatial skills training, they are more likely to develop their skills as well as their confidence to consider a future in a STEM field and to persist in that field. Likewise, in the past it was considered that girls were less capable and thus less successful than boys in mathematics, but recent data suggest that these trends are changing, changes that suggest that an individual's abilities in mathematics may be more heavily influenced by culture than underlying biology (Hill et al., 2010).

Research Based Actions to Eliminate Gender Inequities in Science

In answer to their question as to "Why are so few women in science, technology, engineering, and mathematics?", Hill et al. (2010) explain that the paucity of women is largely due culture's perceptions and unconscious beliefs about gender in mathematics and science. In contrast, the progress women have made in STEM fields over the last 50 years does indicate that these perceptions and beliefs are flawed and open to change. Indeed, as they describe, "often the very act of identifying a stereotype or bias begins the process of dismantling it" (Hill et al., 2010, p. 90). Based on their meta analysis, Hill and colleagues offer the following recommendations to increase the role of women in science, and we focus our discussion on aspects of their recommendations that can and should be realized in the K-12 setting--that is the need to cultivate girls' achievement and interest in science and engineering.

In order to cultivate girls' achievement and interest, Hill et al., (2010) suggest that educators must tackle "head on" the stereotype that men are better than women in STEM areas, as this stereotype has been found to negatively affect girls' performance. To challenge this stereotype, educators must:

- Expose girls and boys to female role models in STEM careers,
- Highlight the numbers of girls and women who are succeeding in STEM subjects,
- Emphasize the lack of gender "barriers" to success in STEM subjects.

Hill et al. (2010) further suggest that educators must be clear that the intellectual skills, including spatial skills that are needed for success in STEM are acquired through hard work, not inherited. Educators must emphasize that "passion, dedication, and self-improvement, not simply innate talent, are the road to achievement" in STEM (p. 35). To encourage students' engagement, and allow for further learning, educators should praise girls (and all students) for their efforts in the classroom rather than their intelligence. Overall, instruction in STEM in the K-12 setting should educate students about stereotype threat, that is the threat of being viewed through the lens of a negative stereotype or the fear of doing something that would confirm a negative stereotype (Steele & Aronson, 1995). Indeed, helping students understand the very real influence of a stereotype threat can result in better performance for girls.

Because spatial skills are particularly important in STEM fields, and because girls and boys with good spatial skills may be more confident about their abilities and express greater interest in pursuing certain STEM subjects, all learners, but especially girls, should be encouraged to develop their spatial skills. Opportunities should be provided for all children to assemble and disassemble objects, play with construction tools, and work with their hands. Likewise, girls should be encouraged to take calculus, physics, chemistry, computer science, and engineering classes in high school as these courses will be necessary to successfully pursue STEM in college.

It is interesting that the recommendations offered by Hill et al. (2010) sidestep some of the earlier research findings that have identified differential treatment of girls by their teachers as part of the reason for girls' absence in STEM. Clearly, as stereotypes are challenged and dismantled, teachers' expectations of the girls in their classes must change, and the manner in which girls are engaged in science class must be brought more in line with the treatment of boys (i.e., being asked challenging questions, receiving more attention, given more comprehensive answers). In short, girls like their male counterparts, must be pushed to excel throughout their K-12 experiences, if they are to be successful in STEM fields.

THE ACCOUNTABILITY MOVEMENT IN THE UNITED STATES

For years, the K-12 educational system in the United States has struggled with issues of equity. As one marker of this struggle, the *Elementary and Secondary Education Act (ESEA)*, first enacted in 1965 under President Lyndon B. Johnson, was designed to reduce the achievement gap for children living in poverty. Over the years, the intent of this legislation as been retained and honed, and in the second Bush administration, the ESEA was renamed No Child Left Behind (NCLB), a name that emphasized the central goal of this legislation –that of closing 'the achievement gap between nonmainstream and non-minority students and between disadvantaged children and their more advantaged peers' (NCLB, 2001, Sec. 1001[3] p. 3).

NCLB is a national policy in the US that focuses squarely on student achievement, with its requirements of standardized academic standards for all students, its specification of the knowledge and skills students are to master, and its reliance on state-based student achievement testing as a means of monitoring students' achievement (McDonnell, McLaughlin, & Morison, 1997). What made NCLB so very different from its precursors are its requirement of state administered assessments and its broad jurisdiction across all students in the public schools. NCLB mandates the reporting of test scores in core subjects (first reading and mathematics, followed in part by science), and it holds schools accountable for adequate progress of all students (known as Adequate Yearly Progress [AYP]) on these tests. NCLB motivates compliance by the states by instigating sanctions when AYP is not met, sanctions that included reduced funding and/or removal of administrators or teachers (Penfield & Lee, 2010). Sanctions are central to the theory of action of NCLB, as they were thought to motivate schools and districts to allocate resources so that all designated groups of students could meet the established levels of progress (Marx & Harris, 2006; Supovitz, 2009).

Initially, a wide range of individuals and groups—spanning the political spectrum—embraced NCLB. This embrace was due to one of the central features of NCLB, that is its requirement that students from all demographic groups were to meet the same academic standards. Because NCLB required the disaggregated reporting of test scores by students' social class, race and primary language use, it was hoped this close attention to the success of different groups of students would provide the impetus to improve classroom instruction. Given the emphasis on the disaggregation of data, NCLB gave the appearance of requiring the equality of educational opportunities (Kantor & Lowe, 2006). By requiring standardized assessments to be systematically administered, and by requiring the disaggregated reporting of student performance on these measures, and by tying these requirements to federal funding, NCLB held the promise of changing the education of students traditionally underserved in education, and the science education community hoped that was true also in science (Marx & Harris, 2006; Penfield & Lee, 2010; Pringle & Carrier Martin, 2005).

Unintended Consequences of Accountability Policies and Science Teaching & Learning

It is important to point out that NCLB carries with it no clear direction in terms of how teaching and learning should be approached. Instead it is an accountability system, requiring states to closely attend to the results of their instructional efforts. But the legislation itself offers no clear description of what those instructional efforts should look like. In addition, the attention to science in NCLB has been delayed and limited, so that science has taken a "back seat" to reading and mathematics. Because of this, administrators have urged teachers to almost exclusively focus on the reading and mathematics core of AYP. Because early years of NCLB focused on reading and mathematics, and because science scores are not factored into AYP determination with the same weight as reading and mathematics once they were considered, NCLB has diverted the attention of schools away from science learning.

In the context of NCLB, when science is addressed, it often trivializes science, and instead focuses on reading and answering science questions, ignoring much of the research on effective practice (Buxton, 2006; Settlage & Meadows 2002). Within the high stakes world of NCLB, teachers avoid the use of effective teaching practices such as inquiry because of the time and energy they require (Shaver et al., 2007). Decision-making about science instruction is focused on the test rather than on science learning (Buxton & Lee, 2010). In many settings science instruction is designed to familiarize students with the structure and content of the test (Saka et al., 2009).

Southerland et al. (2007) describe that the vast scope of the current science standards, the need for "quick improvements" so that schools can obtain AYP, and limited instructional time work together to prohibit teachers from closely considering the way they teach science. Indeed, because of the interaction of broad standards and high stakes testing, NCLB has pushed teachers to rapidly cover science content (Upadhyay, 2009; Saka et al., 2009), something that is in direct opposition to the kinds of science teaching that research suggests is essential to support students' science learning.

Most damaging, given the initial goal of equity in education, the structure of NCLB has forced teachers to focus on test preparation to the exclusion of teaching all of their students science (Shaver et al., 2007). Instead of fostering an increased attention to quality in their teaching, Settlage and Meadows (2002) describe that NCLB policies have caused many teachers to adopt a "triage" mentality—in which teachers are focusing their attention on those students whose scores show the greatest potential for increase, at the expense of less promising students. Pringle and Carrier (2005) describe that scripted lessons, which have become a common reaction to high-stakes measures, prevent teachers from responding to their students' particular needs in science.

Explaining the Unintended Consequences

One-way to understand the unintended consequences of NCLB policy, we have applied Cuban's (1988) idea of first order and second order changes in education (Southerland et al., 2007). First order changes include small changes to existing practices, changes designed to increase the effectiveness of existing teaching practices (i.e., after school tutoring, review sessions, changing tests). In contrast, second order changes require transformation of the fundamental structure of teaching (i.e., moving from lecture to practices that require students to do the conceptual work in a lesson). Second order changes, because they require the transformation of the structure of schooling, are difficult to implement and support, and they often require a long period of time to produce desired results. NCLB is a system to support first order changes, as it simply requires changes on the part of school without providing a goal for instructional change. Because of the way in which AYP can result in sanctions, teachers must often resort to take the most expedient route to raising students' achievement on the standardized measures. Thus, teachers are pushed by administrators to focus on test preparation, drilling vocabulary, investing their energy in only the most promising students. The high stakes nature of NLCB force school systems to invest their limited resources in these first order changes, leaving no resources available for actually changing the manner in which science is taught and learned.

Anticipating Unintended Consequences of Accountability for Girls

As the previous discussion highlights, in the US the attention schools and teachers devote to science has lagged behind the overwhelming attention devoted to mathematics and reading. This is because science testing similarly lagged behind testing in the other subjects and because the results of science test for schools are not factored in to determinations of AYP with the strength of the other two content areas.

An analogous situation can be found when addressing the attention to girls in NCLB legislation. Although NCLB requires states to make test results open to the general public, only a few report testing data disaggregated by gender (Hyde et al., 2008).

> The NCLB Act is designed to help all students meet high academic standards by requiring that states create annual assessments that measure what children know and can do in reading and math in grades 3 through 8. ... Data will be disaggregated for students by poverty levels, race, ethnicities, disabilities, and limited English proficiencies to ensure that no child—regardless of his or her background—is left behind. (Paige, Hickok, & Neuman, 2002, p. 9)

Indeed, as the above quote suggests, gender groups are not used as separate sub-population in AYP determinations. Thus, a central facet of the theory of action of NCLB, that of holding schools accountable for the achievement of a particular subgroup, is missing when the subgroup of interest is girls.

It is our argument that the results of the first order nature of NCLB actions have been mixed, and this situation is even more negative for those learners who do not excel in traditional classrooms. Given limited time, funding and lack of coherent vision of science teaching and learning in NLCB policy, an unintended consequence of this legislation is a new embrace of an old concept—a deficit view of diversity. Although *NCLB* does focus attention on achievement gaps of particular demographics groups, it does not provide schools the vision or resources necessary to meet the requirements it imposes. Because of resource limited/high stakes nature of NCLB, any need to alter from traditional practices can be seen as "bringing down" a school's success—a view that does not support or allow teachers to focus on the particular needs of the students in her class or alter instruction to best captivate a students' interest or ability. Given the misalignment of the US' accountability system, teachers begin to understand any student that requires deviation from set norms to be a detriment.

In classrooms in which teachers are struggling to "cover" wide bodies of content in a limited amount of time, in which they need to focus their energies on bringing as many students as possible up to an acceptable level of achievement, and in which they are not held accountable specifically for the achievement of girls, it seems unlikely that they will focus on the manner in which they question, respond, and challenge the girls in those classrooms. It seems equally unlikely that teachers will be able to devote time to focus on science careers, scientists and the knowledge and skills needed to join those scientists. NCLB has narrowed the curriculum to those topics tests, and because stereotype threats are not listed on science standards, and the understanding of subtle effects of gender bias will not be tested, it is unlikely that their discussion will become a staple of science classrooms. Already the research suggests that the context of NCLB has diminished the use of activities and inquiry in instruction, as in the context of NCLB science success is understood as the ability to read and answer questions. Thus, the need to provide hands-on activities, which will also further students' spatial abilities, seems to be a thing of the past. In a world in which a teacher's success is measured in large part by the short-term measure of their students' success on standardized measures, it is unclear that the long term successes of fostering girls' interest and abilities in science will be seen as priorities.

How Can We Better Support the Education of the Next Madame Curies?

We began this chapter by asking, as much of the world moves toward systems of accountability as a lever for change in schools, are we building a system that only allows for the occasional anomaly, or are we challenging the norms so that the science learning of all girls is fostered? We suggest that the former is true, and that the ways in which accountability has been operationalized in the United States has worked to limit the attention girls' science learning receives. Lynch (2001) warns against the potential of current educational policy as supporting a "one size fits all" approach to teaching. We agree and suggest that the misalignment of accountability legislation combined with its rapid, high stakes nature can be understood to push science teachers and science classrooms to become more uniform, fast-paced, and one-dimensional. Thus, the specific context of NCLB pushes us back to first wave feminist discussions, but without the necessary resources (i.e., time, energy, programs) to help girls excel in these classrooms. Paradoxically, while NCLB and other approaches to accountability were designed to support the learning of those students traditionally underserved in instruction, such efforts may force teachers to become more *difference blind* as they are pushed to meet a host of first order changes. We suggest that such legislation and its attendant difference-blindness moves us away from a reality in which girls are supported in becoming scientists. Without radical changes in the way we approach accountability (i.e., alignment of standards, assessment and professional development), the manner in which it is enacted (i.e., time for changes to take effect, the provision of useful information to inform instruction) and how it is supported (i.e., the provision of resources of professional development, further investment in producing assessments that actually represent useful and applicable science knowledge), we fear that future Marie Curie's will remain anomalies.

REFERENCES

AAUW (1998). Gender gaps: Where schools still fail our children, Washington, DC: Author. Retrieved from http://www.aauw.org/learn/research/upload/GGES.pdf

AAUW. (2008). *Where the girls are: The facts about gender equity in education*, by C. Corbett, C. Hill, & A. St. Rose. Washington, DC: Author. Retrieved from http://www.aauw.org/learn/research/upload/whereGirlsAre_execSummary.pdf

AAUW (2010). *Why so few: Women in science, technology, engineering and mathematics*, by C. Corbett, C. Hill, & A. St. Rose. Washington, DC: Author. Retrieved from http://www.aauw.org/learn/research/upload/whysofew.pdf

Baker, D. (2002). Where is gender and equity in science education? *Journal of Science Teacher Education, 39*(8), 659–663.

Barton, A. C. (1998a). *Feminist science education.* New York: Teachers College Press.

Barton, A. C. (1998b). Teaching science with homeless children: Pedagogy, representation, and identity. *Journal of Research in Science Teaching, 35*(4), 379–394.

Brickhouse, N. (2001). Embodying science: A feminist perspective on learning. *Journal of Research in Science Teaching, 38*(3), 282–295.

Brickhouse, N., Lowery, P., & Schultz, K. (2000). What kind of a girl does science? A construction of school science identities. *Journal of Research in Science Teaching, 37*(5), 444–458.

Buxton, C. (2006). Creating contextually authentic science in a low performing urban elementary school. *Journal of Research in Science Teaching, 43*(7), 695–721.

Buxton, C. & Lee, O. (2010). Fostering scientific reasoning as a strategy to support science learning for ELLs. In D. Senal, C. Senal, & E. Wright (Eds.), *Teaching science with Hispanic ELLs in K–16 classrooms* (pp. 11–36). Charlotte, NC: Information Age Publishing.

Ceci, S. J., Williams, W. M., & Barnett, S. M. (2009). Women's underrepresentation in science: Sociocultural and biological considerations. *Psychological Bulletin, 135*(2), 218–261.

Cuban, L. (1988). A fundamental puzzle of school reform. *Phi Delta Kappan, 69*(5), 341–344.

Curie, M. (1923). *Pierre Curie* (translated by C. Kellogg & V. Kellogg). New York: The Macmillan Company.

De Welde K, Laursen S, Thiry H. (2011). SWS Fact Sheet: Women in Science, Technology, Engineering and Math (STEM). Sociologists for Women in Society. http://www.socwomen.org/index.php?ss=25.

DeWandre, N. (2002). Women in science: European strategies for promoting women in science. *Science 295*(5553), 278–279.

Kahle, J. B. (2004). Will girls be left behind? Gender differences and accountability. Journal of *Research in Science Teaching, 41*(10), 961–969.

Kantor, H. & Lowe, R. (2006). From New Deal to no deal: No Child Left Behind and the devolution of responsibility for equal opportunity. *Harvard Educational Review, 76*(4), 474–502.

Hallman, L. D. (2009). *Women and girls in STEM: A comprehensive approach to achieving equity.* A report presented to the National Science Foundation's Committee on Equal Opportunities in Science and Engineering, Oct. 26, 2009.

Harding, S. (1998). *Is science multicultural? Postcolonialisms, feminisms, and epistemologies.* Bloomington, IN: Indiana University Press.

Hyde, J. S., Lindberg, S. M., Linn, M. C., Ellis, A.B., & Williams, C. C. (2008). Gender similarities characterize math performance. *Science, 321*(5888), 494–495.

Jones, M. G. & Wheatley, J. (1990). Gender differences in teacher-student interactions in science classrooms. *Journal of Research in Science Teaching, 27*(9), 861–874.

Lynch, S. (2001). "Science for all" is not equal to "one size fits all": Linguistic and cultural diversity and science education reform. *Journal of Research in Science Teaching, 38*(5), 499–627.

Marx, R. W., & Harris, C. J. (2006). No Child Left Behind and science education: Opportunities, challenges, and risks. *Elementary School Journal, 106*(5), 467–477.

McDonnell, L., McLaughlin, M., & Morison, P. (1997). *Educating one and all: Students with disabilities and standards-based reform.* Washington, DC: National Academy Press.

National Science Foundation. Division of Science Resources Statistics. (2008). Science and engineering degrees: 1966–2006. Detailed Statistical Tables) (NSF 08–321). Arlington, VA: Author. Retrieved from www.nsf.gov/statistics/nsf08321/pdf/nsf08321.pdf

National Science Foundation (2009). Women, minorities, and persons with disabilities in science and engineering: (NSF 09–305). Arlington, VA: Author. Retrieved from http://.www.nsf.gov/statistics/wmpd

No Child Left Behind Act of 2001, Pub. L. No. 107–110, 115 Stat. 1425 (2002). Retrieved from http://www.ed.gov/legislation/ESEA02/

Paige, R., Hickok, E., & Neuman, S. B. (2002, September). No child left behind: A desktop reference. Jessup, MD: Education Publications Center, U.S. Department of Education. Retrieved from http://www.ed.gov/offices/OESE/reference

Penfield, R. D., & Lee, O. (2010). Test-based accountability: Potential benefits and pitfalls of student assessment with student diversity. *Journal of Research in Science Teaching, 47*(1), 6–14.

Pringle, R. M & Carrier Martin, S. (2005). The potential of upcoming high-stakes testing on the teaching of science in elementary classrooms. *Research in Science Education, 35*(2–3), 347–361.

Rosser, S. V. (1995). *Teaching the majority: Breaking the gender barrier in science, mathematics & engineering.* New York: Teachers College Press.

Sadker, M., & Sadker, D. (1994). *Failing at fairness.* NY: Simon & Schuster.

Saka, Y., Southerland, S. A., & Brooks, J. (2009). Becoming a member of a school community while working toward science education reform: teacher induction through a CHAT perspective. *Science Education, 93*(6), 996–1025.

Settlage, J., & Meadows, L. (2002). Standards-based reform and its unintended consequences: implications for science education within America's urban schools. *Journal of Research in Science Teaching, 39*(2), 114–127.

Shaver, A., Cuevas, P., Lee, O., & Avalos, M. (2007). Teachers' perceptions of policy influences on science instruction with culturally and linguistically diverse elementary students. *Journal of Research in Science Teaching, 44*(5), 725–746.

Simpson, R. D., & Oliver, J. S. (1985). Attitude toward science and achievement motivation profiles of male and female science students in grades six through ten. *Science Education, 69*(4), 511–526.

Simpson, R. D., & Oliver, J. S. (1990). A summary of major influences on attitude toward and achievement in science among adolescent students. *Science Education, 74*(1), 1–18.

Sorby, S. A., & Baartmans, B. J. (2000). The development and assessment of a course for enhancing the 3-D spatial visualization skills of first year engineering students. *Journal of Engineering Education, 89*(3), 301–307.

Southerland, S. A., Golden, B., & Enderle, P. (2011). The bounded nature of science: An effective tool in an equitable approach to the teaching of science. In M. Y. Khine (Ed.), *Advances in the nature of science research: Concepts and methodologies*. Dordrecht, The Netherlands: Kluwer Academic Publishers.

Southerland, S. A., Smith, L. K., Sowell, S. P., & Kittleson, J. M. (2007). Resisting unlearning: Understanding science education's response to the United States' national accountability movement. *Review of Research in Education, 31*(1), 45–77.

Sowell, S. (2004). *Doing gender/Teaching science: A feminist poststructural analysis of middle school science teachers' identity negotiations*. Unpublished doctoral dissertation, Florida State University, Tallahassee, FL.

Steele, C. M., & Aronson, J. (1995). Stereotype threat and the intellectual test performance of African Americans. *Journal of Personality and Social Psychology, 69*(5), 797–811.

Supovitz, J. (2009). Can high stakes testing leverage educational improvement? Prospects from the last decade of teaching and accountability reform. *Journal of Educational Change, 10*(2), 211–227.

Tobin, K., Kahle, J. B., & Fraser, B. J. (Eds.) (1990). *Windows into science classrooms: Problems associated with higher-level cognitive learning*. London: Falmer Press.

Upadhyay, B. (2009). Negotiating identity and science teaching in a high-stakes testing environment: an elementary teacher's perceptions. *Cultural Studies of Science Education, 4*(3), 569–586.

Weinburgh, M. (1995). Gender differences in student attitudes toward science: A meta-analysis of the literature from 1970 to 1991. *Journal of Research in Science Teaching, 32*(4), 387–398.

Wennerås , C., & Wold, A. (1997). Nepotism and sexism in peer-review. *Nature, 387*(22), 341–343.

Sherry A. Southerland
Professor and Co-Director, FSU-Teach
Florida State University
ssoutherland@fsu.edu

Sibel Uysal Bahbah
Science Education Researcher
Florida State University
sibel.uysal@gmail.com

BIOGRPAHICAL SKETCHES OF AUTHORS AND EDITORS

Pnina Geraldine Abir-Am

Dr. Pnina Geraldine Abir-Am, historian of science with special expertise in the history of biomolecular sciences in the 20th century, has a Ph.D. in History of Science and M.Sc. in philosophy of science and B.Sc. in chemistry. Since 2007 she has been a Resident Scholar at the Women's Studies Research Center, Brandeis University. She served as Director of Research at CNRS, Paris, and as Principal Investigator on various US grants from NSF and NIH. She is the recipient of a prize for outstanding research from the History of Science Society and of various research awards including from the Welcome Trust of London.

Sibel Uysal Bahbah is a researcher in the Biological Science Department at Florida State University, Tallahassee, FL. She received her M.S. in botany from Anadolu University, Turkey, her M.Ed. in science education from the University of Missouri-Columbia, and her Ph.D. from Arizona State University in science education. Currently, she works for the Research in Experience for Teachers (RET) Project at FSU. The objective of the project is to explore the effect of inquiry-based teacher professional development workshops on students' ideas with regard to inquiry in science. Her research interests also include gender education in science in different cultures.

Ron Blonder is a Senior Researcher at the department of Science Teaching at the Weizmann Institute of Science in Israel. She is involved in the professional development and training of chemistry teachers and teaches a course in nanotechnology and science education. Her research interests include understanding teaching self-efficacy and its inflection on students' gains, and integrating modern topics in chemistry and nanotechnology for high school teachers and students. She is a member in a committee of the Ministry of Science dealing with regional science laboratory centers for youth in Israel and a deputy of the head of the National Chemistry Teachers' Center in Israel.

Mei-Hung Chiu is a Professor of Science Education at National Taiwan Normal University (NTNU). She taught secondary school chemistry in Taiwan before completing her doctorate at Harvard. Her research interests include better understanding and promoting students' conceptual constructions and changes in science as well as developing effective science instruction materials for learners at various developmental levels. She received the Federation of Asian Chemical Societies Award for Distinguished Contribution to the Advancement in Chemical Education in 2009. She was the International Coordinator for National Association for Research in Science Teaching (2008-2010). Currently, she is the Associate Editor of the journal, *Journal of Research in Science Teaching,* and chair of Sub-committee on Chemistry Education for Development and a titular member of IUPAC Committee on Chemistry Education.

Yehudit Judy Dori is the Dean of Continuing Education and External Studies and a professor at the Department of Education in Technology and Science at the Technion – Israel Institute of Technology, Haifa, Israel. She is also Visiting Scholar at the Center for Educational Computing Initiatives at Massachusetts Institute of Technology. Her research interests encompass scientific visualizations, higher order thinking skills, educational assessment at high school and university levels, and distance education. Professor Dori is a member of the editorial board of *Journal of Research in Science Teaching* and *Journal of Science Education and Technology*; in 2010, she founded TIDES– Technion International Distance Education & Studies Center.

John K. Gilbert was Professor of Education at The University of Reading, where he was concerned with the training of research students in the School of Education and with undergraduate courses in science communication in the Faculty of Science. He has been Editor-in-Chief of *International Journal of Science Education* since 1991 and, jointly with Susan Stocklmayer of Australian National University, recently introduced the new journal '*IJSE(B): Communication and Public Engagement*'. His present research interests are in the use of informal approaches to the public communication of the ideas of chemistry, especially the role of models in that process. He is currently Visiting Professor of Science Education at King's College London and was the 2001 recipient of the NARST award for 'Distinguished Contributions to Science Education through Research'.

Penny J. Gilmer is the Nancy Marcus Professor Emerita of Chemistry & Biochemistry at Florida State University. She engaged in both biochemistry and science education research for 33 years. She retired in 2010 but is still active with an NSF grant to advance the status of academic women faculty in chemistry, physics and engineering and a US Department of Education grant to develop formative assessments in science for teachers with middle school students. She is a former President of the National Association for Research in Science Teaching (2006-2008). In 2010 Springer published her book, *Transforming Undergraduate Biochemistry Teaching Using Collaborative Learning and Technology: Ready, Set, Action Research*. Gilmer is a Fellow of the American Association for the Advancement of Science, elected in 1994.

Anita Hussénius is Associate Professor in Organic Chemistry at the University of Gävle and Director of the Centre for Gender Research at Uppsala University, Sweden. She also coordinates the research program Nature/Culture Boundaries and Transgressive Encounters, the aim of which is to study empirically and reflect theoretically on the ways in which knowledge about gender and gendered knowledge are produced in the intersection between the natural and cultural sciences. Her main research interest concerns gender perspectives on science education and more specifically, how an increased awareness of gender issues in science and in science teaching influences teachers' identities as teachers and their teaching of science.

Julie Des Jardins is an Associate Professor of History at Baruch College, City University of New York. She teaches American history, focusing on women and gender, and has written *The Madame Curie Complex: The Hidden History of Women in Science* (Feminist Press, 2010) and *Women and the Historical Enterprise in America: Gender, Race, and the Politics of Memory, 1880-1945* (University of North Carolina Press, 2003). Currently she is completing a biography of Lillian Gilbreth for college courses and a study of American masculinity at the turn of the 20th century.

Rachel Mamlok-Naaman is a senior staff scientist and coordinator of the Chemistry Group in the Department of Science Teaching at the Weizmann Institute of Science. In addition, she is the head of the National Centre for Chemistry Teachers at the Weizmann Institute of Science, and coordinator of a special M.Sc. program for chemistry teachers. She is engaged in the development, implementation, and evaluation of new curricular materials, and research on students' perceptions of chemistry concepts. Her publications are in the areas of scientific and technological literacy, teachers' professional development, cognitive aspects of students' learning, assessment, and curriculum development.

Catherine Milne is Associate Professor at New York University with research interests in sociocultural studies of science education, the role of history and philosophy of science and science teaching, and the role of multimedia and game in learning science. She has just authored, *The Invention of Science* (Sense Publishers, 2011), which uses cases from history to explore the nature of science, is co-editor-in-chief of the journal, *Cultural Studies of Science Education,* and coordinates a large research project exploring the development of scaffolds within simulations for chemistry education.

Marilyn Bailey Ogilvie is Professor Emerita and Curator of the History of Science Collections at the University of Oklahoma. She is the author of several biographies of women in science including one of Marie Curie, two biographical dictionaries of the history of women in science, numerous chapters in books, and papers in scientific journals. As Curator of the History of Science Collections she traveled extensively to buy books in the history of science, taught numerous courses, was a member of many graduate students' M.A. and Ph.D. committees, and is active in professional organizations.

Bill Palmer obtained his doctorate from Curtin University, Australia in 2003 and he continues with research in the history of science as an associate at Curtin. Bill was a senior lecturer in the Faculty of Education, Health and Science at Charles Darwin University, Australia from 1989 to 2007 when he retired formally after nearly 50 years in science education. Bill has worked in Britain, Australia, Nigeria, Papua New Guinea, Western Samoa and Tanzania. He is a Fellow of the Royal Society of Chemistry and of the Royal Australian Chemical Institute.

Kathryn Scantlebury is Professor in the Department of Chemistry & Biochemistry and Director of Secondary Education in the College of Arts & Sciences at the University of Delaware. She taught high school chemistry, science and mathematics in Australia before completing her doctorate at Purdue University. Her research interests focus on gender issues in various aspects of science education, including urban education, preservice teacher education, teachers' professional development, and academic career paths in academe. She recently co-edited two books, *Re-visioning Science Education from Feminist Perspectives: Challenges, Choices and Careers* (Sense Publishers, 2010) and *Coteaching in International Contexts: Research and Practice.* Scantlebury is the Research Director for the *National Science Teachers Association* and a Fellow of the American Association for the Advancement of Science.

Sherry A. Southerland is Professor in the College of Education and Co-director of FSU-Teach at Florida State University in Tallahassee, FL, USA, where she has taught courses on learning theory, history and philosophy of science, educational research methods, and diversity and science teaching and learning. Her research interests include the influence of affect and culture on conceptual change in science, the role of educational policy in influencing science education reform, and teachers as agents of change in science classrooms. She has served on the editorial board for *Journal of Research in Science Teaching, Science Education* and *International Journal of Science Education* and was selected as Fellow of the American Association for the Advancement of Science in 2007 for distinguished contributions in describing the cultural and affective dimensions of science learning and understanding the barriers to systemic reform in science education.

David F. Treagust is Professor of Science Education at Curtin University in Perth, Western Australia where he teaches courses in campus-based and international programs related to teaching and learning science. His research interests include understanding students' ideas about science concepts and how these ideas relate to conceptual change, the design of curricula and teachers' classroom practices. He is a former President of the National Association for Research in Science Teaching (1999-2001) and in 2011 was the recipient of the American Chemical Society Award for Achievement in Research for the Teaching and Learning of Chemistry.

Nadia Y. Wang is currently attending the International Health Program (M.S. degree) at National Yang-Ming University, Taiwan. She graduated from the Department of Public Health at Kaohsiung Medical University, Taiwan, and has participated at the IUPAC International Conferences on Chemical Education (ICCE). She will present a paper on Marie Curie at the IUPAC World Congress in Puerto Rico in August 2011.

INDEX

Printed in the United States
By Bookmasters